358.503 380.03

KER

Ref.

385.03

901790

-5. MAY 1988

KT-234-683

380.5

00001703

The Hamlyn Colour
Encyclopedia
of
Transport

The Hamlyn Colour
Encyclopedia
of
Transport

Robin Kerrod
Christopher Pick
J. D. Storer

Hamlyn
London · New York · Sydney · Toronto

CONTENTS

Published 1983 by
The Hamlyn Publishing Group Limited
London · New York · Sydney · Toronto
Astronaut House, Feltham, Middlesex, England
© Copyright The Hamlyn Publishing Group Limited 1983

ISBN 0 600 38837 9

Printed and bound by Graficromo s.a., Cordoba, Spain

WATER

SHIPPING TERMINOLOGY

For centuries sailors have employed a special vocabulary to describe different parts of a ship, and this tradition, developed in the days of sail, is maintained on modern vessels.

The left side of the ship is known as the port side, the right as the starboard side. (The difference is easy to keep in mind if you remember that the word 'port' has the same number of letters as the word 'left'.)

The front part of a ship is called the *fore end*, and someone going to the fore end of the vessel is said to be going forward; the very front is known as the *bow*. A ship moving forwards is described as moving ahead. The back part of the ship is known as the *after end* or the *stern*. A person going to the after end is going aft, and the ship herself moves astern. *Amidships* is the part of

the vessel between the fore and after ends. *Beam* is the word used to describe the widest part of the ship, found amidships. Also usually amidships is the bridge, from which the ship is controlled.

A ship's speed is measured in knots. One knot is 1.85 kph (1.15 mph) and so a ship travelling at 20 knots has a speed of 37 kph (23 mph).

Markings

All ships must display their name on each side of the bow and also on the stern. In addition, the name of the port at which they are registered must also be shown on the stern.

Glance at any vessel and you will see a number of other signs and symbols.

Draught marks – displayed on each side of the bow and stern and sometimes amidships as well – indicate the depth of water required to float a ship. Thus, a ship's draught is the distance between its keel, or bottom, and the waterline. Many harbour and estuary entrances are quite shallow, and vessels above a certain draught are unable to enter as there is insufficient water to accommodate them.

Load lines, which appear amidships, are a guide to the amount a cargo vessel may carry at different times of the year and in different waters. The more heavily loaded a ship is, the lower it sits in the water and, in consequence, the smaller its freeboard. A vessel's *freeboard* is the vertical distance between the main deck and the waterline, measured amidships. In general, the

Below: Bird's eye and profile views of a steamship. The various parts of the hull (the ship's superstructure) are always known by these names.

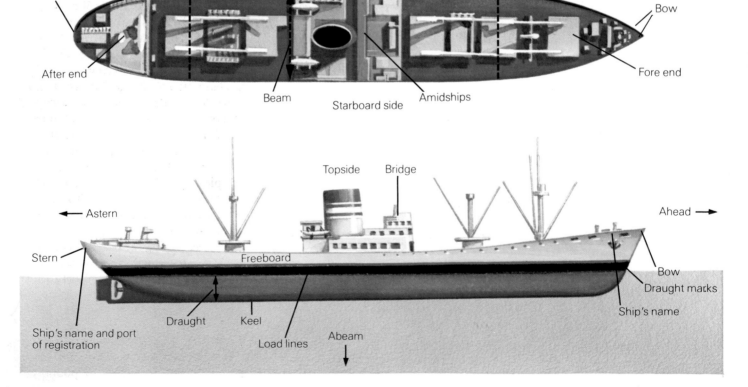

6

larger the freeboard – that is, the more of the ship that appears above water – the more easily the vessel can cope with bad weather. The load lines indicate the minimum freeboard permitted in different conditions. From the bottom upwards, the first four marks refer to Winter North Atlantic (WNA), Winter (W), Summer (S) and Tropical (T). Thus a ship making a North Atlantic crossing in winter, during which bad weather and stormy seas are virtually certain, may carry a much lighter load than a vessel making a voyage in tropical waters, in which calm seas are to be expected. (The WNA line is compulsory only on vessels less than 100 metres long.)

The top two load lines, Fresh (F) and Tropical Fresh (TF), are applicable when an ocean-going vessel is being loaded in a freshwater port. As fresh water is less dense than sea water, such a ship floats deeper in the water than a similar vessel being loaded with the same amount of cargo in a salt-water harbour. A ship loaded to TF in fresh water will thus rise to T when it reaches the open sea, and one loaded to F will rise to S. Maritime charts indicate the different parts of the world to which each load line applies.

Separate regulations, with a different set of load lines, apply to passenger-carrying vessels.

The third marking found on every vessel is the *tonnage mark*, which is also positioned amidships.

A ship's tonnage may be expressed in a number of different ways. The two most commonly used are *deadweight tonnage* and *gross tonnage*. Deadweight tonnage (dwt) refers to the total weight that a vessel can carry, not only its cargo but also stores (provisions for crew members, spare equipment), fuel, crew, passengers and so on. Whereas dwt is a measure of weight, gross tonnage – known officially as gross registered tonnage (grt) – is a measure of volume. To state a ship's gross tonnage is to describe her total capacity below the

Above: Lucerna *being delivered by her builders to Quebec. The ship is high in the water, showing one blade of the screw propeller.*

main deck and also that of any permanently enclosed spaces there may be above the main deck. The different measurements are used according to the type of cargo the ship is built to carry. Heavy cargoes are charged for per unit weight, whereas bulky cargoes are charged for per unit volume.

A vessel has to pay numerous charges during a voyage. Some, such as the fees charged by pilots for bringing a ship into harbour and charges for time spent in dry dock, are based on gross tonnage. Others – some harbour and port dues, for instance – are based on *net registered tonnage*. This measurement represents the volume of those parts of the ship occupied by cargo: that is, the vessel's gross registered tonnage less the space occupied by the engine, bridge, crew accommodation and so on.

To make things yet more complicated, the ton itself is not a constant measurement of weight. A short ton – known as an American ton – is 2000 pounds (907 kilograms), whereas a long (British) ton is 2240 pounds (1016 kilograms). Deadweight tonnage is often expressed in long tons. (A metric tonne is 1000 kilograms, 2204 pounds.)

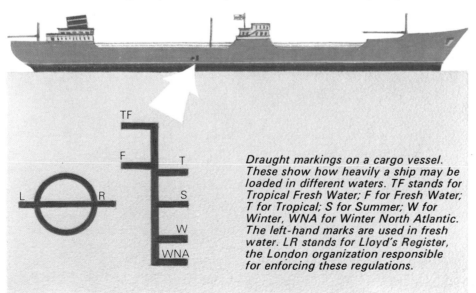

Draught markings on a cargo vessel. These show how heavily a ship may be loaded in different waters. TF stands for Tropical Fresh Water; F for Fresh Water; T for Tropical; S for Summer; W for Winter, WNA for Winter North Atlantic. The left-hand marks are used in fresh water. LR stands for Lloyd's Register, the London organization responsible for enforcing these regulations.

SHIP POWER

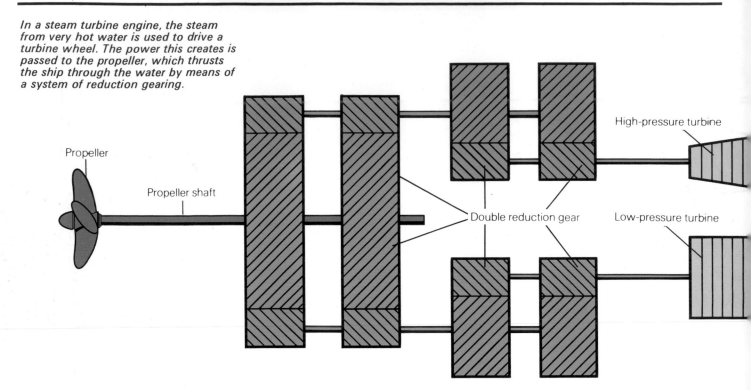

In a steam turbine engine, the steam from very hot water is used to drive a turbine wheel. The power this creates is passed to the propeller, which thrusts the ship through the water by means of a system of reduction gearing.

Propeller

Propeller shaft

Double reduction gear

High-pressure turbine

Low-pressure turbine

Nowadays, the vast majority of ships are powered either by a steam turbine or by a diesel engine.

A steam turbine creates power in the following way. Water is heated in a boiler, and the steam thus produced is brought to high pressure by being compressed as it passes along a series of tubes that run through the boiler. The high-pressure steam is then ejected through a nozzle on to the angled blades of a turbine wheel. The nozzle is so shaped that the steam rushes out of it extremely quickly. The force with which the steam hits the blades causes the turbine wheel to rotate at a very high speed. Although coal was once always used to heat the boiler, practically every steamship now uses oil.

In general, the diesel engines used aboard ships are like those used in other forms of transport (*see pages 70 and 96*). Fuel is burnt in enclosed cylinders, and the resulting gases drive pistons, whose *reciprocal* (up and down) motion

is converted to *rotary* (circular) motion by a crankshaft. Unlike the diesel engines used in lorries and railway locomotives, which follow a four-stroke cycle, marine diesel engines work on a two-stroke cycle. They are also supercharged to make them more efficient, a process that involves forcing air into the cylinders under pressure.

Traditionally, marine diesel engines are slow-speed. More recently, however, medium-speed engines have also been employed, in particular on roll-on/roll-off (*ro/ro*) ferries (*see pages 30–31*).

The main advantages of steam turbines are that they are quiet – they hardly vibrate at all – and extremely powerful: they can produce up to 75 000 horsepower. In consequence, they are mostly used in very large, powerful vessels such as passenger liners – on which the comfort and ease of travellers is a prime consideration – and large tankers. On both these types of ship people are willing to pay the

high fuel costs that fast speeds make necessary. In 1978, about 33% of the world's gross tonnage was powered by steam turbines, but this represented only 3.5% of the total number of ships worldwide.

Diesel engines, by contrast, are the workhorses of the world's merchant navies and in 1978 were to be found in some 63 000 of the 69 000 vessels registered (65% of the world's gross tonnage). Although both types – slow- and medium-speed – are more expensive to build than steam turbines, they are cheaper to install. Because they are less powerful (the most powerful slow-speed diesel engine can only produce about 48 000 horsepower, which is in fact sufficient for all but the most rapid vessels), fuel costs are lower; furthermore, less fuel has to be carried on board, which leaves more space for money-earning cargo. The main disadvantage of diesels is that they are very noisy and vibrate a good deal.

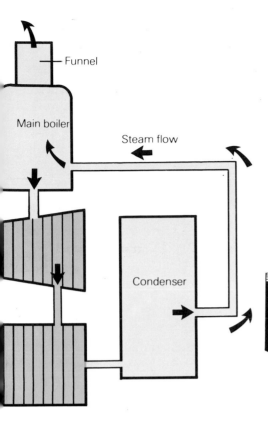

Funnel

Main boiler

Steam flow

Condenser

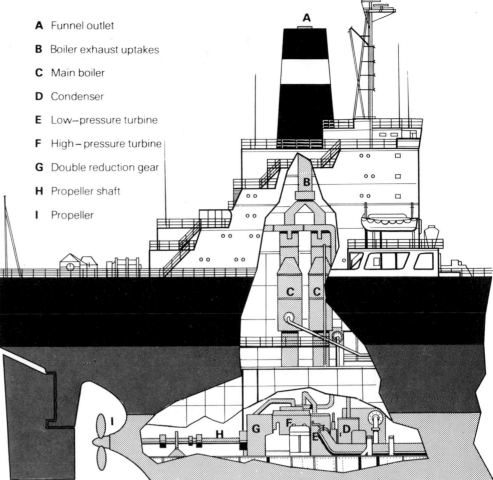

A Funnel outlet

B Boiler exhaust uptakes

C Main boiler

D Condenser

E Low–pressure turbine

F High–pressure turbine

G Double reduction gear

H Propeller shaft

I Propeller

The propeller

In a car, power has to be passed from the engine to the wheels before the vehicle will move. In a ship, it is the propeller that provides the thrust that pushes the vessel through the water. The commonest type of propeller – known properly as a marine screw propeller – has several broad blades (usually four, five or six on large vessels) made of manganese bronze. As the blades turn, the water passing between and over them is accelerated, and the force of this acceleration thrusts the vessel forwards.

On conventional propellers, the pitch, or angle, of the blades is fixed and cannot be altered. As a result, the ship only operates most efficiently when she is running at her normal cruising speed, that is, the speed for which the propeller has been designed. On controllable pitch propellers, by contrast,

each blade can be individually adjusted by a hydraulic mechanism operated from inside the ship. This means that the pitch of the blades can be altered according to the speed required and the weather conditions encountered.

Whichever type of propeller is used, power is transferred from the engine to the propeller along the propeller shaft, which runs from the engine room to the propeller itself. If the engine room is amidships the shaft has to be enclosed in a tunnel as it passes through the vessel's holds.

Steam turbines run most efficiently at a fairly high speed, considerably faster than the best operating speed of a propeller. Therefore, the power produced by the engine cannot be transmitted direct to the propeller shaft and thence to the propeller, and a system of gears – like those used on a car (*see pages 99–100*) – is placed between the engine and the propeller shaft to reduce the speed to that most suitable for efficient

working of the propeller. On slow-speed diesels no gearing is required, and the engine can be coupled directly to the propeller shaft; medium-speed diesel engines, by contrast, do require a gear box.

A controllable pitch propeller: each blade can be individually adjusted.

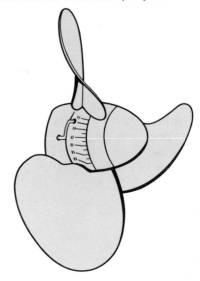

Other forms of power

Other types of propulsion used in ships include diesel-electric and turbo-electric drive and gas turbines.

In vessels equipped with turbo-electric drive, the steam turbine does not power the vessel directly. Instead, it drives an electric generator. This in turn powers a driving motor connected to the propeller shaft and thus to the propeller. The same thing happens with diesel-electric drive. Only about 1150 ships have these types of drive.

Although gas turbines are the latest type of engine to be installed in merchant ships, they have been used in naval vessels since the late 1940s. The gas turbine works rather like the steam turbine, but, in contrast with the steam turbine, the turbine blades are turned not by the force of high-pressure steam but by the hot, expanding gases generated when compressed air mixes with fuel in a combustion chamber and burns.

The advantages of gas turbines are considerable. They are small, light, powerful, and easy to maintain and repair, but consume much fuel.

Some experts believe that by about 2000 coal – cheaper and more plentiful than oil – might come into use again.

It seems possible that an increasing number of high-speed vessels will be equipped with gas turbines during the 1980s and 1990s. Nuclear power may also be more frequently used. Although nuclear submarines are now quite common, only a few experimental nuclear-powered surface vessels have been constructed. The first was a Russian ice-breaker, the *Lenin*, built in 1957; the second, the American *Savannah* (1962), with a gross tonnage of 12 200 tons, was the first nuclear-powered merchant vessel.

The nuclear-powered vessels built so far work in much the same way as conventional steam-turbine ships. The only difference is that a nuclear reactor, rather than oil, is used to produce steam. The great advantage of nuclear-powered vessels is that they virtually never have to stop to refuel: a modern nuclear warship, for instance, may have a range of up to 640 000 kilometres.

Above: *The* Savannah *from the United States, the world's first nuclear-powered merchant vessel, which was built in 1962.*

Right: *This four-blade propeller produces a speed of about 16 knots. Each ship's propeller is very carefully designed.*

Finnjet

Although four container ships were equipped with gas turbines in 1972, the engine has so far been most successful in the *Finnjet*, which went into service in 1977.

Finnjet was planned to replace older, slower vessels on the Baltic route between Helsinki, the Finnish capital, and Travemünde in the Federal Republic of Germany. Previously, 35 hours had been the quickest time for the 960-kilometre journey. However, it was found that a ship with gas turbines could maintain a constant speed of 56 kph (35 mph, 30 knots), thus completing the round trip in less than 48 hours.

NAVIGATION

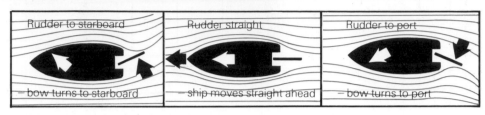

Rudder to starboard — bow turns to starboard | Rudder straight — ship moves straight ahead | Rudder to port — bow turns to port

Once power has been produced by the ship's engines and transmitted to the propeller, thus causing the vessel to move, it is necessary to be able to control the direction in which the ship moves – in other words to steer it. This is done by means of the *rudder*.

In essence, a rudder is an extremely simple device. It consists of a steel plate attached by hinges to the stern of the vessel and hanging down into the water. As the ship's wheel is turned, information is electrically transmitted to steering engines which turn the rudder. The movement of the rudder controls the direction in which the ship travels. If the rudder is at an angle of 90° from the point at which it is fixed to the stern, the vessel will move straight ahead. This is because the water exerts equal pressure on each side of the rudder. If, however, the

Above: *The effect of the rudder on the water flow around the hull.*

rudder is turned to the right, the pressure created by the water on the right-hand side of the rudder will be greater than that created on the left-hand side. In consequence, the stern of the vessel will be pushed to the left, and the vessel itself will turn to the right. If the rudder is not returned to its normal position, the vessel will turn in circles.

Some liners and large cargo vessels such as tankers and bulk carriers are equipped with a device known as a

Right: *Although the great circle route looks longer on a chart, it is in fact the most direct.*

bow-thruster. This is a controllable pitch propeller mounted in a water tunnel built across the ship near the bows and below the waterline. It enables the bows of the ship to be turned either to port or to starboard. Many other forms of steering are available.

Shipping routes

Equipped with engines, screw propeller and rudder, a ship does not simply cast off and sail where she will. Seamen have to be able to navigate: that is, to decide the best route to follow to their destination and then to direct their vessel along it.

One might think that to decide on a route between port A and port B would be an easy matter: the ship would simply leave harbour and then position herself so as to sail in a straight line to her destination. But, because the Earth's surface is curved, a curved line – not a straight one – is in fact the shortest distance between two points. In nautical terminology, this is known as the *great circle route*.

More often than not, ships do not follow the great circle route and instead they use a system known as *weather routeing* to establish the best route. A number of meteorological offices in different maritime nations run weather routeing services. The one operated from Britain covers the whole of the northern hemisphere. Meteorologists and scientists use information assembled from 1300 land and ship

Below: *A bow-thruster, seen in bird's eye and profile views. It is used to turn a vessel to port or starboard.*

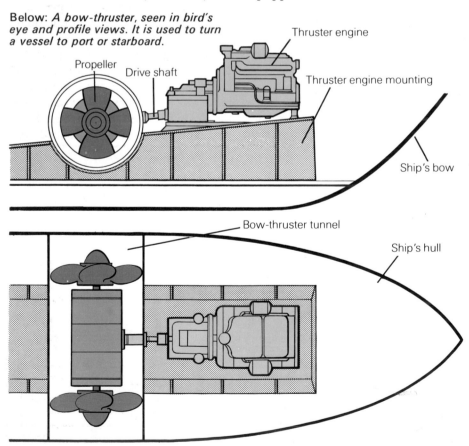

Thruster engine

Thruster engine mounting

Propeller

Drive shaft

Ship's bow

Bow-thruster tunnel

Ship's hull

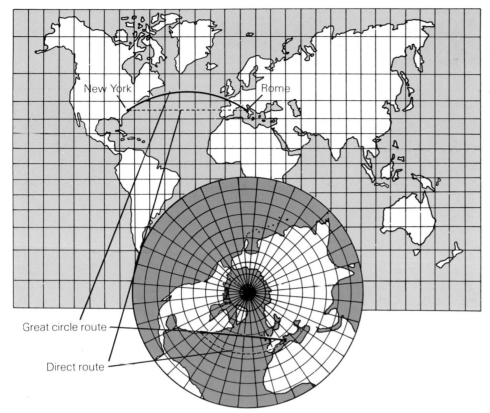

Great circle route

Direct route

weather stations; from equipment carried in balloons at heights up to 35 kilometres; and from weather satellites, to forecast weather conditions for up to 3 days ahead. The best route for a particular vessel is then worked out by computer. The route will avoid the worst weather conditions, take advantage of surface currents and avoid fog and ice. In consequence it will save fuel, reduce the time spent on the voyage and may well, in bad weather, minimize or avoid damage to the ship and her cargo.

In many busy parts of the world's oceans, ships have to follow a different kind of routeing system, one that keeps vessels travelling in different directions apart from each other so as to minimize the risk of collision. There are 73 such schemes in operation all over the world, no less than 22 of them in western European waters, between the mouth of the River Elbe in northern Germany, the coast of Brittany in France, and southern Ireland. In principle, they work rather like a motorway: ships travelling in opposite directions have to keep in separate lanes. These are divided by an area of sea known as a

separation zone which may not be entered. Ships crossing the traffic lanes must do so at right angles to them.

Buoys are used to mark special channels that ships must follow, whether in mid-ocean or in estuaries and harbours. Additional safety features at sea are lighthouses and lightships. Both are equipped with flashing lights and foghorns that guide vessels and also warn

them off dangerous coasts. Many lighthouses and lightships are also used to transmit radio and radar signals.

Navigation

There are a number of ways in which a navigator can determine the position of a vessel at sea. *Dead reckoning* (the word dead is a shortening of deduced) enables a navigator to deduce (find out) the ship's position merely from the speed and direction of the vessel, without referring to any fixed points.

Information about the direction of travel comes from the ship's compass. Information about the speed at which the vessel is travelling comes from the log. (The first logs were exactly that: a small log thrown out astern at the end of a rope into which knots were tied at regular intervals. As the ship moved along, the rope was paid out, and the number of knots was measured against a sandglass. This is the origin of the nautical unit of speed, the *knot*. One knot equals one nautical mile per hour, the nautical mile being an international unit equal to 1.85 kilometres.) A modern log consists of a propeller towed in the water behind the ship and connected to a dial marked in nautical miles: the faster the speed of the vessel, the quicker the propeller rotates. Having thus determined the speed and

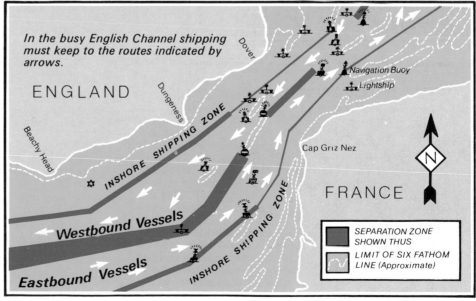

In the busy English Channel shipping must keep to the routes indicated by arrows.

ENGLAND

Dover

Dungeness

Beachy Head

Navigation Buoy

Lightship

INSHORE SHIPPING ZONE

Cap Griz Nez

FRANCE

N

Westbound Vessels

Eastbound Vessels

INSHORE SHIPPING ZONE

SEPARATION ZONE SHOWN THUS

LIMIT OF SIX FATHOM LINE (Approximate)

direction, and knowing the time that has passed since the ship left port, the navigator can calculate the ship's position on a chart.

The problem with dead reckoning is that it is difficult to be at all precise. *Astro-navigation* involves accurately determining a vessel's position by reference to the Sun, Moon or stars. Using an instrument called a sextant, the navigator measures the altitude of two or three stars above the horizon. With this information, and using a nautical almanac, which gives accurate information about the position of stars and planets, the vessel's position can be calculated exactly.

Within sight of land, a navigator can use a compass to take a *bearing* on any visible landmark which is also marked on the chart. A position line is then drawn on the chart at the appropriate angle from the landmark. A second bearing is taken on another landmark, and another position line is drawn. The point at which the two position lines cross marks the position of the vessel. Bearings can also be taken on buoys, lighthouses and lightships.

Equipment

All merchant ships must carry both a magnetic and a gyro compass. The magnetic compass was the first to be developed, but the Earth's magnetic field and also the magnetic field created by the steel with which the ship's hull and fittings are made mean that it is liable to error. The gyro compass always shows true, rather than magnetic, north. Detailed correction tables for magnetic compasses are available.

Maritime charts, covering harbours, coastal waters and oceans, are another extremely important piece of equipment that all vessels must carry. Charts provide detailed information about everything seamen need to know in order to complete a voyage safely: the position and depth of channels, wrecks, sandbanks, lighthouses; plans of harbours; and so on.

The oldest electronic navigation

technique is *radio direction-finding*, introduced in 1912 and now compulsory on all vessels with a gross tonnage of more than 1600 tons. In radio direction-finding, aerials which can determine the direction of a radio signal are used to take bearings along the radio waves transmitted by radio stations on land, and with this information the vessel's position can be found.

Navigational *satellites* orbiting the earth are a more recent aid to position-

finding. The radio signal emitted by the satellite can be used to determine a vessel's position extremely accurately; very often the calculations are done by a computer on board. A 'fix' can be taken whenever the satellite passes overhead, usually every 80 minutes.

Modern merchant vessels also make considerable use of *radar*, which is now compulsory on all vessels above a gross registered tonnage of 1600. Radar is chiefly a safety device that indicates the

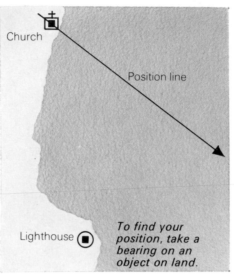

To find your position, take a bearing on an object on land.

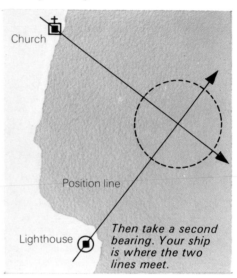

Then take a second bearing. Your ship is where the two lines meet.

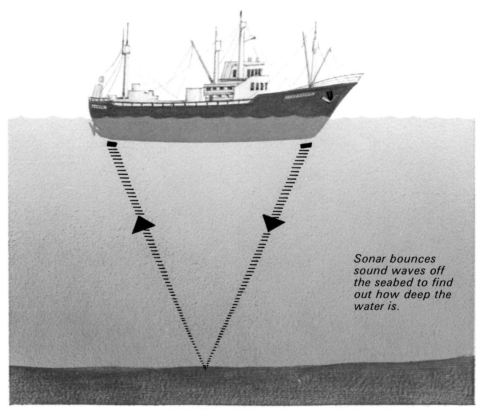

Sonar bounces sound waves off the seabed to find out how deep the water is.

position of other vessels nearby and thus allows a ship to proceed – although slowly – even in thick fog. Radar can also be used to determine a ship's position.

In addition to finding out where they are, mariners often need to discover the depth of water beneath their vessel. The technique used is called *sonar* (short for SOund NAvigation Ranging and often also known as echo-sounding). As the name suggests, sound waves are utilized to measure the depth of water.

Vessels over 300 gross registered tonnage must also be equipped with some form of radio transmitter. VHF (very high frequency) radio-telephones are used for communicating over short distances, often with other vessels and pilot boats and tugs in harbours, and over longer distances by means of the conventional land-based telephone system. Wireless telegraphy, in which messages are transmitted by Morse code, is still used a great deal.

Many ships also have teleprinters, and some use communications satellites for long-distance communications.

Below: *A sextant, used in finding a ship's position at sea.* Inset bottom: *A radar screen. Modern navigational equipment is very sophisticated and is often linked to satellites and computers so that the best route can be plotted very rapidly.*

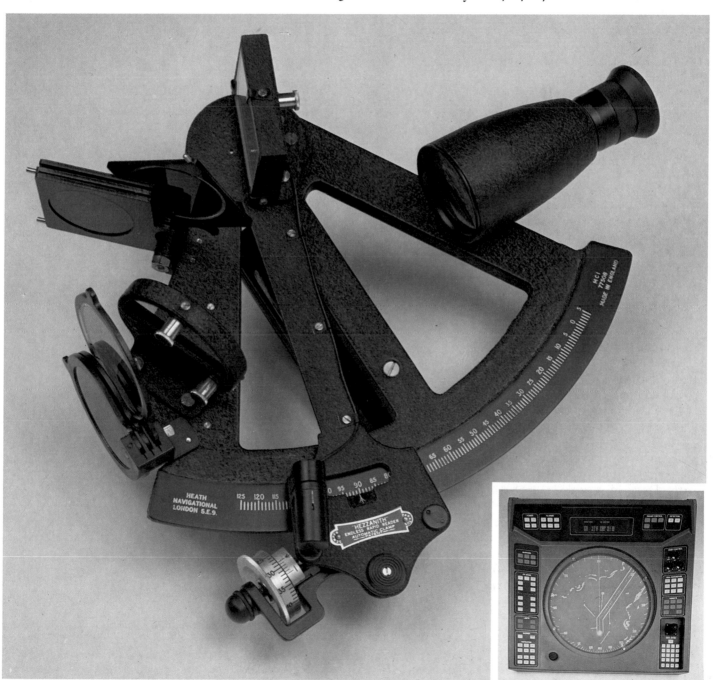

PORTS

The words port, harbour and dock tend to be used as if they mean the same thing – which they do not. A harbour is a sheltered area of water where one or more vessels may moor. The word port describes not only a harbour but also the town that lies behind it; unlike a small harbour used only by fishing and pleasure vessels, a port normally has storage facilities and connections with road or rail transport. A dock is the area of a port in which ships load and unload passengers or cargo.

Harbours may be either natural or artificial. Whenever practicable, a harbour is built in a bay or an inlet or at the mouth of a river, so that the coastline gives some protection from the full force of the wind and the sea. Breakwaters, often called *moles*, may have to be built; these are long arms that stretch around most of a harbour entrance, leaving a fairly small gap through which vessels can enter. Made of concrete, stones and rubble, or of cement blocks, they provide a barrier against the waves and thus create an area of calm water within the harbour. Dover, on the coast of the English

Channel at its narrowest point, is an artificial harbour; the breakwater there is no less than 3.2 kilometres long.

No matter what type of vessel will visit the port, a number of different facilities must be provided. Most important of all are wharves and quays built either along the shore or out into the harbour. Vessels come alongside these to discharge and stow cargo. The wharves and quays must be equipped with cranes able to lift a variety of

Below: *Dockside gantry cranes, used to load and unload ships.*

cargoes into and out of ship holds. Storage facilities are also necessary, both under cover and in the open air, so that cargoes can be assembled to await loading and also stored until taken away by road or rail.

Loading and unloading cargo

The increasing number of specialist vessels now being built means that special facilities have to be provided at docks. Container vessels usually berth at huge purpose-built container terminals. Although covered warehouses are not needed, a large area is necessary to assemble the containers. Good land transport connections are essential, preferably a railway line and a good road or a motorway. Giant gantry cranes are used to load and unload the containers. Sometimes these are large enough to span both the assembly area and the vessel; if they are not, a variety of mobile equipment, such as tractors and trailers, is used to bring the containers to and from the quay.

Bulk vessels carrying such cargoes as coal, iron ore and grain often dock alongside an offshore jetty, linked to the shore merely by a conveyor belt system. Tankers often tie up alongside a similar structure and discharge their cargo straight into a pipeline which carries the oil to the shore and thence to large storage tanks. Alternatively they use single-point moorings (*see page 40*).

A range of equipment and buildings is necessary for cargoes destined for dry cargo vessels. The cargoes are kept in large warehouses until they are ready to be stowed; valuable and hazardous cargoes are kept apart in separate areas. Whenever possible, general cargoes are palletized – that is, placed on wooden boards called pallets. This means that a fork-lift truck can easily move them from the warehouse to the quay. General cargoes may be packed in any number of ways–in bales, bags, cartons, crates or boxes. Larger items – tractors, for instance – may not be packed at all.

Although a great deal of automation has been introduced into cargo-handling operations, especially for containers and bulk loads, general cargoes are still positioned by dockers working in the holds of the vessel. After a crane has deposited a load in the hold, they manoeuvre it into the position laid down on the stowage plan (a plan that sets out exactly where each item should go in the holds), using crowbars and handhooks. Cargoes must be correctly stowed: their weight must be evenly distributed throughout the holds so that the ship remains stable and they must be secured so that they do not shift during the voyage.

Inland ports

The construction of inland waterways large enough to accommodate ocean-going vessels means that not all ports nowadays are on or even very near the coastline. The Manchester Ship Canal in Britain enables large ships to travel

Above: *Dockside unloading. The lift descends into the ship's hold, where a seaman puts a crate on each platform.*

The biggest port in the world

In the Netherlands, the port at Rotterdam (near the mouths of the Rivers Rhine and Maas), which in terms of the amount of goods handled is by far the biggest port in the world, has also moved further downstream. In 1978, 268.7 million tonnes of sea-borne goods passed through the port, almost twice as many as at Kobe, Japan, its nearest rival. Rotterdam has expanded downstream in three stages since 1945 and now has 2148 hectares of water, more than four times as many as in 1945.

58 kilometres inland to Manchester, and in the USA the harbour at Houston, Texas, reached by means of the Houston Ship Canal, is 84 kilometres from the Gulf of Mexico. By contrast, other ports such as London, that were once some way inland, have moved downstream towards the sea. The main reason for the move is to enable them to accommodate the very large ocean-going vessels for which the water further inland is too shallow and the docks too small. In London's case, there was no room for the large container terminals and storage areas necessary in modern docks in the 19th century port near the centre of the city.

Pilots are experts in a particular stretch of water: they literally know every metre and will advise the ship's master on the best route by which to enter port. Usually they are taken out to an incoming vessel by a fast motor launch or a helicopter. Pilots have to be taken on board in many harbours and difficult stretches of water.

Above: *A harbour pilot clambers up a rope ladder from his launch to guide a ship into harbour.*

Maasvlakte, the most recent extension, which stretches 5 kilometres out into the North Sea, can accommodate the largest bulk carriers and tankers up to 300 000 dwt.

No less than 30 000 ships visit Rotterdam every year, and a complex system of traffic management is necessary to ensure that they all reach their berths safely. A harbour radar system is already in operation, and a computerized Vessel Traffic Management System (VTMS) is being developed. Many vessels are towed into port by tugs, and pilots are also available to guide a vessel into its berth.

SHIP DESIGN

Although it may vary a great deal in important details, the basic design of all the many different kinds of ship in operation today is the same.

The shell of the ship is known as the *hull*. With a very few exceptions, modern hulls are made of steel. They have to be extremely strong to withstand the continual pressure they receive, especially in heavy seas. The hull must be shaped in such a way that the ship can travel through water as easily as possible and to make her as manoeuvrable as possible.

Besides a main deck, many ships have additional decks. Their number, and whether they are sited above or below the main deck, depends on whether the vessel is designed to carry passengers or cargo, and on the type of cargo. Additional decks above the main deck form part of what is known as the ship's superstructure. On some cargo vessels, freight, usually in the form of containers (*see pages 34–7*), is carried on the main deck. Part of the main deck also consists of large steel hatch covers leading to the holds, in which cargo is stored. On most modern ships the hatch covers are operated mechanically.

The one part of the superstructure that is common to all ships, whatever their function, is the bridge. Although the traditional place for the bridge is amidships, on many modern vessels it is placed aft. The bridge is the operational centre of the ship. The wheelhouse contains the wheel, with which the ship is steered, and the ship's compasses and other navigational equipment. Also on the bridge are the chartroom, where the ship's route is worked out, the radio room, and the master's living quarters. Good all-round visibility from the bridge is essential, since the officers and crew members working there must be able to see where the ship is going when they are in very busy waters. The bridge can communicate with the other parts of the ship.

Below decks

The space inside a cargo ship is divided into a number of holds, in which cargo is stored. The number of holds and the sort of cargo for which they are suitable varies from one type of ship to another. Cargo is usually – though not always – stowed (loaded) and discharged (unloaded) through hatchways, and again the number and size of these varies.

Inside a passenger-carrying ship everything is quite different, with cabins, lounges, restaurants and so on. The number of these and the different facilities available depends on whether the vessel is a ferry, on which the journey may take at most about 36 hours, or a cruise liner, on which passengers may spend a two- or three-week holiday.

Below: On the bridge of a ferry, which has an autopilot, to hold it on a pre-set course, and radar.

All vessels must by law incorporate a number of watertight steel *bulkheads*. These run across the ship transversely (from one side to the other) or from the bottom up to the main deck, thus dividing the vessel into a number of watertight compartments. These stop water flooding in if the hull is holed, and so they reduce the risk of the ship sinking; they also help to prevent fire spreading. In addition, the bulkheads support the main deck and stop the hull buckling under the weight of the cargo or the pressure of the sea. All cargo ships have a collision bulkhead and bulkheads to protect the engine room. Passenger vessels have additional bulkheads because there are stricter safety regulations.

Other safety features with which every vessel must be equipped include lifeboats and lifebelts and fire-fighting equipment. In addition, regular surveys of the ship's equipment and general condition must be carried out.

In the engine room (often below the bridge) are the engines that power the ship, plus a great deal of other machinery, including generators for the vessel's lighting and refrigeration systems and for operating other equipment. The funnel – which is painted in the colours of the shipping company that owns the vessel – is usually above the engine room. The traditional place for the engine room was amidships, but nowadays it is more often positioned aft. This leaves more space for cargo in the middle of the ship, the widest part, and also reduces the length of the propeller shaft tunnel.

Ships are designed to be stable when they are fully loaded. If, therefore, they undertake a voyage either partly loaded or without any cargo on board at all they have to take on ballast to make up the necessary weight and keep level. Ballast was once pebbles and sand but now usually consists of sea water. This is pumped into the two main ballast tanks, known as the fore and aft peak tanks.

Vessels with large holds are constructed with a double bottom – that is, two separate layers of steel plates. If a vessel with a double bottom runs aground and is holed – which happens at a rate throughout the world of two ships per day – water is much less likely to penetrate into the cargo holds. (Ships such as oil tankers, in which the holds are divided into a number of separate small tanks, do not have a double bottom.) The space created by the double bottom is used for seawater ballast or for storing fuel or fresh water.

Stabilizers help to reduce the amount a vessel rolls in heavy seas. This is important both for the comfort of passengers and, on cargo ships, for the stability of the cargo in the holds. Fins projecting from the hull, one on each side below the waterline, are the most common type of stabilizer. Instruments automatically tilt each fin according to the amount and direction of the roll. The fins resist the pressure of the water as it tries to roll the vessel over and thus they help to keep it upright. When they are not being used, the fins are retracted into watertight boxes in the hull. Other types of stabilizer include bilge keels and anti-rolling tanks.

Below: *Stabilizers projecting from the hull help to stop a ship pitching in heavy seas. They are retracted into the ship when not in use.*

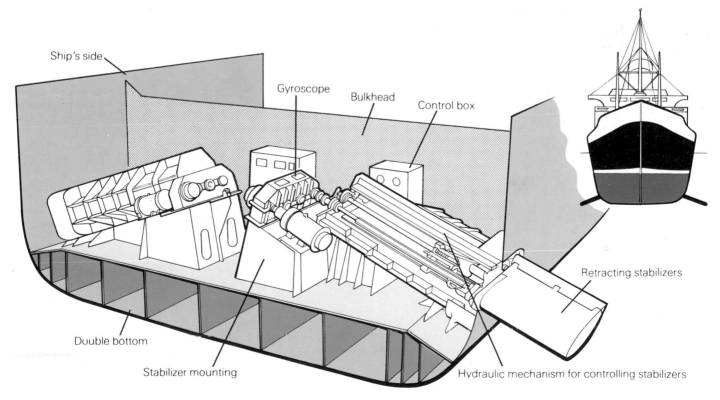

Ship's side

Gyroscope

Bulkhead

Control box

Retracting stabilizers

Double bottom

Stabilizer mounting

Hydraulic mechanism for controlling stabilizers

21

SHIPBUILDING

Building a ship is a long, complicated and expensive process. It falls into three main parts: deciding whether to build a new vessel and then what type and size to build; detailed planning and design; and actual construction work.

In many ways, the first of these three parts is the most difficult of all. It takes several years to plan and construct a ship, and so a shipping company has to try to predict demand several years ahead. That can be tricky, for the amount of cargo sent overseas depends at least to some extent on how prosperous countries are. Since cargo ships are becoming increasingly specialized, shipping companies also have to be confident that the particular type of cargo to be carried by the new vessel will continue to be in demand. Further-more, they have to forecast how far other means of transport will succeed in competing with ships (an increasing amount of traffic between western Europe and the Far East, for instance, travels overland via the Trans-Siberian Railway).

Nor is that all: even if the shipping company does decide to build a new vessel, decisions about its size and

speed have to be made. If it is to travel through one of the maritime canals (*see page 53*), that immediately restricts its size. Other factors have to be taken into account as well. Put simply, a 200 000-dwt tanker is not four times more expensive to run than a 50 000-dwt tanker. The extra running cost may be relatively small: only a small increase in crew numbers will be necessary, and fuel costs will not be much greater, whereas the return – that is, the money earned – will be much higher. Construction costs, of course, will be much greater. The greater profit

can only be achieved, however, if the vessel is fully loaded, or at least nearly so, on every voyage: empty space in the holds means a lower profit, or even a loss, for the ship's owners.

Once a decision has been made about what type of ship to build, first a general plan and then detailed plans of the new vessel are prepared, often with the assistance of a computer. These are the working drawings that will be used in the construction of every part of the vessel. Sometimes a scale model of the finished ship on a much smaller scale is tested in a tank.

Then the ship actually begins to take shape in its berth in the shipyard. Ships used to be built from the keel upwards and would gradually rise higher and higher. Now different sections of the hull are built in different parts of the yard and are then assembled in the building berth, where they are welded to the neighbouring sections. Assembly usually starts with the stern and progresses towards the bows of the vessel.

While all this is happening, plans are

Below: *A tanker under construction in a Japanese shipyard. Japan is now one of the world's major shipbuilding nations.*

drawn and orders are placed for those parts of the ship – the propeller, anchors and many other items – that are built outside the shipyard. As many as 300 different manufacturers may be involved in constructing a 250 000-tonne tanker, and it has been estimated that out of every five people who work on a ship only one is actually employed in the shipyard. A great deal of detailed organization and control is needed to ensure that every part is ready in time.

When the shell of the vessel – that is, the hull and the superstructure – is completed and has been painted it is ready to be launched. This is usually done amid great celebrations. Launching can be a tricky operation. The vessel has to slide down the slipway into the river at exactly the correct speed: if she moves too fast she may hit the opposite bank or even keel over, but without sufficient momentum she will not be able to move at all.

After being launched, the vessel is fitted out. This is almost the equivalent of furnishing a house. The engines and other machinery are installed, together with the electrical, plumbing and navigational equipment; lifeboats and deck gear are fixed in place; cabins are furnished, and the entire interior is decorated.

There remains one final stage before the vessel enters service. This is the ship's trials, which take place first in

Above: *Models of new ship designs are tested in this tank at the National Maritime Institute, London.*

Below: *This model of the Suez Canal was used to find out how much the canal needed to be enlarged to take big modern tankers.*

Floating docks

Another type of dry dock is known as a floating dry dock. Unlike a conventional dry dock, this does not have to be constructed as part of the harbour facilities. Instead it is built elsewhere and is then towed to where it is required. A floating dock works as follows. When a vessel is to be admitted, ballast tanks in the bottom and side walls of the dock are filled, so that the entire structure is almost completely submerged. The ship enters the dock, whereupon water is released from the ballast tanks. As the floating dock rises out of the water, the ship settles on the keel and bilge blocks. Eventually the entire dock is floating on the surface of the water, and the ship herself is surrounded by a completely dry area.

Ballast tanks

Quayside

dock and then in the open sea. Their purpose is to check that all the equipment is working properly and that the vessel herself is performing as she should. Once the trials have been completed satisfactorily, the ship is handed over to her owners.

Ship repairs

Minor repairs can be made while a vessel is underway, or at the dockside during loading and unloading operations. When a major overhaul is necessary, however, or if repairs have to be made to the hull below the waterline, the ship must come into dry dock.

A dry dock is a dock from which the water can be emptied. The ship enters through lock gates and comes to rest on bilge and keel blocks. These will support her when the dock is dry. The lock gates are then closed behind her, sealing the dry dock from the rest of the port, and the dock is emptied. Modern bilge and keel blocks run on guide rails and can be positioned by remote control to fit the shape of the ship. The older type has to be set by hand; this

means that after one ship has left the dry dock the blocks can only be reset by emptying the dock and filling it again.

Some very large dry docks are now being built: at Rotterdam in the Netherlands there is one suitable for 500 000-tonne tankers. At the moment, floating docks are only capable of accommodating vessels of up to about 70 000 dwt.

Below: An empty dry dock. It is filled with water, the ship enters through the lock gates then the dock is emptied.

Lock gates

Bilge blocks

Keel blocks

Gantry crane running on rails

PASSENGER CRAFT

In general, ships may be described in one of two ways, either according to what they carry or according to the type of service they offer. Vessels may carry either passengers or cargo, and a few carry both. They operate on either liner or tramp services. Liner services, which may carry passengers or cargo, run regularly on fixed routes, whereas tramp ships carry any cargo that they can accommodate to any ports they are able to enter.

Liners

Until relatively recently, if you wanted to travel overseas you had to go by boat. Every major maritime nation had sev-

eral large shipping companies that ran services to different parts of the world.

The development of aircraft, and in particular of jets during the 1950s, changed all that. In 1957, for the first time more people crossed the Atlantic

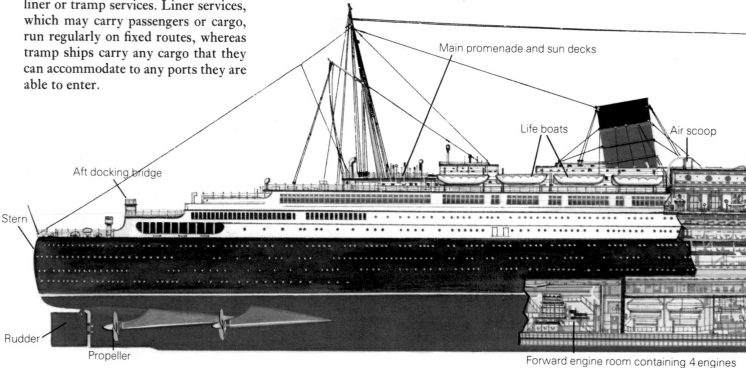

Main promenade and sun decks

Life boats

Air scoop

Aft docking bridge

Stern

Rudder

Propeller

Forward engine room containing 4 engines

by air than by sea. Since then aircraft have become faster and larger, and in consequence, despite the increase in fuel costs, fares have fallen. Travel has become more popular too.

The same trends that benefited the airlines injured the shipping companies. The big liners were very labour-intensive – that is, they required a large crew to operate them and to attend to the passengers. As a result, rapidly increasing wages meant that fares had to rise; higher fuel costs increased them still further. Moreover, people became increasingly unwilling to spend several days travelling on a liner when the same journey by air took a few hours.

As a result of all these factors, there are now virtually no passenger liner services anywhere in the world. From Britain, the last service to South Africa sailed in 1977 and the last one to

The last four great luxury transatlantic liners. Below: The Queen Mary (launched 1934). Bottom left: Queen Elizabeth I (1938). Bottom centre: United States (1952). Bottom right: France (1961). For travel in style, there was nothing to beat these vessels: five days of rich food, attentive service and high society. (The two Queens also served as troopships in the Second World War, under very different conditions.) However, by the mid-1960s the ships could no longer compete with faster, cheaper jet aircraft, and now most people cross the Atlantic by plane.

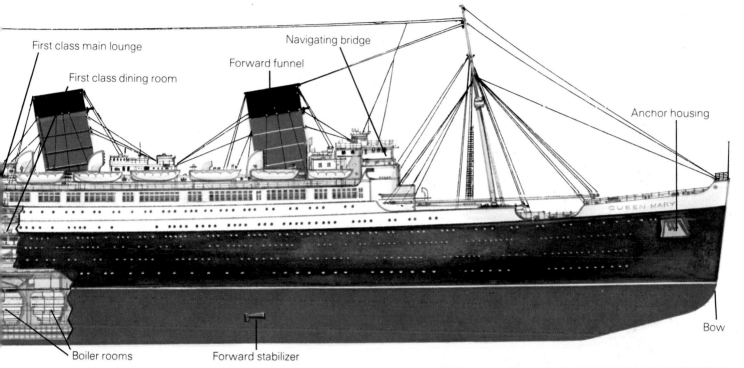

First class main lounge
First class dining room
Forward funnel
Navigating bridge
Anchor housing
QUEEN MARY
Bow
Boiler rooms
Forward stabilizer

Australia in the same year; in the 1980s there are only a few sailings across the Atlantic to North America.

Although many celebrated and much loved liners have been sent to the breaker's yard, liners, as a class, have adapted remarkably well to changing public demand. Cruises lasting between about 10 days and 6 weeks or even more (a round-the-world voyage on P & O's *Canberra* lasts 13 weeks) are now a popular form of holiday. Usually cruises are in sunny areas such as the Mediterranean or the Caribbean, and they enable prosperous holidaymakers to combine good food; pleasant surroundings, company and entertainment; and visits to interesting places on shore.

A typical modern purpose-built cruise liner might be 18 000–20 000 grt and accommodate between about 750 and 1000 passengers. This is smaller than the older liners. The reason is that, whereas traditional liner services sailed between major ports, cruise ships often have to put in to small harbours near places of interest. Another major difference is in the number of classes (or types) of accommodation. The older liners had as many as four or five different classes, each with its own dining-rooms, bars and so on, and passengers in one class never mingled with those of any other class. Modern cruise vessels, by contrast, are usually one-class: although the standard, and therefore the cost, of different types of cabin may vary, everyone uses the same facilities.

And the facilities on a cruise ship can be really sumptuous. There will almost certainly be several different restaurants; bars; a bank, cinema, hairdresser, gymnasium, swimming-pool and library; games rooms and play centres for young children. In the evening there will be elaborate dinners, dancing, gambling and other entertainments.

Left: *The Double Room is one of two big public rooms on board the QE2. So-called because it is on two levels, it serves as a lounge during the day and in the evenings is used for cabaret, dancing and entertainment.*

All these services are extremely labour-intensive although not as much as they were on the older liners. However, modern technology means that the size of the crew working on deck and in the engine room is much smaller than it used to be.

Modern cruise liners travel fast, and they frequently have to travel quite long distances at night between different ports, so that shore visits can be made each day. They are usually, though not always, powered by steam turbines. Safety precautions are extensive: watertight bulkheads divide the ship into tiny sections to prevent flooding, and there are elaborate fire detection and sprinkler systems.

Above left: *Launched in 1961 for the regular run between Britain and Australia, the* Canberra *now offers luxury cruises all over the world. There are shops, restaurants, bars, games rooms, night clubs, discos – everything the fashionable holiday-maker could want.*

Above: *The main pool on the* Canberra, *one of three on board.*

Below: *The Cunard flagship* Queen Elizabeth 2 (QE2), *launched in 1967, has also done duty as a troopship. Together with* Canberra, *she carried troops to the South Atlantic in the 1982 Falkland Islands crisis.*

FERRIES

Ferries are passenger-carrying vessels that operate on what are known as short-sea routes. (A short-sea voyage is one that lasts no longer than about 36 hours. From Britain, the short-sea trade includes sailings to Ireland, parts of Scandinavia, Holland, Belgium and France.)

Like liners, ferries have had to adapt a great deal to changing travelling habits in the last 20 years or so. Until about 1960, it was quite rare to take a car abroad by boat. If you did do so, it was loaded into the cargo hold by crane, a procedure that could take a long time, especially if there were a number of cars to be stowed. On the whole, ferries catered for passengers travelling by train; quite often they also carried general cargo too.

All that has now changed, and most ferry services are operated by what are known as ro/ro (short for roll-on/roll-off) vessels. Although some joker has claimed that the first ro/ro ship was Noah's Ark, in fact the idea came from landing craft used during the Second World War. Most modern roll-on/roll-off vessels work on a drive-through principle. There are two large ramps, one at each end of the vessel. A car drives on over, say, the stern ramp,

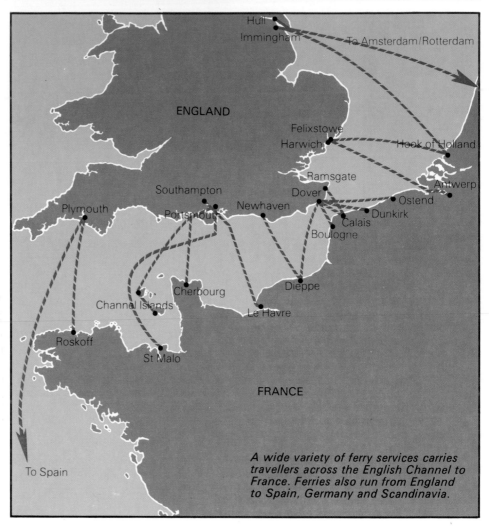

A wide variety of ferry services carries travellers across the English Channel to France. Ferries also run from England to Spain, Germany and Scandinavia.

parks, and at the end of the voyage drives off over the bow ramp, having literally driven through the ship. Vehicles park behind each other in narrow lanes; blocks placed in front of and behind each vehicle keep it in position during the voyage. On modern ro/ro vessels parking is on at least two levels, sometimes more, so that the ship is rather like a floating multi-storey car-park. The roll-on/roll-off arrangement means that turn-round time in port is extremely short, often as little as one hour.

Left: *Trucks loading on to a cross-Channel roll-on/roll-off ferry. They will make the journey on deck or in the hold.*

Ro/ro ships are extremely fast and manoeuvrable. Many of them are double-ended: that is, they have a rudder and propeller at each end. This saves a great deal of the time usually spent manoeuvring to come alongside, for the vessel simply docks, say, stern first and sets sail again bows first. Ro/ro vessels are usually equipped with two or three diesel engines, although the *Finnjet* (*see page 10*) has gas-turbine engines. Stabilizers and bow-thrusters are standard equipment.

Some of the latest ro/ro vessels to enter service on the routes between England and France are 8000 grt. Their cruising speed is 22 knots and they take just 75 minutes for the 35-kilometre voyage from Dover to Calais. They have a crew of 80 to 90, more than half of whom work in the restaurants and other passenger facilities.

Services

On the shorter ferry routes, elaborate facilities for passengers are not required. Vessels plying between England and France, for example, have bars, shops, a restaurant and a self-service café; on many there are no cabins. On ships serving the longer routes, there are some cabins.

The short-sea trade is often extremely competitive, and companies have to provide as fast, efficient, punc-

Above: *One of the many ferries that runs between Dover and Calais, the nearest French port to England.*

Below: *Roll-on/roll-off ships can accommodate coaches as well as cars.*

tual, cheap and comfortable a service as possible to attract passengers. There is considerable rivalry between different shipping companies on such routes – no less than four companies were operating 16 different routes between England and France in 1981. Ferries also have to compete with the faster hovercraft (*see page 58*), which can carry cars, and hydrofoils (*see page 62*), both of which are designed to operate on short-sea routes. In mid-summer 1981 there were no less than 77 sailings on a single Saturday between England and France.

On the more popular short-sea routes, such as the crossing between England and France, freight-only ro/ro vessels are also operated. The passenger-carrying vessels can accommodate 1300 passengers and have space for 350 cars or their equivalent: a typical load might be 200 cars or caravans, 10 coaches and 30 lorries. The freight-only vessels have far less space for passengers, who consist only of the lorry drivers. Such vessels can accommodate a total length of 1000 metres of freight, the equivalent of about 60 large lorries, plus a number of cars for export. Often unaccompanied trailers are also carried.

Although ferry crossings on busy sea routes are mostly operated nowadays by ro/ro vessels, there are of course numerous other smaller ferries that carry passengers, and sometimes a few vehicles as well, across rivers, estuaries, bays and so on.

CARGO VESSELS

Specialization has been the keynote of changes in freight transport on water in the last 25 years. This specialization has taken two forms. It has brought the construction of many more types of ship designed to handle a single or a few kinds of cargo. It has also brought the development of containers, which are often described as revolutionary. Container ships carry nothing but containers. What those containers hold has no effect on the vessel or her crew or the loading and unloading operations on the dockside.

Accompanying this shipboard specialization have come increasingly sophisticated systems of transporting loads to and from their vessels: liquids are loaded and unloaded by means of pipelines or conveyor belts, and containers can be lifted bodily on to trucks or railway flat cars for immediate onward transportation.

Dry cargo vessels

All this means that the traditional cargo ship, the dry cargo vessel, has lost much of the importance it once had. In 1978, such vessels made up less than 60% of the world's fleet – 20% of the gross registered tonnage.

A typical modern dry cargo vessel is between 6000 and 15 000 dwt with a capacity of up to about 21 237 cubic metres and a cruising speed of up to about 20 knots. Bulkheads divide the hold into several sections vertically, and two 'tween decks (the upper and lower) running the entire length of the vessel, between the main deck and the bottom, do the same horizontally. 'Tween decks make it possible to distribute heavy cargo throughout the ship and also prevent goods stowed at the bottom being crushed by the weight of the cargo above. In addition, they enable different types of cargo, and loads for different destinations, to be kept separate. There may also be accommodation for a limited number of passengers.

Many dry cargo vessels have an additional deck above the main deck, known as a shelter deck. This provides additional space for bulky cargoes such as cotton, hay or straw. There are two types of shelter deck, open and closed. On the closed deck all the bulkheads throughout the ship are continued up as far as the shelter deck, whereas in the open version all but the collision bulkhead stop at the main deck. Instead of the extra shelter deck, some dry cargo vessels carry a limited number of containers on the main deck. Dry cargo vessels usually carry their own derricks (deck cranes) for stowing and discharging cargo.

Most dry cargo vessels are powered by slow-speed diesel engines. The engine room and the bridge are both placed amidships, and there are often two more superstructures on the main deck, the fo'c'sle (forecastle) at the bows and the poop at the stern. In rough weather, these diminish the force of waves breaking over the deck and so protect the cargo stowed on deck.

Dry cargo vessels operate both liner and tramp services. One major American shipping company, whose headquarters are at New Orleans on the Gulf of Mexico, has a fleet of 38 dry

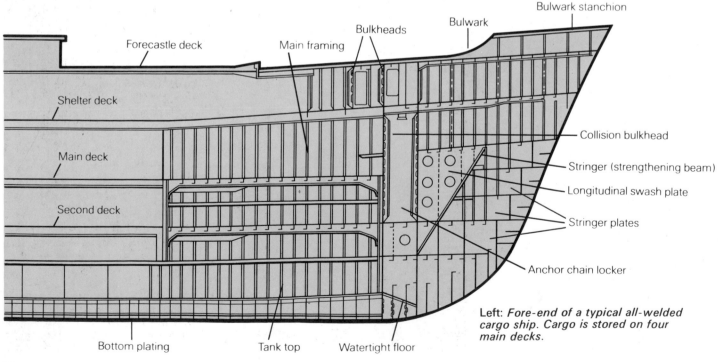

Left: *Fore-end of a typical all-welded cargo ship. Cargo is stored on four main decks.*

Forecastle deck — Bulkheads — Bulwark — Bulwark stanchion — Main framing — Shelter deck — Main deck — Second deck — Collision bulkhead — Stringer (strengthening beam) — Longitudinal swash plate — Stringer plates — Anchor chain locker — Bottom plating — Tank top — Watertight floor

cargo ships. It offers regular sailings from the USA Gulf ports to the Far East and also to the west coast of South America; from the Gulf ports and south Atlantic ports of the USA to the Mediterranean; to the Mediterranean from the Great Lakes via the St Lawrence Seaway in Canada; and also to the Far East from USA west coast ports. Thus, for example, on the Mediterranean route there is a sailing to Egypt every 7 days, to Israel every 14 days and to Spain and Italy every 15. In addition, whenever there is sufficient cargo, sailings are made to France, Lebanon, Tunis, Turkey, Morocco, Algeria, Yugoslavia and Greece.

Bulk carriers

Bulk carriers are designed to carry large quantities of a single bulk cargo. Iron ore, coal and grain are probably their most important cargoes, but they also carry sugar, bauxite, potash and fertilizer. Bulk carriers have only one deck; since they do not carry a variety of goods to a variety of destinations, more than one deck would only reduce the size of the load that could be carried. Vertical bulkheads divide the cargo space into a number of holds, and a double bottom strengthens the hull against the often considerable weight of the cargo above.

On many bulk carriers the engines are aft, so leaving space amidships for cargo. Smaller bulk carriers usually carry their own deck cranes, but frequently the larger vessels, which tend to use only major, well-equipped ports, do not. The hatch covers are normally very large so that the cargo can be loaded and unloaded quickly. Engines are diesel, with a cruising speed of perhaps 15 or 16 knots.

Bulk carriers come in a number of different classes (sizes). Coal and iron ore are often shipped in vessels of about 100 000 dwt, and it has been forecast that 1000 bulk coal carriers of over 100 000 dwt each will be required by the end of the century. Bulk carriers are becoming increasingly important.

Designed for inland travel

Between 25 000 and 28 000 dwt is the maximum size of bulk carrier that can pass along the St Lawrence Seaway and hence reach the Great Lakes and the ports of the American mid-west. The Panamax class is between 50 000 and 60 000 dwt; these are the largest vessels that can be accommodated in the Panama Canal.

Resolution Bay, *which runs on a regular service between Europe, Australia and New Zealand, passing through a lock on the Panama Canal.*

CONTAINER SHIPS

The essence of container transportation, and the reason why it has developed so successfully and so quickly in recent years, is its extreme simplicity and adaptability. A container is nothing more than a large box into which virtually any kind of goods can be packed, and a container ship is simply a large vessel designed to carry as many containers as possible. Furthermore, containers are not only conveniently transported on ships; the same container can equally well be loaded on to a lorry or a railway flat car, without its contents having to be handled at all.

What happens in container transportation is as follows. A factory manufacturing, say, one type of part for a car loads the finished parts into a container. The container is transported by road, rail, or inland waterway to the port, where it is put on board a container vessel. At the end of the voyage, the container is unloaded and transported directly to its final destination, where the car parts are unpacked, ready to be used on the production line. Throughout the journey it is the container itself, rather than its contents, that is handled.

The advantages of container operation are enormous. The containers themselves are easy to handle. They come in standard sizes and so it is far easier, and far quicker, to stow and discharge containers than dry or bulk cargo, which may be an awkward shape and may have to be manhandled. Some docks can load as many as 400 containers in a working day. Because loading and unloading time is shorter, a container vessel can make more voyages than a bulk vessel of an equivalent size, and hence earn more money for her owners, even though her cruising speed

Liverpool Bay *in Hong Kong harbour. This vessel, which can carry 2500 containers, takes 24 days to make its regular run from Europe to the Far East. Container ships like this now serve major ports throughout the world.*

may be no faster. In addition, because the container contents are inaccessible, there is less danger of pilfering, and therefore lower insurance charges.

Perhaps most important of all is the way in which the sea stretch of a journey can be made to link with the parts on land. Because containers can be moved equally easily by road or rail, shipping companies can co-operate with road transport concerns and railway companies to offer their customers a complete service, using whatever form of transport seems best for each stage of the journey. This means that a container vessel need only call at one or two ports in each country, from which its containers can be dispatched by road or rail; a dry cargo vessel might have to call at a far larger number of ports. Often, the land section of a journey is as important as the sea section. Sometimes Japanese goods destined for Europe will travel by sea to the west

coast of the USA, then cross the continent by rail and finish the journey in another container vessel.

Container transportation does have some disadvantages, mainly to do with the cost of establishing the service. Special berths have to be built for container vessels, and the dockside hand-

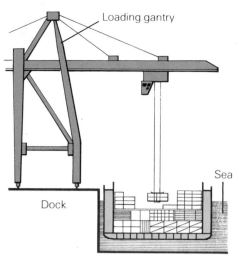

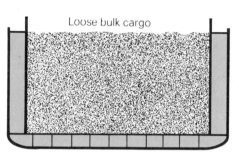

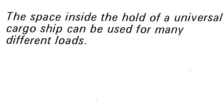
The space inside the hold of a universal cargo ship can be used for many different loads.

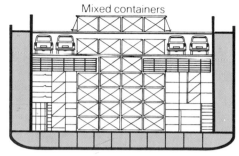

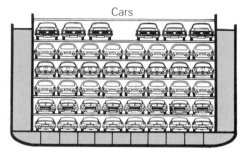

ling equipment is extremely expensive; computers are also used to keep the flow of containers running as smoothly as possible. In addition, a large number of containers is needed if the service is to be run efficiently.

Container transportation is not restricted to companies producing enough goods to fill an entire container. Part loads delivered to an inland container terminal are combined with other part loads of similar goods for the same destination to fill a complete container.

Equipment

The containers themselves are made, usually from steel or aluminium, in a variety of sizes and designs for various purposes. For example some containers are refrigerated.

On the container vessels themselves, the engine room, bridge and crew accommodation are all placed aft, thus

Left: *Tilbury Docks, now one of London's main ports. Containers are waiting to be loaded on to ships.*

releasing as much space amidships as possible for cargo. The containers are lowered through large hatch covers into the hold. A grid of cell guides divides the hold into a large number of small compartments, or cells, and helps to hold the containers in place. When the hold is full, the hatch covers are closed, and one, sometimes two, layers of containers are stowed on deck, secured to the hatches with steel rods or wires. Container vessels, which do not carry their own lifting gear, are normally equipped with diesel engines; their cruising speed is often 20 knots or more.

Container vessels are built in a number of different sizes; some may carry only 300 containers, others 2500. The first purpose-built container ship went into service in 1964 and regular transatlantic services only began two years after that. Now, however, there are nearly 600 in operation. Regular liner services carrying a wide range of cargoes – consumer goods, steel, liquids, light machinery, powdered materials, fruit, vegetables, meat – are run between most of the world's major ports.

TANKERS

Whereas bulk carriers transport dry goods, tankers, as their name implies, carry liquids. Although the majority of tankers afloat are designed to carry petroleum products, others carry liquid petroleum gas (LPG) or liquid natural gas (LNG); parcel tankers are specially designed to transport chemicals; and there are also combination carriers, designed to transport both liquids and dry goods in bulk.

Oil tankers

Oil tankers are single-deck vessels with the engine room, bridge and crew accommodation situated aft (passengers are never carried on tankers for safety reasons). They are normally equipped with diesel engines; a typical cruising speed is about 16 knots.

Oil can be a very unstable cargo, and unless the tanks are full it may move about a good deal; bad weather in particular may set up a wave-like motion. Therefore, two bulkheads running the length of the vessel divide the hold of an oil tanker into three main tanks called the centretank and the port and starboard wing tanks. Transverse bulkheads subdivide these three tanks into still smaller tanks. Safety is another reason for these subdivisions,

which restrict the amount of oil that will spill into the ocean if a tank is holed. Tankers rarely have double bottoms. An additional safety measure is an empty space called a *cofferdam* which separates the tanks from the rest of the vessel.

There are two main types of oil tanker, *crude carriers* and *products carriers*. Crude carriers take unrefined oil from the oilfields to a refinery. A typical voyage might be from Ras Tanura in Saudi Arabia to the big refineries at Milford Haven in South Wales.

Crude carriers are some of the largest vessels in the world. Almost all of them are more than 100 000 tons deadweight; indeed a standard size is 250 000 dwt. Tankers over 150 000 dwt are known as Very Large Crude Carriers (VLCCs) and those over 350 000 dwt as Ultra Large Crude Carriers (ULCCs). The largest tanker now afloat has a deadweight tonnage of about 550 000. Products carriers, by contrast, are far smaller, usually about 20 000 to 30 000 dwt. They carry up to seven or eight different grades of refined oil from the refinery to smaller distribution centres and individual customers.

Unlike other cargoes, oil is not loaded and unloaded by cranes or derricks but is pumped on and off ship through a complex series of pipes leading to each separate tank. On some VLCCs and ULCCs the pipelines are replaced by a 'free flow' system by means of which the crude oil flows through sluice gates in the bulkheads; this system is only possible when one grade of oil is being carried. To stop the oil becoming cold, and therefore difficult to pump, the tanks are fitted with a steam heating system.

British Patience, *a 250 000-ton oil tanker owned by British Petroleum.*

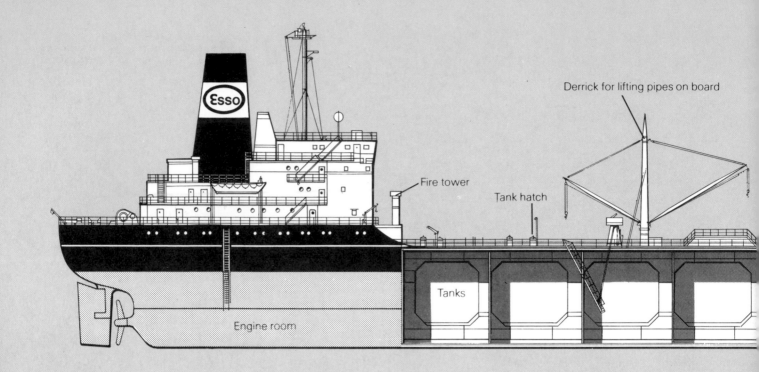

Derrick for lifting pipes on board

Fire tower

Tank hatch

Tanks

Engine room

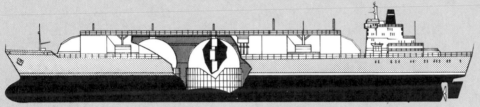

Above: *Liquefied natural gas tankers carry gas at the correct pressure and at a very low temperature. They were introduced to meet the growing demand* *for natural gas as a source of energy. The cut-away diagram shows the storage cylinders.*

In contrast with most other cargo-carrying vessels, oil tankers do not have to come alongside a quay to stow their cargo. Because many oilfields are located offshore, often far out in an ocean (as are, for example, the North Sea oilfields), various kinds of offshore loading points have been developed. Although these differ in detail, basically they all consist of one or more buoys, which the tanker comes alongside. Oil is pumped through the buoys into the tanker direct from the wellhead or from storage tanks; or the vessel moors at a jetty in the usual way.

Other types of tanker

In essentials, LPG tankers are much like oil tankers. The liquified gases travel in hemispherical or rectangular tanks. An empty space filled with an inert gas must be left between the tanks and the hull to prevent leaking gas mixing with oxygen and exploding. In LNG carriers the natural gas has to be transported at an extremely low temperature, between − 160 and − 258°C, in internally insulated tanks.

Parcel tankers are designed to carry a large number of different chemicals, often as many as 40. They also carry other liquid cargoes such as lubricating oils, animal, vegetable and fish oils. The cargo-handling arrangements on a parcels tanker are much more complex than on a conventional oil tanker. Often the products carried may be incompatible with each other, and precautions have to be taken to prevent them mixing; some of them are also danger-ous. Therefore, parcel tankers are divided into a large number of small tanks, all carefully segregated from each other and filled independently. There are also void spaces between the tanks, and in addition the vessel has a double bottom so there is no risk of water mixing with the chemicals.

The chief problem with tanker operations is that, by and large, trade is one way. As a result, every second journey is made in ballast (i.e. without cargo, carrying only sufficient ballast to keep the vessel stable). Combination carriers – of which the two most important are O/O (ore/oil) vessels and OBOs (ore, bulk, oil) – have been developed to carry more than one type of bulk freight and overcome this problem. O/Os always carry either oil or ore, never both at the same time.

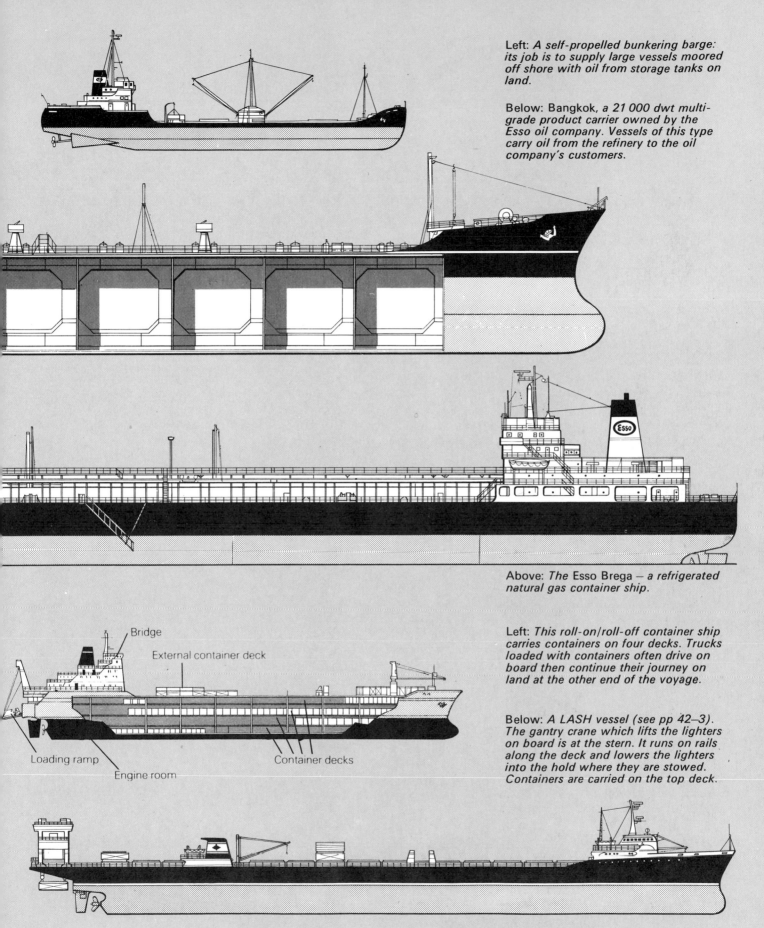

Left: *A self-propelled bunkering barge: its job is to supply large vessels moored off shore with oil from storage tanks on land.*

Below: Bangkok, *a 21 000 dwt multi-grade product carrier owned by the Esso oil company. Vessels of this type carry oil from the refinery to the oil company's customers.*

Above: *The* Esso Brega — *a refrigerated natural gas container ship.*

Bridge

External container deck

Loading ramp

Engine room

Container decks

Left: *This roll-on/roll-off container ship carries containers on four decks. Trucks loaded with containers often drive on board then continue their journey on land at the other end of the voyage.*

Below: *A LASH vessel (see pp 42–3). The gantry crane which lifts the lighters on board is at the stern. It runs on rails along the deck and lowers the lighters into the hold where they are stowed. Containers are carried on the top deck.*

WATER FREIGHT

Coastal craft are small cargo-carrying vessels that operate tramp services along major inland waterways and around a nation's coasts and also undertake short-sea voyages.

Traditional *coasters* have a fo'c'sle, poop, and a bridge between them, and are equipped with their own derricks. These vessels will carry more or less any type of bulk cargo. Other coastal vessels are *colliers*, which only carry coal, and *tankers*, which transport oil from coastal refineries to storage depots, power stations, factories and even to other, larger, ships. On colliers and tankers the engine room and bridge are aft and the vessels have no derricks. Modern coasters have a low bridge aft, giving more space for cargo and enabling them to work inland waterways.

The size of coastal craft varies a great deal. Some may carry as few as 250 tonnes, whereas others may be able to accommodate as many as 2000. The crew is usually about three or four.

The importance of coastal craft diminished as railways and roads came to be used for transporting freight. There are, however, a number of cargoes, mainly bulk loads for which rapid delivery is not essential, that can be transported more cheaply on water than on land, and coastal craft will probably continue to be used for these.

Barge-carrying vessels

Barge-carrying vessels are a connecting link between two different types of water transport: long-distance ocean voyages made by dry cargo vessels or bulk carriers, and the journeys made on inland waterways.

The chief vessel used on inland waterways is the *lighter*, often also called a barge. Modern lighters have a capacity of up to about 1000 tonnes. Some are self-propelling, while others have to be towed or pushed. In harbours that are too shallow for ocean-going vessels, cargo may be unloaded on to or loaded from lighters which carry it between the dockside and the vessel, or take it further inland along waterways. Lighters also serve deep harbours by carrying cargoes between towns and factories along inland rivers and canals and ocean-going vessels.

Barge-carrying vessels are a logical development of this process, designed to make it cheaper and quicker. Like container vessels, they do not carry individual cargoes but rather the units in which those cargoes are stowed. As with containers, the cargo itself is not handled, and what the cargo consists of makes no difference to the handling operations.

The main type of barge-carrying vessel is known as a LASH ship. LASH stands for Lighter Aboard SHip, which explains in essence how the ships function. As on a container vessel, bulkheads divide the hold into a number of separate cells. On the deck is a large travelling gantry crane. The crane, which runs on rails on each side of the deck and extending beyond the stern, lifts the lighters one at a time from the water and lowers them through one of the hatch covers into the hold. They are returned to the water in the same manner. It takes 15–20 minutes to load or unload one lighter. Vertical barge guides in the holds help to keep the lighters secure during the voyage.

Some LASH vessels also carry lighters on the deck, stacked two high on top of the hatch covers, while others

Acadia Forest

A typical LASH service is the one operated by the first LASH ship built, the *Acadia Forest*, which carried cargoes of raw materials for the paper industry from the USA to Europe. The products of paper mills along the Mississippi and Arkansas rivers and the Gulf Intracoastal Waterway were stowed in lighters, which then joined their mother-ship at New Orleans. The *Acadia Forest* crossed the Atlantic, calling first at London and then at Rotterdam, where lighters were unloaded, for final delivery to factories located along the rivers Thames, Medway and Rhine.

Acadia Forest *moving downstream helped by two tugs. Note the gantry crane at the stern with lighters next to it.*

can also carry containers, liquids in tanks, lengths of steel and other cargoes. The number of barges that can be accommodated varies from 60 to 89. Total deadweight tonnage is 41 000 to 43 000 tons. The barges themselves are 18.7 metres long and 9.5 metres wide and have a deadweight tonnage of 320 to 370.

On the mother ship, the crew accommodation and bridge are placed forward and the engine room semi-aft.

LASH ships are powered by diesel engines, often with a cruising speed of approximately 19 knots.

The first LASH vessel went into service in 1969, and in 1980 there were 24 in operation all over the world. A large variety of routes is worked, many connecting ports on the west, Gulf and east coasts of the USA with Europe, the Mediterranean and the Far East. Sheerness in Kent is one of the central points for LASH ships in northern Europe.

Above: *A barge-carrying vessel from the United States about to hoist a lighter on board.*

The chief problems with LASH ships are that they are expensive to build and that the gantry crane does not always work very well. In addition their very size means that quite extensive traffic is necessary to make the service profitable. Therefore other versions of LASH have also been developed.

BARGE-CARRIERS

Another important type of barge-carrying system is known as SEABEE. The SEABEE mother ship is 267 metres long and 32.3 metres wide; her cruising speed is 20 knots. She can accommodate 38 SEABEE barges, each of which is 29.7 metres long and 10.7 metres wide and is 840 dwt. Each barge is the same width and half as long as the 'jumbo' barges used on American inland waterways. This means that the SEABEE barges can be accommodated in tows on rivers such as the Mississippi (*see page 55*).

The SEABEE barges are floated two at a time on to a submersible elevator at the stern of the mother ship which lifts them to one of three decks. An electrically-operated transporter on rails then moves the barges into position two abreast. Loading or unloading time is 12 hours, 10 times as fast as to load a dry cargo vessel of the equivalent size.

The SEABEE mother ship can also carry 160 twelve-metre containers stowed on top of the barges on the upper deck. Alternatively the upper deck can be entirely filled with several hundred containers, although when this is done the ship has to go alongside to load and unload. The mother ships are extremely versatile and can easily be converted to roll-on/roll-off operation or to transport three-storey buildings, large road-building and construction equipment and so on.

Three SEABEE mother vessels are currently in operation, providing regular services between the Gulf ports of the USA and Europe.

One of the newest barge-carrying vessels is the BACO-LINER (BACO stands for BArge/COntainer), the first

Right: *SEABEE in action.* Top: *A barge being pushed into place on the submersible elevator on the mother ship.* Centre: *The elevator in operation (only one barge is being lifted instead of the normal two).* Bottom: *The mother ship at sea, with a load of containers on the top deck. The barges are inside.*

44

of which came into service in 1979. The vessel functions on the float-on/float-off principle (like a floating dry dock – *see page 25*) and can accommodate 12 BACO barges or four LASH barges. In addition, 500 containers can be carried. BACO barges are 24 metres long, 9.5 metres wide and have a deadweight tonnage of 800. The mother ships are 204.1 metres long, 28.5 wide and have a remarkably small draught, only 6.7 metres.

The two BACO-LINERS currently being operated have been built for the Europe to West Africa run. Their small draught enables them to serve ports such as Warri, in Nigeria, that are too shallow for conventional vessels. The BACO barges are planned to travel inland on rivers such as the Niger and the Senegal.

Also introduced in 1979 was a Russian version of the SEABEE named the *Julius Fuchik*. These vessels (the first has already been joined by a sister-ship) carry 26 DANUBE barges, which at 38.2 metres long and 11.0 metres wide, with a deadweight tonnage of 1100, are rather larger than the SEA-BEE equivalents. The *Julius Fuchik* is planned to operate between the Black Sea ports of the eastern bloc and India, Pakistan and the Far East, but when the Main–Danube canal (*see page 51*) has been completed they will probably also be seen in western European waters.

Although there are many different systems, barge-carrying vessels only play a small part in world shipping. In 1978 there were just 29 mother vessels in existence with a total gross tonnage of 773 000, a tiny proportion of the world's fleet and of its total tonnage. None the less, the flexibility that they provide, and the fact that new systems continue to be developed, suggests that their importance will continue to increase.

Ocean tug-barge systems

Tug-barge systems are used extensively in the coastal waters of the USA. The barges are either towed or pushed.

Towing is quite difficult, especially in rough weather, and tends to be slower than pushing. There are two main methods of pushing barges. In one, the barges and the tug pushing them are only loosely connected and move in the water independently. In the second, they are joined to form an integral unit which then behaves like a conventional ship. In the former system the tug that does the pushing can be used for other work, whereas the tug part of the integral unit cannot operate alone. The disadvantage of the former is that it cannot sail in rough weather.

About half of all the cargo delivered to Alaska now travels by means of ocean tug-barges, and one company takes only 4.5 days for the voyage from Seattle. Ocean tug-barges are also used on the Great Lakes and in the Gulf of Mexico. In Europe, however, only one regular service is in operation, between Marseilles, in the south of France, and Yanubu, in Saudi Arabia.

Below: *An oil-carrying barge being pushed up the Hudson river in New York State.*

A RETURN TO SAIL

For thousands of years, wind was the only source of power for seamen, but that changed in the 19th century. The first commercially successful steamboat went into service in 1807. In the 1840s and 1850s, the screw propeller was introduced and ships began to be built of iron rather than wood. By the turn of the century, the change was virtually complete, and the steam reciprocating engine was already being replaced by the steam turbine, itself soon to be joined by the marine diesel.

The new ships were far more reliable

Below: *In 1981 a sail-assisted jack-up rig was installed in the North Sea to carry out test drillings. Two sails on the forward leg saved four days on the Atlantic crossing from Galveston, Texas.* Right: *The* Shin Aitoku Maru, *a Japanese sail-assisted tanker, perhaps the shape of things to come on the oceans.*

vessels: except in the worst weather, they kept to a fixed timetable. The fuel they used – coal at first, oil later – was cheap and plentiful. And the crew required was much smaller.

Now, however, there are experimental plans to revive sailing ships on certain types of route for certain cargoes. The main reason for this is economic: oil has become expensive, and shipowners want to reduce costs. The sails will be furled and set mechanically, computers will adjust the rigging according to the weather, and information on future weather conditions from communications satellites will enable the most efficient route to be planned. In consequence, a small crew will be sufficient.

One such sailing vessel has been built in Japan, and there are research programmes in the GDR and USSR. The *Shin Aitoku Maru*, a 680-tonne sail-assisted tanker, was launched in August 1980. Equipped with two sets of sail, each about 12 metres high and 8 metres broad when spread, and a 1600-bhp auxiliary diesel engine, she cost just under £1 million, about 15% more than a conventional coastal tanker that size. However, her makers claim that fuel bills will be 50% lower, so she will repay her additional construction costs in two or three years.

The two forms of propulsion in a sail-assisted tanker will complement one another. Experiments have shown that a vessel using three sets of sails as well as an engine in a 36-kph wind can travel 1.3 to 1.7 times faster than with an engine alone. In difficult conditions the sails will not be used.

Other ideas include the 17 000-tonne German *Dynaschiff*, which, with six masts and a total of 9600 square metres of sail, could exceed 20 knots; a British Sailiner, a traditional tall ship with auxiliary engine power, which could complete a trip from Great Britain to Melbourne via the Cape of Good Hope and back in 104 days (the current time through the Suez Canal for a conventionally-powered vessel is 82 days); wind turbines, which would drive propellers and could operate into the wind; and airborne sails or kites 300 metres above the ship at the end of a long cable.

A return to coal-burning vessels is also very likely – coal is now one third cheaper than oil, and reserves are about four times as great. A new coal-handling system, in which the boilers are automatically supplied by a pipeline leading from the bunkers, dispels the need for a vast crew. Four 75 000-tonne coal-burning bulk carriers are currently under construction.

INLAND WATERWAYS

Above: *The Thames in the 19th century. Before the railways, water was used for freight and passenger transport.*

There are three main types of inland waterway: rivers, canalized rivers and canals.

Rivers are one of the oldest means of transport known to man. There are two main difficulties with river transport, however. Rivers are not always navigable along their entire length; and they do not always go where people want to travel.

The solution to the first of these problems was the canalized river, to the second the canal. A canalized river is a natural river made deeper by being dredged (dredging involves removing earth from the river bed); often locks (*see page 52*) may also be constructed, to overcome problems of the change of level, and the banks will be strengthened to enable them to stand up to the disturbance created by passing vessels. Whereas canalized rivers follow the course of the original river (although bends are sometimes straightened), a canal, by contrast, is a completely artificial waterway that can, within reason, be routed wherever required.

Development of inland waterways

Although a number of canals were built earlier, and of course navigable rivers were used, the present inland waterways by and large date from the late 18th century and the 19th century. Britain was the first country to start building on a large scale, between about 1760 and 1830. In mainland Europe, and also in the USA, canal-building started later and continued longer.

This difference in timing has much to do with the substantial differences between the British and other European inland waterway networks. Britain has relatively few long navigable rivers, and much of the country, especially the north and midlands, where the industrial revolution started, has no direct water routes to the coast. Therefore, a large number of canals were built to bring raw materials to the new factories and take their finished goods away. By today's standards, these canals are narrow, and the locks are very small. The barges that used them – called, for obvious reasons, narrow boats – were 2.13 metres wide and could only carry 25 tonnes. There is very little commercial traffic on the vast majority of these canals nowadays, although they are popular among holidaymakers.

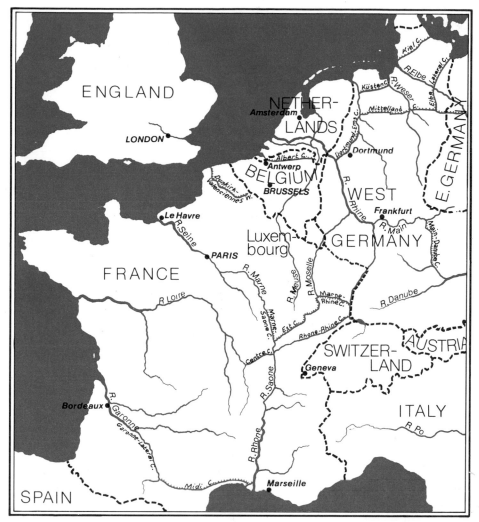

The rest of Europe, by contrast, has a number of large, navigable rivers extending a long way inland, sometimes hundreds of kilometres. The Rhine in Germany and the Netherlands forms the backbone of the network, but also of importance are, in France, the Rhône, Seine and Marne; in Belgium and the Netherlands, the Meuse and Maas (the same river, but with different names in each country); and in Germany, the Main and the Elbe. In consequence, work during the 19th century was concentrated on improving those rivers, to make them more suitable for sizeable vessels, and also on building canals to link them.

In Britain, with the notable exception of the Manchester Ship Canal, opened in 1894, which linked Manchester with the estuary of the River Mersey and the sea, inland waterways were scarcely developed at all after the first railways were built in the 1830s.

In mainland Europe, the network is still being improved even now. Two of the most significant recent developments are the Elbe Lateral Canal in

Left: *The most important inland waterways in western Europe.*

Below: *In their heyday, narrow boats like this carried a wide variety of goods.*

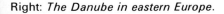
Traffic on the Dortmund-Ems Canal, which leads from the North Sea to the large industrial areas of the Ruhr in Germany.

northern Germany and the Rhine–Main–Danube Canal. The Elbe Lateral Canal, opened in 1976, runs for 115 kilometres between the River Elbe near Lauenburg and the Mittelland Canal near Braunschweig. It provides a direct route between the port of Hamburg and the industrial area around Hanover and Braunschweig and also enables vessels to travel direct via the Mittelland Canal to and from the industrial Ruhr region.

Thus in western Europe inland waterways are thriving and play a significant role alongside roads and railways in transporting freight. In Britain inland waterways, although not completely disused, are not considered a national transport asset.

East–west link

The Rhine–Main–Danube canal is one of the most exciting and ambitious canal works planned for some time. Its aim is to provide a 3500-kilometre direct water link for craft of up to 1350 tonnes between the North Sea and the Black Sea, straight across the heart of western and eastern Europe, serving the Netherlands, the Federal Republic of Germany, Austria, Czechoslovakia, Hungary, Yugoslavia, Romania, Bulgaria and the Soviet Union directly, and even more countries indirectly. The route will follow the Rivers Rhine and Main in the west and the Danube in the east. The new work that has to be undertaken is a 170-kilometre canal from Bamberg to Kelheim in Germany and substantial improvements to the Danube between Kelheim and Regensburg. The 70-kilometre stretch from Bamberg to Nürnberg was opened in 1970, and Nürnberg, several hundred kilometres from the sea, is already an important port. The latest forecast is that work will be completed towards the end of the 1980s. In addition two locks will enable vessels to pass through the Iron Gates – a series of dangerous rapids on the border between Yugoslavia and Romania – quickly and easily.

Right: *The Danube in eastern Europe.*

WATERWAY STRUCTURES

A river is a natural route whose waters descend towards the sea. As long as it is deep enough, vessels will have no difficulty navigating it, and no special engineering structures are needed to help them do so. Bridges and tunnels may have to be built for roads and railways that cross the river, but these do not affect traffic on the river. River banks may have to be protected against erosion, however, and the central channel along which vessels move may have to be enlarged from time to time.

On canals, and to a lesser extent on canalized rivers as well, things are very different. The bed (bottom) and sides have to be kept watertight. Puddled clay was the material originally used to keep the water in, but nowadays a variety of other materials is available, including sheet polythene, concrete, and ash mixed with cement. Often reeds or willows planted on the banks will be sufficient to prevent erosion, but sometimes, especially on relatively narrow canals which carry considerable traffic, the sides have to be protected by steel or concrete piles.

Locks

Since canals are not natural routes, some means has to be found to enable them to change level. This is the function of a lock. A lock is like a step: it enables a vessel to climb or descend from one level stretch of water to another. (The level stretches of water between locks are known as *pounds*.) Modern locks can usually accommodate several vessels at a time. They have fixed walls, and gates at each end that can be opened to admit vessels and to allow them to leave.

Locks work in the following way. A vessel travelling upstream enters the

Right: A barge passing through a lock. On modern canals, locks can accommodate large vessels.

lock. The gates are closed behind it and water is let into the lock either through sluices in the lock gates or through channels set in the lock walls. The level of the water in the lock gradually rises until it reaches that of the canal on the upstream side of the lock, whereupon the lock gates on that side are opened and the vessel can continue its journey. If a barge is travelling downstream, exactly the same thing happens, except that the lock lowers the vessel rather than lifting it.

Things are rather more complicated if a vessel reaches a lock and finds the chamber empty, if it is travelling downstream, or full, if it is travelling upstream. In these cases it has to wait while the chamber is filled or emptied. If there is a water shortage it may even have to wait until a vessel travelling in the other way passes through the lock.

On many British and French canals the locks are very narrow and can only accommodate one narrow boat at a time. These locks are usually worked by hand. Furthermore their rise – that is, the amount by which they raise or lower a vessel – is small, usually between 1 and 5 metres. On modern,

commercial waterways locks are much larger and have room for several barges at a time. The rise on modern locks is also much greater. On the Mississippi system in the USA, for instance, one lock has a rise of 29 metres, and there are many of over 10 metres. Naturally enough, the greater the rise of an individual lock, the fewer locks there need be and hence the time spent passing through them is reduced. Modern locks are worked by hydraulic, mechanical or electric power, which also saves time.

Most modern locks have reservoirs to one side of the lock chamber. When the chamber is being emptied, water is let into them, and, conversely, water is drawn from them to fill the chamber. This system can save up to about 60% of the water needed to fill the lock.

Where a canal rises and falls steeply, there may be a group of locks placed close together. A group of locks separated by very short pounds, perhaps as little as 100 metres long, is known as a *flight*. A *staircase* is an inter-connected group of locks, in which the front gates of the first lock are also the rear gates of the second, and so on.

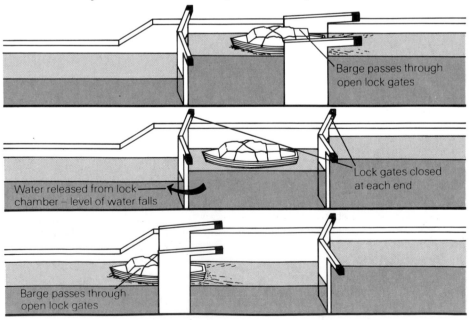

Barge passes through open lock gates

Lock gates closed at each end

Water released from lock chamber – level of water falls

Barge passes through open lock gates

Maritime canals

There are three important maritime canals in the world – the Suez, Panama and Kiel Canals. Although, like conventional inland canals, they are artificial water routes, they serve a very different purpose: in effect they provide maritime short cuts across relatively narrow stretches of land, where otherwise much longer sea journeys would be necessary.

The Kiel Canal runs for 95 kilometres from Brunsbüttel on the North Sea to Haltenau on the Gulf of Kiel on the Baltic, reducing the journey between the two seas – sometimes a very dangerous passage – by several hundred kilometres. Locks at each end of the canal control access into it.

Impressive as the Kiel Canal is, its engineering is overshadowed by that of the Suez and Panama Canals. The Suez Canal links the Red Sea and the Mediterranean, the Panama the Atlantic and Pacific Oceans, and both cut thousands of kilometres off the alternative sea routes, around the Cape of Good Hope and Cape Horn respectively. The Suez Canal, which is 169 kilometres long, has no locks, unlike the 85-kilometre Panama Canal. Both canals cannot accommodate the largest vessels now being constructed, and ship-designers working on vessels likely to use either route must try to fit in as much cargo as possible within the maximum dimensions permitted.

Below: *Ships waiting to enter a lock on the Kiel Canal in northern Germany.*

Lifts and inclined planes

In a number of cases the rise required is too great to be achieved by even a series of locks, or so many would be needed that traffic would be delayed unduly. To overcome this problem, canal engineers can either construct a vertical lift or an inclined plane. Both lifts and inclined planes are found on the earliest canals; in principle their modern counterparts differ little in the way they function, although they are of course designed to take much larger vessels.

A vertical lift raises or lowers a barge in a vertical plane: that is, at the end of the lift the barge is exactly above or below the point at which the lift began. The barge enters a steel tank filled with water, known as a *caisson*. The end of the caisson is then sealed off, and the caisson is either raised to the higher level or lowered to the lower one, whereupon the vessel leaves it and continues its journey. The twin vertical barge lifts at Lüneburg on the Elbe Lateral Canal in Germany are the largest lifts in the world, rising and falling no less than 38 metres.

An inclined plane raises vessels not only vertically but also in a horizontal plane. Thus a vessel being raised ends up not only above where it started but also some way forward. The inclined plane at Ronquières on the Charleroi–Brussels Canal in Belgium has two tanks filled with water, positioned at opposite ends of the plane. The tanks, each of which is fitted with no less than 236 wheels, can each accommodate one 1350-tonne barge or four 300-tonners. Two tracks, one for each tank, link the opposite ends of the plane. When both tanks are loaded, one begins to ascend, while the other starts to descend. The balancing principle is the same as that on a funicular railway (*see page 74*).

The Ronquières plane raises or lowers vessels 68 metres on a gradient of about 1 in 21. The plane replaced no less than 17 locks and greatly reduces travelling time over this stretch of the canal. There are two other inclined planes still in use in Europe – in France and the USSR.

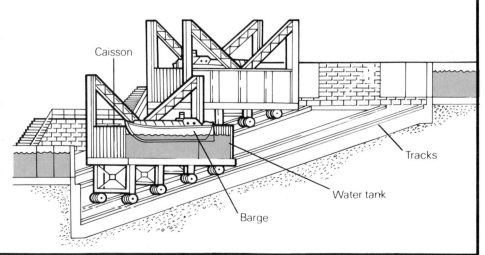

Caisson

Tracks

Water tank

Barge

WATERWAY NETWORKS

In Britain, most of the navigable waterways used by commercial craft are near the coast along rivers such as the Thames, Trent, Severn, Colne and Wear and on canals such as the Aire & Calder Navigation, the Manchester Ship Canal and the Sheffield & South Yorkshire Navigation. Many of these are also used by coastal craft. Inland, canals are only used by pleasure craft, with very rare exceptions.

In Germany, the Netherlands and Belgium, by contrast, there is a substantial network of major inland waterways. In 1976, 25% of all bulk freight was carried on the 4408 kilometres of waterways in Germany; 64% on the 4803 kilometres in the Netherlands; and 23% on the 1535 kilometres in Belgium. The equivalent figure for Britain is less than 3%. France has some modernized waterways, especially in the north and east, and a number of old, small canals rather like those in Britain. In 1976, 8% of all bulk freight was carried on the 6931 kilometres of waterways in France.

In Italy there are a number of waterways based on the River Po, many of which have been included in a modernization programme. Because of the Alps, the Italian system is not linked with that of any other country. Scandinavia has two major canals: the Saimaa in south-east Finland; and the Göta, which runs across Sweden from the east coast to the west, linking Stockholm with Gothenburg.

There are also a number of important inland waterways in eastern Europe. Although it reaches the sea in the Federal Republic, for much of the time the River Elbe runs through the German Democratic Republic (East Germany), reaching Magdeburg and Dresden. Other important rivers are the Vltava, a tributary of the Elbe, in Czechoslovakia, and the Oder, whose

Below: *A barge on the Mississippi River. The red light is the vessel's starboard running light.*

source is in Czechoslovakia but which later forms the border between Poland and the German Democratic Republic.

The Soviet Union has a number of great rivers which are important transport routes – among them the Dnepr, Dvina, Don, Vistula and Volga – and these are connected by canals. There are two routes between the Baltic and the Black Sea, and a third will become available when the Rhine–Main–Danube Canal is opened. The Caspian Sea can also be reached from the Baltic. Among other inland waterways in the USSR is the 225-kilometre White Sea Canal, which links Leningrad and Belomorskiy on the White Sea, reducing the sea journey between Leningrad and Archangel by 4000 kilometres. New canal-building in the USSR is mostly taking place in the Asian territories in the east of the country.

Waterways in North America

The USA has an extensive network of inland waterways, most of which are navigable rivers rather than canals. The biggest part of the system is based on the River Mississippi, which is navigable for 1800 kilometres from Minneapolis south through the heart of the mid-west and the south to the Gulf of Mexico at New Orleans. Flowing into the Mississippi are numerous tributaries, most important among them the Rivers Arkansas, Tennessee, Ohio and Missouri, bringing cities as distant as Tulsa, to the west, Chicago and Milwaukee on Lake Michigan, and Pittsburgh in the north-east into direct contact with ocean-going vessels at Gulf ports. The Mississippi system carries all kinds of raw materials and manufactured goods on the first stage of their journey to customers elsewhere in the USA or overseas and is vital to the economic prosperity of the mid-West.

The St Lawrence Seaway, completed in 1959, enables ocean-going vessels with a capacity of up to about 27 000 tons to reach the Great Lakes

Neither river nor canal

Two other important waterways in the USA are the Gulf Intracoastal Waterway and the Atlantic Intracoastal Waterway. These routes are neither rivers nor, strictly speaking, canals, since they run entirely at sea level. The Gulf Intracoastal Waterway runs for 1600 kilometres from Brownsville, Texas, around the shore of the Gulf of Mexico to Apalachee Bay, Florida, providing a protected channel sheltered by barrier beaches and offshore islands. It crosses a large number of river estuaries (including that of the Mississippi) which give access to ports a short way inland and it is used a great deal by barge traffic.

The Atlantic Intracoastal Waterway follows the east coast from Boston to Key West, some 2600 kilometres, and provides a similar channel through bays and sounds and some stretches of open sea. It is used by both commercial and pleasure traffic. There were once plans to link the two waterways by means of a canal across Florida, but this has not been built.

Below: *The port at Daytona Beach, Florida, used by vessels travelling across the Atlantic and along the Atlantic Intracoastal Waterway.*

and thus makes it possible for some of Canada and the USA's most important manufacturing and agricultural centres to trade directly with overseas customers. Among the cargoes carried are grain, cars, steel products and meat – all for export – and iron ore is brought from Quebec and Labrador in eastern Canada to the steel mills of the mid-West. The Illinois Waterway, which runs from Milwaukee and Chicago to join the upper Mississippi at St Louis, links the Great Lakes with the network of waterways based on the Mississippi, and both systems are connected to New York and the Atlantic coast via the New York State Barge Canal and the Hudson River.

Two major waterways on the west coast of the USA are not linked with any other part of the national system. These are the Sacramento Deepwater Ship Canal and, further north, the Columbia River, which is navigable for over 800 kilometres from the Pacific to Lewiston, Idaho.

Excluding traffic on the Great Lakes, some 10% of internal freight movements in the USA take place on waterways.

CANAL CRAFT

Flat-bottomed, straight-sided barges are the craft mainly used for commercial operations on inland waterways. The amount of cargo they carry depends on the size of the waterway. A capacity of 1350 tonnes is standard on many waterways in western Europe. On major rivers such as the Rhine and, in the USA, on the Mississippi and some of her tributaries, greater capacities, of up to about 3000 tonnes, can be accommodated. On many of those British waterways that are used by commercial traffic, the maximum may be only a few hundred tonnes.

Barges may be either powered or unpowered. Powered barges have their own engine, while unpowered and unmanned barges or lighters (sometimes also known as dumb barges) do not and must either be towed or pushed. Powered barges either travel independently or, as often happens, may tow one or more dumb barges.

A frequent way of moving dumb barges is to group them together under the control of a tug. There are two ways in which this can happen. The tug may tow a line of dumb barges strung out behind it. Alternatively, the dumb barges may be lashed together to each side of, and in front of, the tug, which then pushes them through the water. This is known as a *push-tow*, a somewhat confusing term since the dumb barges are not towed at all but pushed; the tug is called a *push-tug*. Push-tugs, which are powered by diesel engines, are equipped with radar and also have crew accommodation so that they can remain in operation day and night. Dumb barges can only be used on navigable and canalized rivers.

Push-tows are frequently seen on major inland waterways in both Europe and the USA, since they are a cheap way of moving substantial amounts of cargo, and a relatively small crew is required. In Europe push-tows usually consist of six dumb barges. In the USA, however, things are done on a much larger scale, and on the Mississippi, for example, as many as 40 dumb barges may be assembled, with a total capacity of as much as 60 000 tonnes.

Once their mother ship has arrived at her destination, the lighters carried

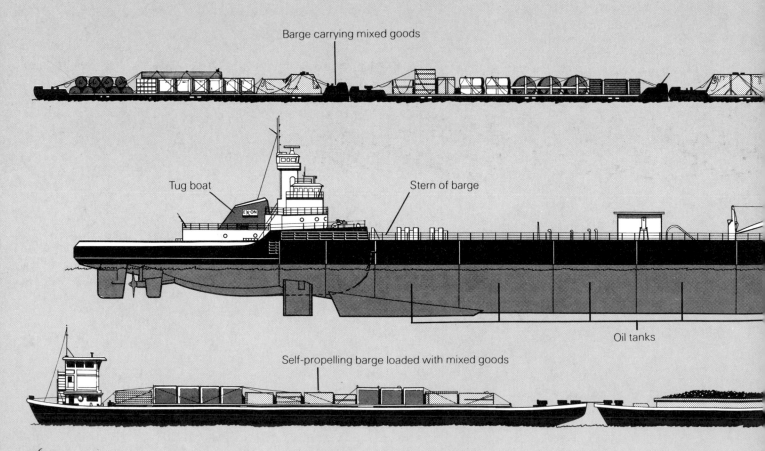

Barge carrying mixed goods

Tug boat

Stern of barge

Oil tanks

Self-propelling barge loaded with mixed goods

aboard barge-carrying vessels such as
LASH and SEABEE (*see pages 43–4*)
are transferred to push-tows to be taken
to their destinations further inland.

Transport on inland waterways is
cheap but relatively slow. In consequence, bulk cargoes such as coal, coke,
steel materials and products, refuse,
aggregates, grain, cement, fertilizers
and chemicals are most frequently
carried. The barges used for such
commodities have large hatch covers to
make loading and unloading easy and
in many respects are inland waterways'
versions of the much larger ocean-
going bulk carriers. Petroleum products
are also carried in tanker-barges, and
on the Rhine a number of companies
also offer regular services for containers,
each dumb barge carrying ninety 6-
metre containers. Inland waterways are
also especially suitable for the transportation of outsize loads such as trans-
formers, turbines and so on.

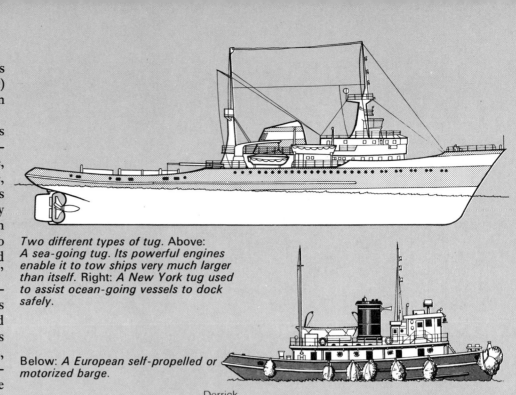

Two different types of tug. Above:
*A sea-going tug. Its powerful engines
enable it to tow ships very much larger
than itself.* Right: *A New York tug used
to assist ocean-going vessels to dock
safely.*

Below: *A European self-propelled or
motorized barge.*

Derrick

Hatch

Push boat

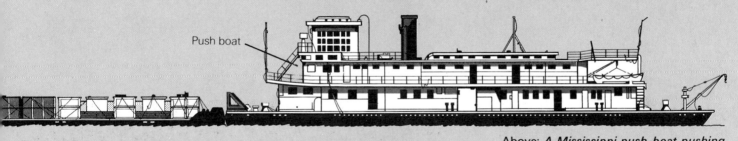

*Above: A Mississippi push-boat pushing
a string of barges. Goods made in the
mid-West travel this way to the
southern ports.*

Left: The tug Exon Sunshine State,
*operating in the Gulf of Mexico. Her
prow fits into a notch in the stern of the
barge she pushes.*

*Below: A tug pulling a dumb barge and
a self-propelling barge on the Rhine.*

Dumb barge loaded with coal

Tow rope

Tug

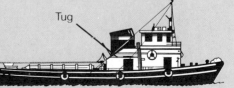

HOVERCRAFT

The main problem with conventional vessels is that high speeds are difficult to achieve. Because most of a ship's hull is under water, much of the power created by its engines goes towards overcoming the resistance of the sea and the waves – that is, towards pushing the vessel through the water. Only a small proportion goes towards increasing the vessel's speed. As a result, ships move fairly slowly, certainly in contrast with trains, planes and cars. Only a few vessels travel at more than about 30 knots. Other than in exceptional circumstances, higher speeds are uneconomic, because of the large engines needed and the large amounts of fuel they require.

Two types of vessel – hovercraft and hydrofoils – developed relatively recently, overcome this problem in a spectacular way. In both, the hull is lifted clear of the water. As a result, most of the power produced by the engines can be used to develop high speeds, much faster than those possible on a conventional ship.

The proper name for a hovercraft, *Air Cushion Vehicle* (ACV), describes the craft exactly. The hull sits on a large inflatable cushion of air which skims over the surface of the water (or land). Because the vessel moves on the water, not through it, high speeds can be reached. The fastest hovercraft so far built can travel at 90 knots, and the normal cruising speed of the latest models used commercially is 60 knots.

Most hovercraft are equipped with gas turbine engines (*see page 10*). Propulsion is provided by four air propellers, like those used on aircraft. These are mounted on swivelling pylons on the roof of the craft. Because they are variable-pitch (*see page 9*) they can be used to help to steer the hovercraft and also to propel it backwards.

Hovercraft are not easy to steer, mainly because there is so little grip between the craft and the surface over which it is moving. In addition to the propellers, there are aircraft-type rudders on the tail of the craft. The propellers on one side can also be given more thrust than those on the other, which helps the craft to turn.

The air cushion – known as the *plenum chamber* – is kept inflated by fans powered by the gas turbine engines. Air is blown in through a *momentum curtain*. This consists of a series of jets so angled as to prevent air already in the plenum chamber escaping. The air cushion is surrounded by a flexible skirt made of several hundred plastic or rubber fingers. This helps to trap air and also makes a much deeper cushion possible, which in turn means that the craft can travel through high waves, over sand banks and so on. When the craft is turning, the flow of air through the jets on the inside of the turn – that is, the jets on the left side of the craft if it is turning left – is reduced. As a result the craft sinks slightly on that side and banks rather like an aircraft.

In an emergency, the craft can be stopped very quickly – within about 160 metres – by cutting out the fans and reversing the pitch of the propellers. The air cushion provides buoyancy and so the craft will not sink.

The great advantage of ACVs is that they can travel on both land and sea and can move from one surface to the other without even having to slow down. The craft simply drives from the sea straight on to the beach. Loading and unloading

Opposite: *Hovercraft like this can take only 30 minutes to cross the Channel but cannot operate in bad weather.*

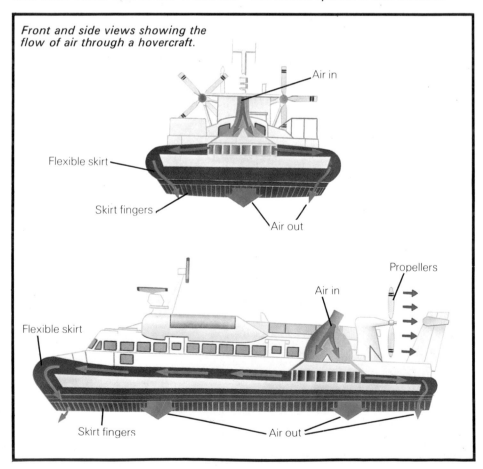

Front and side views showing the flow of air through a hovercraft.

Air in

Flexible skirt

Skirt fingers

Air out

Propellers

Air in

Flexible skirt

Skirt fingers

Air out

58

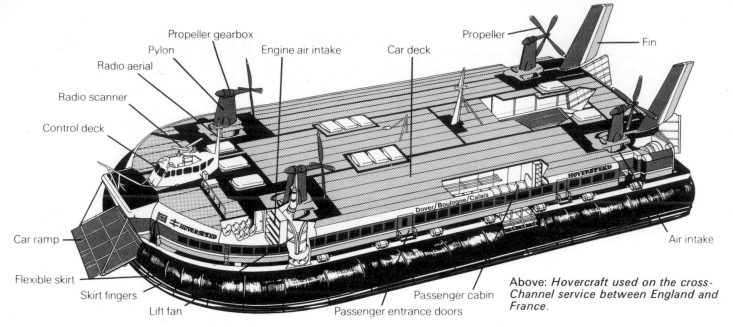

Propeller gearbox
Pylon
Radio aerial
Radio scanner
Control deck
Engine air intake
Car deck
Propeller
Fin
Car ramp
Flexible skirt
Skirt fingers
Lift fan
Passenger entrance doors
Passenger cabin
Air intake

Dover/Boulogne/Calais

HOVERSPEED

Above: *Hovercraft used on the cross-Channel service between England and France.*

does not have to take place at a dock-side. A large concrete apron is all that is necessary.

Hovercraft have several disadvantages. Although they can travel on reasonably flat land as well as on water, they cannot cross rocky ground or wide ditches nor climb steep hills. Since they overturn easily, they also cannot be used when waves are more than about 3 metres high. They also use large amounts of fuel, and in fact at low speeds conventional ships are cheaper to run. To make a profit, they have to be kept in use for as much of the time as possible, and turn-round time between trips has to be reduced to the absolute minimum. Perhaps the worst thing as far as passengers are concerned is that the ride is extremely noisy and bumpy.

Hovercraft services

A number of hovercraft are used to provide ferry services on popular routes, such as the crossing between England and France. The most recent craft to enter service there can carry 416 passengers and 55 cars and take only 35 minutes for the 35-kilometre trip. These craft are equipped with two radar systems. One has a range of 16 kilometres, the other, used for identifying fishing vessels, sand banks and so on, of 1.2 kilometres. They also have a Decca Navigator (which is a sophisticated form of radio-direction finding) and log. On the whole, however, hydrofoils are more successful in providing this kind of ferry service.

The value of hovercraft lies in their versatility. They can travel on most kinds of terrain, whether land or water. They are used in the Arctic regions of Alaska, Canada and the USSR to cross ice in winter and the boggy tundra that replaces it in summer. They are used high in the Andes on Lake Titicaca, where reeds impede the progress of conventional vessels. One hovercraft even took explorers to the headwaters of the Andes.

Hovercraft also have a large number of non-commercial uses. Their role in military operations is becoming increasingly important, and a large number of armies are equipped with them.

An important advance in hovercraft design and technology was made in May 1981 when a new model was unveiled to the public. The craft, known as the AP1-88, is much cheaper to build

Above: *This BH.7 fast attack hovercraft is in service with the British navy.*

Opposite: *Hovercraft loading at Calais hoverport.*

Right: *The API-88.*

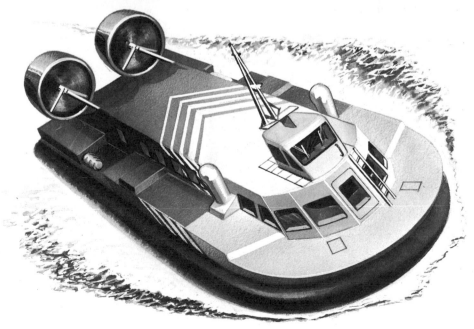

and to operate than its predecessors and will also be much quieter. It will be equipped with two marine diesel engines and propulsion will be by means of two shrouded propellers placed at the aft end and powered by two additional marine diesels. Rudders and bow thrusters (*see page 12*) will steer the craft. The AP1-88 will not only be used to provide passenger services (its seating capacity is 80); it can also be used for search and rescue operations, geographical surveying, anti-smuggling operations, firefighting, providing flood relief and in a variety of military roles.

HYDROFOILS

The hull of a hydrofoil is lifted clear of the water not by a cushion of air, as happens with a hovercraft, but by a number of foils or fins supported on struts. When it is stationary or moving very slowly, the craft floats and the struts and foils are retracted. As it increases speed, the foils raise it out of the water and support it just above the surface. The foils function in the same way as aircraft wings. Water passing over the top, curved, surface of the foil has to travel further than the water passing over the bottom surface, which is flat. Because it travels further it also travels faster. As a result pressure on the top surface of the foil decreases, and this creates the 'lift' necessary to keep the craft out of the water.

If the sea were flat and motionless all the time, it would be simple to keep the hull of the hydrofoil stable. Because it is not, some way has to be found of maintaining a constant amount of lift. This involves controlling the foils very precisely. There are two main types of foil, each operating in a different way.

Hydrofoil with surface-piercing foils.

As you would expect from the name, *surface-piercing foils* partially emerge from the water. When the craft is travelling slowly, a great deal of lift is needed to make the foils emerge and so they remain completely submerged. As its speed increases, the amount of lift created increases, and so the foils emerge from the water. When a wave breaks over the foils, more lift is created, so restoring the hull to its original position. The same thing happens when the craft rolls to one side. There are a number of different designs for surface-piercing foils; a V-shape is the most common.

Although very efficient, surface-piercing foils give a bumpy ride and cannot be used in seas higher than 3 metres. As a result hydrofoils equipped with them are chiefly employed on services in inland or coastal waters.

Unlike surface-piercing foils, which are fixed, the angle of *fully-submerged foils* can be altered. Because the foils remain beneath the water all the time, they cannot respond to the action of the waves in the same way as the surface-piercing foils. Instead, they are controlled by a series of sophisticated electronic devices which continually adjust the foils so that the hull of the craft remains stable. Hydraulic rams alter the angle of the foils, and the rams themselves are controlled by gyroscopes – which sense the craft's pitch, roll, and heave – and by a sonic device which measures the height of the waves.

Hydrofoil equipped with surface-piercing foils in operation off Guernsey in the Channel Islands.

Hydrofoil with fully-submerged foils.

Hydrofoil services

The most modern hydrofoils can accommodate 250 passengers, seated on two decks, and have a cruising speed of about 45 knots. They are equipped with gas turbines, and propulsion is by means of high-pressure water jets. Other less powerful types have marine diesels and conventional propellers.

Hydrofoils are becoming increasingly popular for short-sea journeys and may well come to replace conventional ferries on many services. Their fuel consumption is low and their speed high. The journey from Stavanger to Bergen in Norway, for instance, takes 3.5 hours by hydrofoil, 10 hours by boat. Sometimes, where the distance by water is shorter, they can provide a faster service than trains or buses. At the beginning of the 1980s, hydrofoils were operating in at least 30 countries throughout the world and were carrying some 50 million passengers a year.

Below: *Hydrofoils are replacing ferries for some short-distance services, but they cannot run in rough seas.*

LAND

STEAM POWER

The basic way in which steam locomotives operate has not changed since the first ones were built in the late 1820s. Modern locomotives are much bigger and faster, however, and can carry far greater loads.

The wheels of the locomotives are driven by the energy released when steam is expanded under high pressure. The steam is produced by heating water. The fuel normally used is coal, although wood was common in the USA for most of the 19th century, and more recently oil-fired steam locomotives have been built. The fuel is burnt in the firebox. The flames and hot gases from the fire are then sucked through tubes in the boiler, which is full of water. This heats the water, creating steam which rises into the steam dome at the top of the boiler.

From the steam dome the steam passes through a regulator and enters the locomotive's cylinders. Valves admit steam from the cylinder to the pistons, first on one side, then on the other. The expanding steam pushes the pistons forwards and backwards. The pistons drive connecting and coupling rods and the crank, which in turn

Below: *No. 71 000* Duke of Gloucester, *the last new main-line steam locomotive to enter service in Britain, on the west coast route in 1952. It was withdrawn in 1962 and, after a period abandoned in the scrapyard, is now being reconstructed by the Great Central Steam Trust, at Loughborough in the Midlands.*

Chimney

Smokebox

Steam pipes

Steam dome

Smokebox door handles

71000

DUKE ...ESTER

Buffers

Piston

Leading wheels

Cylinder

Piston valve spindle

Crosshead

drives the wheels, converting the pistons' forwards and backwards movement into a rotary (circular) movement.

The exhaust steam that has passed through the cylinders escapes up the blastpipe, into the chimney and so out into the open air. The smoke from the boiler escapes the same way.

When a locomotive is running at speed, steam does not need to be admitted to the cylinders for the whole of each piston stroke. This is because the pressure of the steam already in the cylinders provides most of the power needed. Usually, steam is only admitted for the entire stroke when the locomotive is starting up.

The power a steam locomotive can develop – that is, the speed at which it can travel and the weight it can pull – depends to a large extent on the pressure of the steam in the cylinders. The first locomotives had tiny boilers, which could only produce steam at low pressure. Gradually, however, bigger boilers were designed and built, making higher pressures possible.

Superheaters were another improvement, introduced at the beginning of the 20th century. After leaving the steam dome, the steam passes through tiny U-shaped pipes within the boiler tubes where it becomes drier and still hotter, often reaching as much as 300–350°C. Because the steam produced by superheaters contains more energy, less steam is needed, and thus fuel and water are saved. Almost all locomotives built after about 1912 had superheaters.

The first locomotives had two cylinders. Later ones were built with three or four. These produce a smoother ride because power is supplied to the wheels almost continuously.

Right: *Cut-away view of a steam locomotive. Steam passes through the cylinders to drive the pistons, which in turn drive the wheels.*

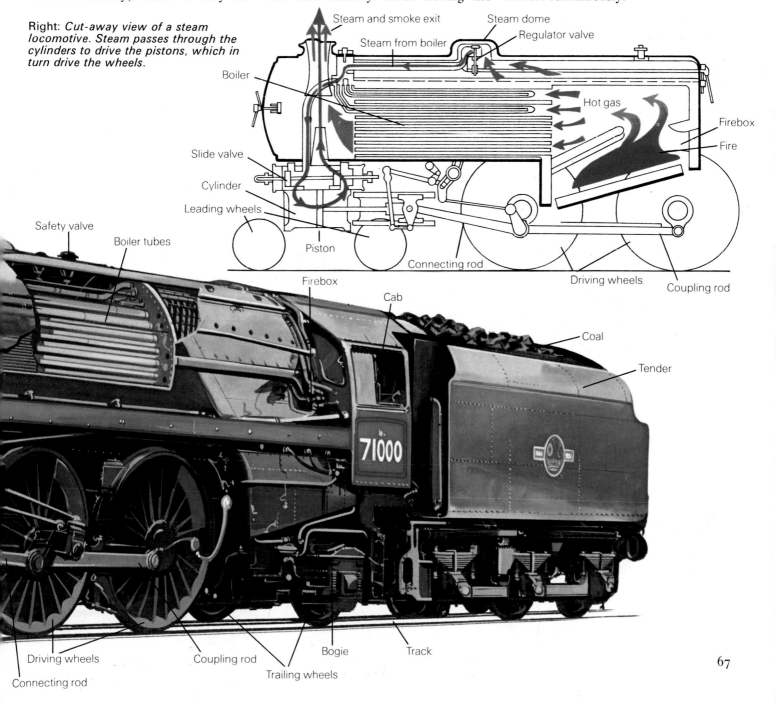

67

Controlling locomotives

Most modern locomotives have three sets of wheels. Only the large centre set, called the *driving wheels*, actually propels the locomotive. The wheels at the front, known as the *leading wheels*, help to guide the locomotive round bends. They are attached to a *bogie*, a frame which swivels as the locomotive changes direction. At the back of the locomotive, the *trailing wheels*, which are also attached to a bogie, help to support the weight of the firebox and boiler. A lip, or *flange*, on the inside rim of each wheel helps to keep them on the track as they go round corners.

Articulated locomotives were designed to pull extremely heavy loads. They have two sets of driving wheels and two sets of cylinders, both of which are powered by one boiler placed between them. The articulated Union

Right: Union Pacific's Big Boy, 1941.

Pacific Big Boys, the largest locomotives ever built, had two sets of eight driving wheels. The front set was mounted on a bogie. The Big Boys were used to pull heavy freight trains through the Rocky Mountains of the USA.

In the English-speaking world, steam locomotives are classified according to the number of wheels they have. Thus the famous British Gresley Pacific locomotives – one of which, *Mallard*, took the world speed record for steam in 1936 – were known as 4–6–2s, because they had six driving wheels and

six carrying wheels (four leading and two trailing). In the rest of Europe the system follows the number of axles (an axle links each pair of wheels, one wheel on each side of the locomotive), and there *Mallard* would have been known as a 2–3–1.

Two people are needed to operate a steam locomotive, a driver and a fireman. The driver watches the line, obeys the signals and operates the brakes and the regulator, which controls the amount of steam admitted to the cylinders, and thus the speed. The fireman's job is to keep the firebox supplied with fuel. This normally involves shovelling the coal in by hand, although some of the largest locomotives have mechanical stokers. Water is automatically supplied to the boiler in a continuous flow from storage tanks.

Coal is stored either on the locomotive itself or in a separate *tender* immediately behind.

0-4-0 T

4-6-4 T

2-6-0 Mogul

4-6-2 Pacific

2-8-0 Consolidation

2-6-2 + 2-6-2 Garratt type

Above: *Common wheel arrangements on steam locomotives. The numbering sequence runs: leading wheels, driving wheels, trailing wheels.*

Below: *The* Mallard's *1938 world steam speed record of over 203 kph (126.5 mph) is still unbeaten.*

TYPES OF POWER

Diesel oil is the fuel used in diesel engines. The power to drive the engine is created when compressed air meets the oil and ignites it.

Most diesel engines work on a four-stroke cycle. On the first stroke, air is let into the cylinder. On the second, the piston compresses the air, making it very hot. On the third, the diesel oil enters the cylinder. As it meets the compressed air, it ignites, and the gases released by the burning oil drive the piston downwards. On the fourth stroke, the exhaust gases are released from the cylinder. The engine is supercharged by a turbo-supercharger (fan) which increases the pressure of the air before it enters the cylinders.

If there were only one cylinder in a diesel engine, power would be produced very unevenly. In consequence, many diesel engines have as many as 12 or 16 cylinders acting in sequence. These may be arranged in a line next to one another, in a V-formation or in a triangle (called a deltic formation).

It is the third stroke of the cycle that actually creates the motive power. In a steam engine, which can be run at varying speeds, motive power can be transmitted directly to the locomotive's driving wheels. A diesel engine, however, runs at a constant speed, and therefore power transmission must be indirect so that it can be controlled at some point.

There are three types of transmission: mechanical, hydraulic and electric.

Diesel engines with mechanical transmission work in the same way as those installed in lorries and buses. Power is transmitted to the driving wheels by means of a clutch and gearbox. The gears can be changed manually or automatically.

In diesel-hydraulic transmission the power from the engine drives a pump which turns the oil in a *torque converter* (the word torque means turning effort) which in turn drives the blades of a turbine. The turbine conducts power to the driving wheels by means of a system of shafts and gears.

In diesel-electric transmission, the engine drives an electric generator. The electric power this produces drives traction motors mounted on axles linking the driving wheels. In effect, a diesel-electric locomotive is an electric locomotive that carries its own source of power. The notation system for diesel-electrics is based on axles.

A diesel engine provides the power that pulls a train. Unlike a steam engine, however, which always forms part of a steam locomotive separate from the rest of the train, a diesel engine can either be contained in a separate locomotive or can form part of a passenger coach. (Diesel-powered freight trains are always hauled by separate locomotives.)

Most diesel locomotives have diesel-electric transmission, although in Germany diesel-hydraulic is popular. There are a large number of different types of diesel locomotive. The least powerful are used for shunting and other light duties, whereas the most powerful are used to move fast long-distance expresses carrying passengers and freight.

Electric traction

Unlike steam- or diesel-hauled trains, trains powered by electricity do not create their own power supply. Instead they take it from the national grid (the national electricity supply system).

Electricity is supplied in one of two ways: either by means of a third rail (sometimes both a third and a fourth)

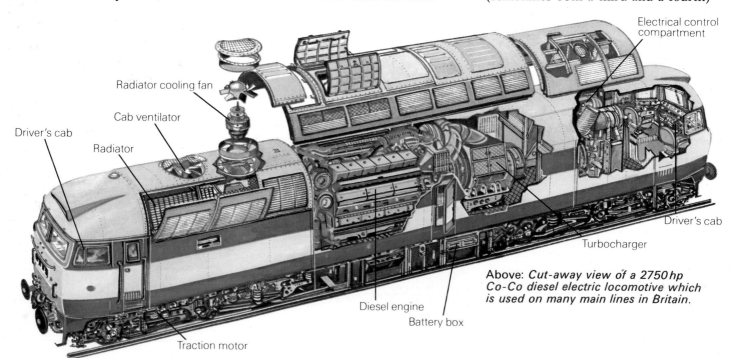

Above: *Cut-away view of a 2750 hp Co-Co diesel electric locomotive which is used on many main lines in Britain.*

Electrical control compartment

Radiator cooling fan

Cab ventilator

Driver's cab

Radiator

Driver's cab

Turbocharger

Diesel engine

Battery box

Traction motor

or by means of overhead wires. In the first case, a shoe running along the rail picks up current from the third rail. For the overhead wires, a *pantograph* (a long spring-loaded arm) is used. In Europe there are no less than four different kinds of electricity supply. To cope with this, the most modern electric locomotives have four pantographs; the change from one to the other is automatic. Overhead supply is by far the more common system and is used on virtually all electrified main lines. The third rail is mostly found on underground and suburban railways.

Once it has reached the power units, the electric power drives traction motors on the wheel axles in exactly the same way as in a diesel-electric. Because they do not generate their own electricity, electric locomotives can take additional power from the national grid to start up or to climb a particularly steep gradient. Electric locomotives can also be coupled to provide more power.

Like diesel locomotives, electric locomotives are mounted on two bogies, one at each end. These guide the locomotives round curves and help to carry their weight.

Gas-turbine locomotives

A number of locomotives powered by gas turbines have been built. These work in the same way as the gas turbines used in aircraft (*see page 141*) but are fuelled by diesel oil. The power the gas turbine produces does not drive the locomotive's driving wheels directly but is transmitted electrically, as in a diesel-electric locomotive.

Gas-turbine locomotives – or turbo-trains as they are sometimes called – operate in several countries. In the USA and USSR they are used to haul long-distance freight trains, while in Canada and France several main-line passenger routes are equipped with them.

Right: *A pre-production TGV (the French high-speed train) near Alsace in France.*

THE END OF STEAM

Until the 1920s, there was a steam locomotive at the head of virtually every train in the world, passenger or freight, local or long-distance. For another 30 years, most trains were still steam-hauled, although there were a few diesels, and suburban lines around big cities and a few main lines were electrified. During the thirty years after that, however – between the early 1950s and the early 1980s – the picture changed completely. Steam was entirely abandoned in western Europe and North America (except for the short private lines run by enthusiasts), and many countries elsewhere, in Africa, Asia and Australasia, only use steam now for their less important services. Only in South Africa, India and China are there a significant number of steam-hauled main-line services, and even these countries also have large fleets of electric and diesel locomotives.

Why did this change happen so rapidly and so completely? The reasons are both technological and social.

To begin with, steam was literally first in the field. The first steam locomotives were built in the late 1820s. However, the internal combustion engine (of which the diesel engine is one type) was not invented until the 1880s, and the public electricity supply only began to be established at about the same time. It took engineers and railway companies many years more to develop reliable, powerful diesel and electric locomotives.

The main advantage of steam was that the locomotives were cheap to build. They were also reliable: there was not a great deal that could go wrong with the engine.

The disadvantages of steam were rather more numerous. Steam locomotives are very wasteful of energy, using only a small amount of the energy produced by the burning fuel to drive the wheels. Often, two or more locomotives were needed and, as each locomotive had a crew of two, this brought the expense of employing more than one crew for a single journey. In addition, steam locomotives needed frequent and regular supplies of coal and water, and a good deal of maintenance – after a run of only a few hours, quite extensive servicing was necessary. It has been estimated that, on average, a steam locomotive was in service for no more than 10 hours out of every 24.

Finally, in the late 1940s and 1950s, coal was becoming increasingly expensive – at least in comparison with oil, which was very cheap and at that time looked as if it would stay that way!

Diesel and electric power – more efficient

In comparison with steam, both diesel and electric locomotives have far greater tractive power. They usually do far less damage to the track; they can accelerate more quickly (which means that in crowded urban areas trains can be run more frequently); and they can pull heavier loads at a greater speed. If two locomotives are needed, they can be coupled and operated from the front cabin, without increasing the crew. In addition, there is no problem with supplying fuel and water and they need less maintenance.

There is now little prospect that any major railway will return from electric or diesel working to steam. It may be, however, that as oil supplies become increasingly expensive and uncertain, some railways will abandon steam less readily, especially if, like South Africa, they have extensive coal deposits.

It is harder to compare the efficiency of diesel and electric engines. Diesel locomotives are more complex and expensive to build and maintain than electric locomotives. They are also more likely to go wrong. Since, in most western countries at least, electricity is much cheaper than oil, the running costs of electric working tend to be lower than those of diesel working.

Against this must be set two major drawbacks to electric working. Electrification itself is extremely expensive; and, once installed, the equipment is costly to maintain. In addition, diesel locomotives are far more versatile: electric locomotives can only be used on electrified lines, whereas diesels can operate anywhere a railway track has been laid.

In general, it is the most heavily used lines that are worth electrifying. These have enough traffic (both passenger and freight) to offset the high cost of electrification. The line between London and Bletchley, leading to the industrial areas in the Midlands and the north of England for instance, carries no less than 400 trains every weekday. In addition the faster and more frequent services which are made possible by electrification may well lead to more people travelling by rail. Electrification also helps railways to compete against

airlines for middle-distance traffic (up to about 500 kilometres). A businessman in a hurry may well choose to take a fast electric-powered train from one city centre to another rather than travel by air, when the time saved on the actual journey is wasted on travelling to and from the airport.

In western Europe, many main lines have been electrified. Most, though not all, of these are in the industrial areas stretching through northern France, Belgium, the Netherlands and the Federal Republic of Germany, and also in northern Italy. Switzerland and much of Scandinavia also have a very high percentage of electric working, mainly because electricity is very cheap in those countries. In the United States, by contrast, there has been hardly any electrification except in what is known as the Northeast Corridor – the busy stretches of line between Washington, New York and Boston. Elsewhere the big cities are too far apart to make electrification worthwhile, and even the fastest trains cannot compete with aircraft's shorter journey times.

Right: *Express steam locomotives on a turntable. Steam trains continue to run in southern Africa and parts of Asia.*

Crossing the Rockies

The most powerful diesel locomotives – some as much as 8500 hp – are mainly used in North America to haul heavy freight trains. However, since this amount of power is not needed very often, on stretches of line where it is required many railways prefer to couple two or more locomotives instead. These can all be controlled by the driver of the front locomotive. In western Canada one line through the Rockies has a regular service of coal trains made up of 105 wagons, each containing 100 tonnes of coal. For part of the journey the train is hauled by 13 3000 hp diesel-electric locomotives. Four at the head of the train are under the direct control of the driver; five 'slaves' in the middle are under the driver's remote control; and the four 'pusher' units near the end are manned by a driver who can communicate by radio with his colleague at the front of the train.

BUILDING A RAILWAY

Modern railway construction engineers are faced with much the same problems as their predecessors who built the first railways 150 years ago. However, modern technology and equipment have made the task of building a railway much quicker and easier.

When railways were first built locomotives were not very powerful, and so hills caused the main difficulty. Having to climb just one steep stretch of line could delay trains considerably. A steep gradient could also mean that the locomotives used would have to be more powerful than was necessary for the rest of the route, which was a waste of money. As a result, whenever possible, engineers built lines so that they curved round hills.

Nowadays, the situation has changed completely. Gradients can be much steeper, since locomotives are much more powerful. However, curves force trains to slow down and so engineers build as straight a route as they can, helped by the fact that modern machinery makes excavating deep cuttings and tunnels much easier than it used to be. Where curves are necessary, they are very gentle.

Sometimes it is impossible, or too complicated, to avoid natural obstacles such as rivers or mountains, and railway engineers decide to take the line across them. Although it is expensive to build a cutting or tunnel, a bridge or a viaduct, the operating cost of the railway may be lower as a result. In some cases, of course, such as the tunnels through the Alps, there is simply no alternative.

Mountain railways

The steepest gradient a conventional locomotive can climb on conventional track is less than 10%. This is because on steep slopes the locomotive's wheels will not grip the track sufficiently to

Above: *Digging a railway tunnel in Budapest. Although tunnelling is costly and takes time, in the long run it is often better to go through a hill than take a detour round it.*

allow a safe journey. However, in very mountainous districts, railway engineers sometimes have no choice other than to construct the line on a very steep gradient. In such cases they may turn to one of the two specialized types of mountain railway: rack-and-pinion railways and cable railways.

On *cable railways*, power is provided by a stationary engine (normally operated by electricity), and the passenger cars are hauled up and down the line on a cable running between the conventional tracks. There is no power source within the passenger cars themselves.

Most cable railways are *funiculars*. This means that two cars, one at each end of the line, balance each other. Both leave their stations at the same time and pass each other halfway up.

Thus the car going down helps to haul the car going up, with the result that the stationary engine has to produce far less power than if it were merely hauling an ascending car. The cars travel at a maximum of about 15 kph (10 mph).

Cable railways are either single- or double-tracked. If there is only one track, a passing spot has to be built at the halfway point.

Passenger cars on lines on the gentler gradients are conventionally designed. On steeper lines, however, the cars have separate, stepped compartments, and one end of the car may be 3 or 4 metres

Rack-and-pinion railways

There are various types of rack-and-pinion railway, but in principle they all work in the same way. As well as its normal wheels, the locomotive has an additional cogwheel (the pinion wheel) which meshes with a third, toothed, rail (the rack) laid between the normal rails. The teeth are on the top of the rail. Together, the additional wheel and rail give the locomotive far greater adhesion (grip) than is normally necessary.

Rack-and-pinion railways like this function quite satisfactorily on gradients of up to 25%. On yet steeper lines, such as the 50% gradient up Mount Pilatus in Switzerland, a variation is used. Here the additional rail has teeth on both sides. Two horizontally mounted pinions, one on each side, grip the toothed rail. Another pair of pinions is used solely on the downward journey, to give additional braking power.

Many rack-and-pinion railways run for long distances through mountainous countryside. Some operate conventionally for part of the trip and merely employ the rack system in the steeper parts of the line.

Although rack-and-pinion railways were originally operated with steam locomotives, almost all have now been converted to diesel or electric working.

Pinion wheel

Rack (third toothed rail)

Conventional rail

higher than the other. The steepest line in existence is in Switzerland, between Piotta and Piora, where the gradient is as much as 88%.

Safety is very important on cable railways, and cars are provided with an extremely powerful braking system which automatically goes into operation if the cable slackens at all. Both the brakes and the cable itself are regularly checked.

However, rack-and-pinion and funicular railways are rarely, if ever, constructed now due to the development of cable suspension lines. Such cableways avoid the complicated and costly problems of laying railway tracks.

Below: *The Brienz-Rothorn rack-and-pinion railway in Switzerland, where many branch lines run through mountainous country.*

TRACK AND GAUGE

Rails alone cannot support the weight of a train, so the first step after the route has been chosen and cleared is to prepare the roadbed. The track is laid on the roadbed, which helps to take the load imposed by the train.

The roadbed is simply a level, stable strip of ground from which the topsoil has been removed. Concrete may be injected to stabilize it. On top of the roadbed comes a layer of ballast, large pieces of stone on the bottom and smaller pieces on top.

Sleepers (known as cross-ties in the USA) are laid across the top of the ballast. The sleepers help to hold the rails in place. Once sleepers were always made of wood, but some countries now use steel or concrete.

Next come the rails themselves, which are made of steel. Until about 1960, rails were fairly short (no more than 30 metres long, and often much

Below: *Close-up views of railway track and the clips used to fasten the track to the sleeper.*

shorter). Nowadays, most main lines have been re-laid with welded rail. Welded rails are between 60 and 400 metres long and are themselves welded (joined together) once they have been laid, to form a single rail several kilometres long. This is easier to maintain since there are far fewer joins between the rails; these are the weakest part of the track and wear out quickly.

The rails are attached to each other by *fishplates*. The flat bottom of each rail is fixed to the sleeper by means of a clip. A baseplate between the rail and the sleeper helps to spread the weight of the train as it passes over the sleeper. Last of all, a layer of small ballast is laid between the rails and tamped (pressed down) around the sleepers.

Track-laying nowadays is a highly mechanized operation. In some cases, complete sections of track – rails, sleepers, baseplates and so on – are laid by one machine. In others, as on the new line between Tarcoola and Alice Springs in Australia, the track is laid

before the sleepers. There, a trolley running at the side of the roadbed laid fourteen 137-metre lengths of welded rail directly on to the roadbed, but outside their final positions. Then a special sleeper-laying gantry that straddled the whole roadbed laid 40 sleepers at a time. This was followed by a small 'threading' machine that shifted the rails on to the sleepers. Finally the rails were fastened to the sleepers with clips, the rails were welded and ballast was laid and tamped.

Paved concrete track (known as PACT) is a recent development that has already been introduced on some stretches of line. Neither ballast nor sleepers are needed, and the rails are laid directly on to a strip of reinforced concrete about 30 centimetres thick. Concrete track is cheaper to maintain than normal track and a paving train can lay as many as 40 metres of concrete track in one hour.

Railway engineers must also decide how many tracks to build. Two tracks – one for trains travelling in each direction – used to be normal, with just one on the smallest branch lines and four, occasionally even more, on the busier main lines. However, modern signalling techniques often permit two tracks to carry the same amount of traffic as four once did and one track the same as two once did.

Points (known as switches in the USA) have to be provided when two or more tracks diverge from one another. The points are controlled from a signal box. The position of the *switch rails* determines whether the wheels of the locomotive will be kept on the same track or guided on to the diverging track. Until recently, even express trains routed on to a diverging line had to slow down to about 70 kph (44 mph) to make the switch. On some lines, however, high-speed points have now been installed, which permit speeds of up to 110 kph (68 mph).

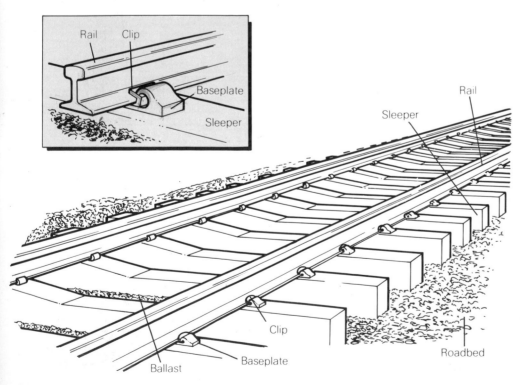

Rail — Clip — Baseplate — Sleeper

Rail — Sleeper — Clip — Baseplate — Ballast — Roadbed

Sulzerlda 28 diesel engine

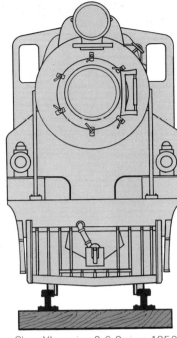

Class YL engine 2-6-2 circa 1952

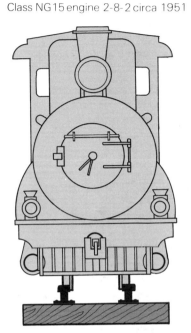

Class NG15 engine 2-8-2 circa 1951

Track and loading gauge

In addition to deciding on a route for the line, railway engineers also have to determine the track gauge (the width between the inside faces of the rails) and the loading gauge (the maximum height and width permitted for rolling-stock).

About 60% of the railway track throughout the world is built on a gauge of 1.435 metres (4 feet 8½ inches). This is known as standard gauge and was used for the first railways in Britain, Europe and North America. Other gauges used fairly frequently are: 1.676 metres (5 feet 6 inches), in India, Sri Lanka, Pakistan, Spain, Portugal and the Argentine; 1.6 metres (5 feet 3 inches), in Australia and Ireland; 1.524 metres (5 feet), in Finland and the Soviet Union; 1.067 metres (3 feet 6 inches), in Australia, Japan, New Zealand, parts of southern and west Africa; metre (3 feet 2 inches) gauge in Swit-

zerland, India, some of Asia, parts of South America and East Africa.

Broader gauges are more expensive to construct but give a more comfortable ride. Narrower gauge tracks mean slower travel but allow the track to curve more sharply; they are also cheaper, as is the rolling-stock built for them. In consequence, the narrower gauges are most often used in developing countries.

What is important is that the gauge should be the same not just in one country but wherever trains run from one country to another so that passengers and freight do not have to change trains. The greatest gauge problem (which is still not entirely solved) was undoubtedly in Australia. There the individual states were responsible for building their own railways, and each state selected a different gauge with the result that trains could not cross the state borders. New lines had to be built, existing ones were converted, and now all the state capitals are linked by

Above: *Different track gauges.* Left, *standard gauge;* centre, *Indian metre gauge;* right, *South African Railways' 0.6096-metre (2-feet) gauge. There are about 440 miles of this narrow track.*

standard-gauge lines.

A few railways built to really narrow gauges exist. Most of these have very specialized industrial uses or are tourist attractions. The narrowest of all are two miniature railways in England – the Romney, Hythe and Dymchurch Railway and the Ravenglass and Eskdale Railway, both of which have a gauge of 38.1 centimetres (1 foot 3 inches).

Loading gauges vary rather more. Britain's is the smallest of any country with standard track gauge. There the width is 3.25 metres (10 feet 8 inches), height 4.55 metres (15 feet). In the USA, a width of 3.3 metres (10 feet 10 inches) and a height of 4.9 metres (16 feet 2 inches) is permitted. The Soviet Union allows the biggest loading in the world: 3.4 metres (11 feet 2 inches) wide, 5.3 metres (17 feet 4 inches) high.

TRAIN SAFETY

Despite all the sophistication of modern technology, trains are still driven by human beings, and people can still make mistakes which sometimes lead to accidents – though it should be pointed out that railways have the lowest accident rate of any form of transport. In consequence, a system of signalling within the driver's cab has been developed in recent years. Like modern signals, the Automatic Warning System (AWS) is based on the track circuit (*see page 81*). At its simplest, the system consists of an audible warning broadcast in the cab at every signal. Sometimes the audible warning varies according to what the signal is indicating. A hooter may continue to sound until the driver acknowledges it by turning a lever. If he fails to do so, thus indicating that something may be wrong, the train's brakes are applied automatically.

In some countries, the speed of the train can also be controlled automatically, and the brakes are applied if it is going too fast. This happens on the high-speed Shinkansen line in Japan (*see page 94*).

AWS is now so far advanced that automatic operation of trains is, in theory at least, already possible (*see also page 92*). It is extremely unlikely, however, that any driverless passenger services will come into operation in the foreseeable future.

Single lines present additional safety problems, since stretches of lines between passing points must only be occupied by trains travelling in the same direction. Often, some kind of staff or token is used to supplement conventional signalling. There is only one token for each section and a train may only enter a section of line if its driver is in possession of the token, which he obtains from the signalman or stationmaster. At the other end of the section he surrenders the token, which is then passed to the driver of the next train wanting to pass through that

section. The disadvantage of this system is that the timetable must be so organized that successive trains run in alternate directions.

Electric token systems can overcome this problem. The token instrument at each end of the stretch of single track contains several tokens, but as soon as one is removed the others are locked in until the first token has been replaced in one or other of the instruments. This

Above: *A level crossing in Normandy, France. The red warning signal and the barrier remind motorists and pedestrians not to cross while a train is nearby.*

procedure ensures that only one train can be present on the single track at a time, but it does not prevent one train following another in the same direction.

Level crossings (or grade crossings as they are known in North America) are points at which roads and the rail-

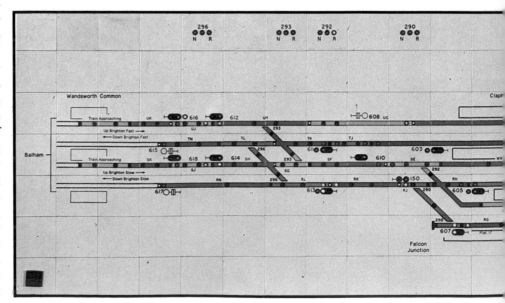

way cross each other. Despite ever increasing safety precautions, they are still notorious accident blackspots. Most modern level crossing gates are operated automatically from the nearest signal box. A few minutes before the train is due to pass, half gates are lowered across the road to block traffic, warning lights start to flash and bells ring. The gates are only raised after the train has passed. The older-fashioned type of barrier consists of two pairs of gates. These were once opened by hand, although most are now operated automatically. The normal position of the gates is across the railway line, but when a train is due they move to block off the road.

Brakes

Brakes are the fundamental safety feature on every train. All the various braking systems in use are controlled by the driver, but as an additional safety mechanism many modern trains have braking systems which can override the driver's controls.

The two main braking systems are air brakes and vacuum brakes. Air brakes consist of an air pipe filled with compressed air which runs the whole length of the train from either the locomotive or the driver's cab; reservoirs also filled with compressed air; and brake cylinders which are linked to brake shoes on every wheel throughout the train. When the brakes are applied, the compressed air in the brake pipe escapes. This causes valves to admit compressed air from the reservoirs which are connected to the brake cylinders. The compressed air makes the pistons in the brake cylinders move out because of the air pressure and press the brake shoes against the wheels. When the brake controls are released, compressed air is admitted into the brake pipe, which causes the compressed air in the brake cylinders to escape and thus releases the brake shoes.

Vacuum braking follows a similar principle, although a partial vacuum, not compressed air, is maintained in the pipe and the cylinders. When the brakes are applied, air is admitted to the pipe and to the underside of the pistons, but the vacuum is maintained above the pistons so that they are forced outwards and press the brake shoes on to the wheels.

Both systems are fail safe. If any part of the train is accidentally uncoupled, the pipe is broken and in consequence the brakes are applied automatically.

Various additional kinds of braking are possible on trains powered by electricity.

Below: *The operation of a train air brake.*

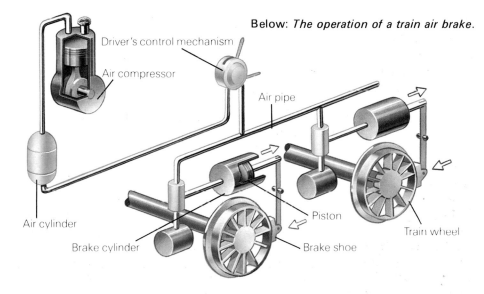

Driver's control mechanism

Air compressor

Air pipe

Air cylinder

Piston

Brake cylinder

Brake shoe

Train wheel

Below: *Diagram of the tracks at Clapham Junction, London, which is the busiest junction in Europe.*

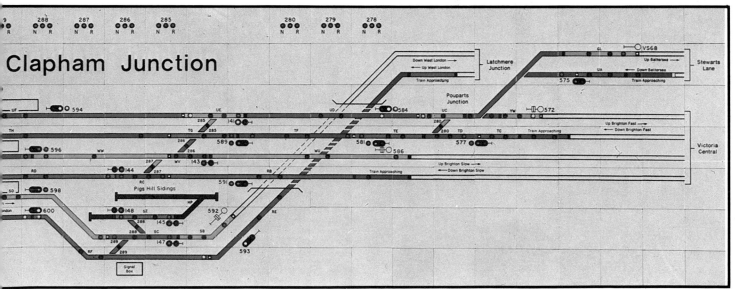

SIGNALLING

A railway signalling system has two purposes. It ensures that the service operates safely, by preventing trains colliding with one another; and, almost as important, it enables the trains to run as fast and as frequently as necessary.

The *block* is the basis of almost all signalling systems. A block is simply a stretch of track in one direction. Only one train may be in a block at any time. If two trains are travelling a short distance apart, the front one must leave its block before the rear one may enter that block.

Entry to a block is controlled by a signal known as the *stop signal*. This tells the train driver one of two things: either to proceed into the block or to stop before entering it. A second type of signal, called the *distant signal*, positioned some way before the start of the block, warns the driver in advance of what the stop signal is indicating. This gives him time to slow down if necessary before he reaches the stop signal.

The length of a block varies enormously. At junctions and around major stations it may be only a few metres, whereas on open stretches of line where there are no points or crossings it may be several kilometres. On these, because trains travelling fast take a long time to stop, the distant signal for the next block but one may be displayed at the same place as the stop signal for the block immediately ahead.

Signals are always placed where they can be seen well in advance. This helps safety, since drivers naturally start to slow down as soon as they see the signal and do not wait to take action until they actually pass it.

Nowadays, most main lines are equipped with colour-light signals. Semaphore signals (which used to be the main type of signal, consisting of a moving arm attached to a signal post) are only used on a few main and some branch lines, where they are gradually being replaced.

Colour-light signals are either three-aspect or four-aspect: that is, they either display one of three or one of four different signals. Three-aspect signals can show, from bottom to top, red (*stop*), yellow (*proceed with caution*) or green (*proceed*). (The red light is always at the bottom so that it cannot be hidden by snow piled up on a lamp hood.) Four-aspect signals have a second yellow light, above the green. This is a preliminary caution, allowing trains to run closer together.

Colour-light signals thus function as both stop and distant signals. Green will not show unless the next signal along the line is either green or yellow; and if the next signal is red then yellow will be displayed. Double yellow on a four-aspect signal means that the next signal is showing a single yellow and the one after that is red. This preliminary caution gives high-speed trains extra time in which to slow down. In many European countries and in North America, signals are also used to inform the train drivers of the speed at which they should travel.

Signalling at junctions, where one or more lines may diverge, and at stations,

Below: *Signals at a busy metropolitan station. The two on the right are four-aspect colour-light signals.*

where a train may be directed into any one of a number of platforms, is far more complicated.

Where colour-light signals have been installed as lines diverge, one signal does service for all the lines. If one of the diverging lines is to be used, one arm of a junction indicator above the signal itself is illuminated to show that the signal refers to that line. If the signal is at stop, or if the train is routed on the direct line, the indicator is not lit.

At converging junctions – that is, where one line joins another – trains on the converging line are controlled by normal signals.

At large stations, where drivers need to know to which platform they are being directed, an illuminated letter or number indicates the route the train is to take.

Controlling the signals

Signals and points are operated by signalmen working from signalboxes and communicating by block telegraph. This instrument indicates the state of the line in the blocks on each side of the box in each direction. For each stretch it can show that the block is occupied by a train, or that a train has been cleared to enter the block, or that no movement has been authorized. The

instruments in neighbouring boxes are linked so that they show the same thing.

When a signalman in box A wants to pass a train up the line to the next block, controlled by box B, he asks signalman B by telegraph whether the line is clear. If it is, he sets his signals and points accordingly. If, of course, the line is not clear, the signalman sets his signals to *caution* or *stop*.

The highly automated techniques of modern signalling, often known as Centralized Traffic Control (CTC), are all based on the principles of track circuiting. Inside a typical modern signalbox, a huge illuminated diagram shows all the lines controlled by the box. A complex system of track circuiting enables the exact position of every single train on the track to be shown as it moves along, so that at any time signalmen know exactly what is happening. As a further aid, each train's

Above: *The modern signal box at a major London terminus, from which signalmen control many miles of track.*

identification number may also be displayed. For much of the time, trains set their own signals as they pass over the various track circuits. When a signalman sets up a route for a train, perhaps across the numerous sets of points outside the entrance to a main station, he simply presses two buttons, one of which controls the entrance to the junction, the other the exit. The exit button sets all the points and signals in the train's favour; once this has been done the entrance signal clears automatically and the train can move forward. Electronic interlocking ensures that no other conflicting route using the same signals or points can be set up until the train has passed.

Overleaf: *Aerial view of Euston station, London.*

Track circuits

For the best part of a century, signalling on stretches of line without any junctions has been greatly assisted by track circuiting. This makes it possible for trains to set signals themselves and so enables the number of signal boxes to be reduced. A track circuit consists of an electric current connecting the track and the signal. The current is passed through a section of track, first along one rail, then across to the other and back to where it started, thus forming an unbroken circuit. When a train enters that section of track, it short-circuits the electric current, which in turn causes the signal to change from *proceed* to *stop*. As the train travels along the line, the signals behind it return automatically to *caution* and then to *proceed*.

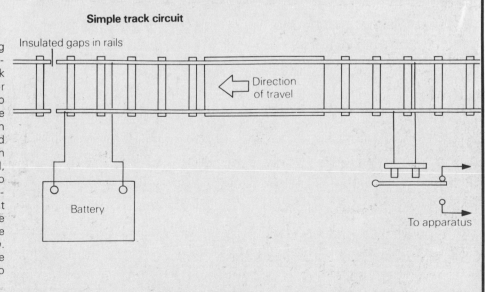

Simple track circuit

Insulated gaps in rails

Direction of travel

Battery

To apparatus

Railways are complex and expensive businesses to run. The equipment needed – locomotives, passenger and freight rolling-stock, signals, track, stations and so on – costs a lot to build and has to be operated by skilled people. In addition, running costs – wages for railway workers, maintenance and replacement of equipment, and so on – are high.

But, despite all this, running a railway would be relatively easy if one sort of service were provided. The ideal railway would consist solely of a regular service between two points carrying exactly the same amount of traffic – passengers or freight – in each direction all the time. But, with the exception of a few specialized industrial railways, the ideal never happens. Running a railway is difficult because so many different services have to be provided – not just passenger trains and freight trains but many different types of passenger and freight service. And often all these trains use the same lines and the same stations.

Stations

At its simplest, a station need only consist of a platform at which a train can draw up. Usually, though not always, there is also a ticket office and a small waiting-room. At its grandest, by contrast, it will contain not just a set of platforms (Waterloo station in London has no less than 21) but also ticket and enquiry offices, a left luggage office, shops, bars, cafés and restaurants, perhaps even a chapel, a cinema and a hotel – everything, in fact, that could possibly be needed by thousands of travellers each day. There will probably also be an underground railway station, bus stops and a car park.

Many stations were erected during the last century, when railways were first built, and are now getting old and

extremely costly to maintain. Because these 19th century stations look old-fashioned and are also not very convenient for travellers, many of them have been rebuilt during the past 20 years. In large cities, where the land on which they stand is worth a lot of money, railways have been able to make a profit by including in the new station an office block which they then let for a very high rent.

Scheduling

Planning a timetable for a railway, especially a busy main line, is extremely complicated. Normally, express trains are given priority. On four-track lines, where one track in each direction is used by slower-moving local and commuter trains and freight trains while the other is left free for fast traffic, this presents a few problems. Things are more difficult on two-track lines, however, and slower trains often have to wait in stations or on loop tracks to let the faster trains through. Often special trains also have to be fitted into the timetable.

British Rail have found an ingenious way of solving this problem on the main line from London to the Midlands and the north of England. Seven fast trains leave Euston station (the London terminus of this line) for different destinations every five minutes between 40 and 10 minutes past each hour. This leaves half an hour clear for local trains to travel and for urgent repair work. Even this arrangement cannot be maintained during the rush hours, however, when commuter trains have to be fitted in with the long-distance services.

At night, it is usual for long-distance freight trains, which travel at up to 120 kph (75 mph), to be given priority, and if necessary overnight passenger sleepers are delayed to let them pass. In any case, night passenger services run

more slowly than their daytime equivalents.

Trains may be delayed for any number of reasons, including bad weather, mechanical breakdown, and longer than usual stops at stations caused by exceptional numbers of passengers. When this happens, traffic regulators working in the signalboxes have to rearrange the order in which trains run so that delays are reduced as much as possible.

Right: *St Pancras station two years after it opened in 1866, a marvellous example of the grand station architecture of the 19th century. The arch is 74 metres wide.*

Below: *Locomotives under repair. Constant maintenance of track and rolling stock is essential for the safe running of a railway.*

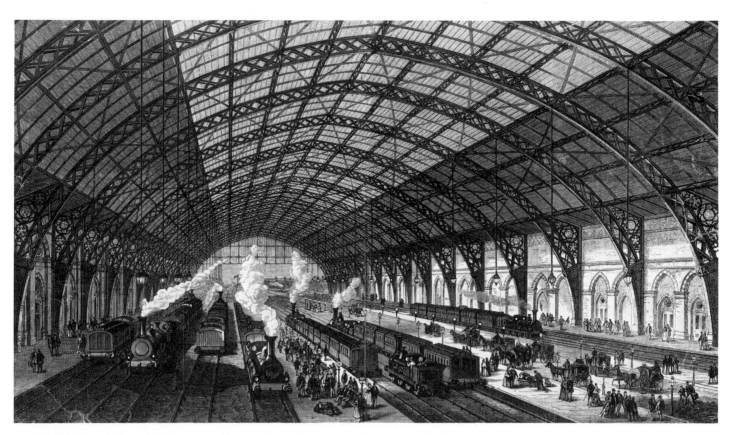

PASSENGER SERVICES

There are three main types of passenger service: commuter trains; branch-line operations; and long-distance services between major cities. (For the new high-speed trains operated in a few countries such as Great Britain, France and Japan, *see pages 93–4.*)

Commuter trains run on lines within about 30 to 50 kilometres of large towns and cities. During the day, when only a few people are travelling, a 'skeleton service' is operated, perhaps one or two trains an hour. But in the mornings and evenings, when crowds of office and factory workers are travelling to and from work, trains have to be run far more frequently and are often very full. No less than 76 000 travellers arrive at Waterloo, one of London's biggest commuter termini, between 7 and 10 a.m. Most commuter services nowadays are operated by diesel multiple units (dmus) or electric multiple units (emus)

Below: *United States Bart train in Oakland West, San Francisco.*

Above: *Branch line diesel multiple unit, a lifeline in country areas. This one is near Micklefield, West Yorkshire.*

which consist of two powered cars and two additional cars. Two or more dmus or emus can be coupled.

Until 30 years ago, sometimes even less, railway maps in most countries showed numerous branch lines reaching the most remote districts. In those days, there were far fewer cars and lorries, and railways were the main form of transport in country districts. Nowadays, all that has changed. It is far cheaper and more convenient to send small amounts of mixed freight by road, so branch railways earn far less from freight traffic. In addition, far more people have cars and no longer make local journeys by train. This has affected literally hundreds of lines in western Europe and North America and many have now been closed.

Travelling long distances

Until about 1950, most people made long-distance journeys by train. Since then, however, car ownership has increased, and air travel has also become much cheaper and more popular. As a result, railways now have to compete for passengers for their main-line services. On middle-distance journeys, however, the railways are more than holding their own, mainly as a result of improvements made during the 1970s. In Britain, a regular service of 'Inter-City' expresses hauled by modern diesel or electric locomotives running every half hour, hour or two hours connects London and all the major provincial towns and the provincial centres themselves. On the east coast of the USA, Amtrak provides a similar service between Washington, New York and Boston.

These trains are designed to appeal to business people in a hurry. Their frequency means that travellers need never wait too long for a train, and the trains themselves are comfortable and fast, with air-conditioning and a buffet or dining car. In Europe, where there is a similar network of expresses, the TEE (*Trans Europ Express*) trains provide an even more luxurious and exclusive service. TEE trains run between many major European cities, usually once a day in each direction.

Of course, not everyone wants to, or can afford to, travel long distances by air. Throughout eastern and western Europe, in much of Asia and Latin America, and in parts of Africa, trains travel enormous distances, often taking a very long time to do so. In yet other countries, such as Canada, Australia and South Africa, travellers often make a transcontinental journey by train part of their holiday. Trains such as *The Canadian* (Montreal and Ottawa to Vancouver), the *Blue Train* (Pretoria and Johannesburg to Cape Town) and the *Indian Pacific* (Sydney to Perth) may take days longer than aircraft, but they offer spectacular scenery and the comfort of a hotel.

Below: *Relaxing in style on the* Blue Train.

Bottom: *A train to Macchu Picchu from Cuzco in Peru.*

Passenger rolling-stock

All passenger rolling-stock, whatever its design, is mounted on bogies, one at each end of the car. In the same way as on locomotives, these guide the car round curves. In addition their springs help to absorb bumps and jolts as the train moves along the track and so give passengers a more comfortable ride.

There are two principal designs of passenger accommodation. In the USA, cars are open inside, with a central gangway and seats on each side. In Britain and the rest of Europe, coaches (the word is taken from the old-fashioned stagecoach) used to have separate compartments entered from a corridor running along one side of the coach, but modern rolling-stock is designed on the American pattern. Double-decker trains are used by some railways in the USA, Canada and Europe.

Most main-line cars have doors at each end. Diesel railcars and diesel and electric multiple units used on crowded commuter lines also have additional doors at intermediate points along the car. More doors mean that passengers can get on and off quickly and so reduce the amount of time the train has to spend standing at a station.

Modern passenger rolling-stock is made of steel. In the USA cars are 26 metres long and weigh between about 60 and 80 tonnes. In Europe and Britain they are made of lighter steel, and the passenger vehicles of the Advanced Passenger Train (*see page 94*) are of aluminium. British carriages are also shorter, usually about 20 metres in length. Heating and lighting are provided by electricity from dynamos on each car, driven by the axle.

Below: *Double-decker train with gallery cars in Chicago.*

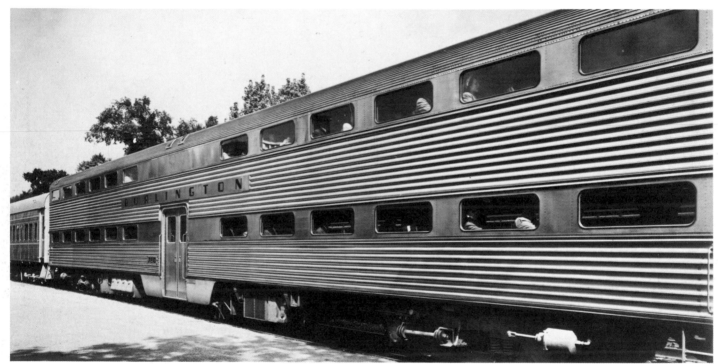

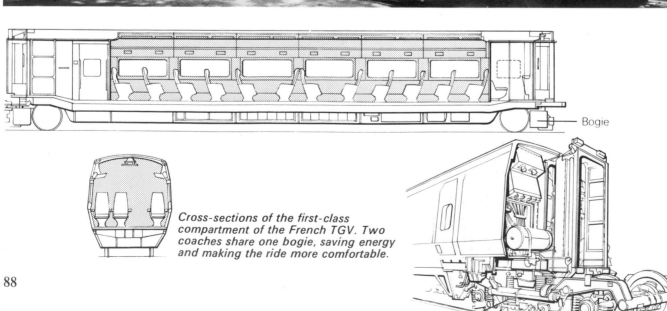

Cross-sections of the first-class compartment of the French TGV. Two coaches share one bogie, saving energy and making the ride more comfortable.

Bogie

Bogie

FREIGHT SERVICES

Carrying freight has always been an extremely important part of railway operations throughout the world: indeed the first railways were built to carry freight, not passengers. While almost all passenger lines (even several main-line services) lose money, many (though not all) freight services make a profit. In the USA, where passenger trains run over only 3% of the track in the country, the different railway companies handed over their passenger services to Amtrak in the early 1970s and they now concentrate entirely on freight traffic.

To fight off competition for freight traffic from road haulage companies and airlines, just as for passenger services, railways have had to revolutionize their freight services. Once freight trains carrying an enormous

German goods train with BRO50 steam engine.

variety of goods in individual small wagons jolted their way slowly across the country; the wagons might only reach their destination after being sorted several times in marshalling yards. Now, with the help of regular, fast freight trains hauled by powerful locomotives, computer-controlled marshalling yards and a large number of different kinds of wagons, railways can give an efficient, competitive service.

There are four main kinds of freight wagon: flatcars, boxcars, gondolas and hoppers. *Flatcars* are simply a flat base on wheels on to which containers or road trailers can be loaded. *Boxcars* are closed boxes in which almost any kind of merchandise can be carried. A large number of special types of boxcar are available. Some have wide doors that make loading and unloading easier. Others have special modifications to enable them to carry certain types of goods without damaging them; the Canadian Pacific Railway, for instance, offers its customers boxcars suitable for car parts, building materials, asbestos, sulphur, packaged sugar, potash and many other items. *Gondolas*, which can have open or closed tops, are mostly used for manufactured iron and steel products and for woodchip. *Hopper cars*, which again can be open or closed, usually carry bulk commodities such as coal, mineral ores, cement, fertilizer and grain. Some hopper cars are designed so their bottoms drop open, and their contents can be unloaded fast.

Other specialized wagons available include refrigerated vans; tanks for oil, chemicals, vinegar, fruit juices, wine and many other liquids; livestock cars; and car transporters (two-deck in Europe, three-deck in the USA).

Specialized freight trains

There are two main kinds of specialized freight train in operation: unit trains and fixed-formation container or piggyback trains.

Unit trains are a very simple idea. They carry a single product from one place to another for one customer and then return empty for the next load in what is virtually a shuttle service. They may be used for all kinds of bulk products, for example coal or grain. Unit trains are unsuitable for companies dispatching loads to a large number of destinations at different times – which is what a factory has to do with its finished goods. For these, container transport is often most suitable.

A *container* is exactly what you would expect it to be: an enclosed space into which goods of more or less any kind can be packed. The containers themselves are then loaded off the road trailer and on to a railway flatcar or – and this is their great advantage – on to a road trailer or on board ship. Thus containers are an extremely flexible and easy means of transporting goods. They can be transferred from one means of transport to another quickly and with very little effort.

Left: *Modern freight stock.*

Piggy-back trains, which operate in North America, where the loading gauge is higher than in Europe, are rather like container trains, except that the entire back part of a road trailer, wheels and all, is loaded on to the flat-car. The French have developed an ingenious version of the piggy-back, called the *kangarou*, in which the trailer wheels rest in special pouches below the level of the rest of the flatcar, so reducing the overall height of the train.

Of course, not every load is large enough to occupy a container. Nor are journeys always between the terminals of the container or piggy-back trains. Therefore, wagons are brought in small trains from the individual depots (where they are loaded) to large marshalling yards. There they are made up into large trains travelling to different parts of the country. Each train runs direct to another marshalling yard where the wagons are sorted into smaller local

freight trains which then deliver them to their final destination.

Marshalling yards are huge sidings with a large number of tracks. The one at Maschen, south of Hamburg in West Germany, is among the largest in Europe. It covers 280 hectares and has 34 reception tracks and 150 sorting sidings.

Below: *The marshalling yard at Maschen in Germany.*

CITY TRANSIT

Underground railway systems (or subways) are now operating in about 70 cities across the world, and in at least 20 more, lines are under construction or being planned. Some systems are huge: New York has over 460 stations; London has 279 stations, with some lines running far out into the countryside. In smaller cities, of course, the system is less extensive.

Whatever their size, all underground systems have the same aim – to move people about as quickly and efficiently as possible. Underground trains are powered by electricity. In most systems a third rail (*see pages 70–71*) provides power, although in the London system a third and a fourth rail are used. There are no separate locomotives. Instead power is supplied to individual motors along the train, which is controlled from a driver's cab at the front.

Because trains run close together, safety is of the utmost importance. As on overground railways, signalling is based on the block system, and track circuiting enables signals to change automatically as trains pass. In addition, an automatic warning system brings a train to a rapid halt should it pass any signal showing red. All the points and signals are controlled from a central office, in which a display panel shows the position of every train in the system.

The most modern underground systems are so automated that they could be operated without a driver on board the train. On the Victoria Line in London, for instance, the first part of which came into service in 1969, electric impulses set off in the rails by one train not only operate the signals but also increase or decrease the speed of the train behind; if necessary they can also apply its brakes and bring it to a halt. A similar system is used by the Metro in Washington DC, by BART (Bay Area Rapid Transit) in the area around San Francisco, USA, and on other lines else-

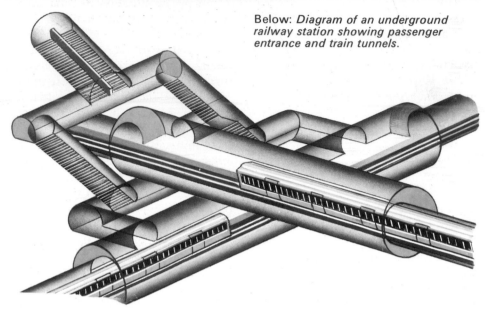

Below: *Diagram of an underground railway station showing passenger entrance and train tunnels.*

where. Nowhere, however, do driverless trains actually run: the authorities believe that, however safe the system may be, driverless trains would worry passengers and discourage them from using the system.

Although individual designs vary from system to system, cars generally have only a few seats (usually sufficient to accommodate daytime passengers) and a large amount of standing room so that the rush-hour crowds can be fitted in. The older rolling-stock in use on many lines is extremely noisy (New York's system is a famous example of one in which conversation is virtually impossible), but recent models give a much quieter and smoother ride – in Washington DC the carriages are even carpeted!

On most underground rolling-stock, steel flanged wheels run on conventional rails, as on overground railways. On some lines on the Paris Metro, however, and also in Montreal, Canada, Mexico City and Santiago, Chile, rubber tyres are used on the wheels. These

Below: *Inside an air-conditioned Washington DC subway car, one of the most comfortable in the world.*

are much quieter and give the impression that the train is gliding along. The rubber tyres run along a concrete track and are kept in place by a set of small horizontal rubber-tyred wheels that press against side guidance rails. Conventional steel wheels, mounted between the rubber-tyred wheels, still have to be used at points, however.

One development from the idea of underground railways is light rapid transit vehicles of LRTVs – conventional subways use 'heavy' rapid transit vehicles. Looking at these vehicles, it is hard to tell whether they are trams or trains. The LRTVs run underground in the city centre, so avoiding the congested streets above, but emerge on to a surface rail system just outside the centre. This provides some of the advantages of a conventional subway but without the very heavy construction and operating costs.

Monorails

Monorails have always attracted a great deal of public attention, but far more have been talked about than have ever been built.

There are two main types, both of which have electric traction. In one, the Alweg type, the cars sit above the single rail (the word mono means 'single'); in the other, the French Safege type, the cars are suspended from the rail.

There are several monorails in operation in Japan, and one in Germany has been in continuous service since 1901. Since their supports take up very little space on the ground, they are particularly suitable for use in urban districts, but it seems unlikely that they will ever replace conventional bus and underground services or the new light rapid transit vehicles.

Safege-type monorail

Alweg-type monorail

Left: *Part of the United States Morgantown 'people-mover' system. A car is always at your disposal.*

Personal rapid transit

Even more exotic than monorails are the various systems of Personal Rapid Transport (PRT) that have been developed in the past few years.

One of the most interesting is the 'people-mover' at Morgantown, a small town in West Virginia, USA. During the morning and evening rush-hours, the service operates in a conventional way with a scheduled service, and the cars, which can seat eight people and can accommodate 13 standing passengers, run every few minutes. During the day, however, a traveller calls up a car by computer. The computer sends the nearest available empty car to that station, the passenger presses a button to show their destination, rather as in an automatic lift — and off they go!

The whole system is operated by just two people based in a central control room. The driverless vehicles, which can travel at speeds of up to 48 kph (30 mph), run on a concrete guideway and are powered by electricity. They have rubber-tyred wheels and lateral guide wheels, rather like those on the Paris Metro. Unlike the Metro, however, there are no rails, and the guide wheels operate in response to computer signals.

HIGH·SPEED TRAINS

During the 1960s, railways faced increasing competition from other forms of transport, especially airlines, for passengers on routes between major cities. The main reason for this was speed. To compete, train speed had to be increased substantially while still giving passengers a safe, comfortable ride.

There were two very different ways in which this could be achieved. One way was to build a completely new line on which only high-speed passenger traffic would run. The other was to make existing lines suitable for high-speed traffic by straightening curves and improving junctions as much as possible and by installing the latest signalling equipment. In Japan and France, the railways chose the first of these alternatives; in Britain, Germany and Italy the second was selected.

In France, the new high-speed line between Melun, outside Paris, and Lyon opened in late 1981. Only specially designed TGVs (*Train Grande Vitesse*, French for 'high speed train') are allowed to run on it. Like the *Shinkansen* trains in Japan, these are electric multiple units, but the TGVs are capable of even higher speeds, up to 300 kph (188 mph), and reduce journey time for the 409 kilometre trip from 3.75 hours to just two, practically halving it.

In Britain it was impractical to build a new line for the route that most needed a high-speed service, the busy west-coast line from London to Glasgow through the industrial Midlands and north. In many areas there simply was not enough space. The solution to the problem was to be the Advanced Passenger Train (APT), but prospects for this seem more and more uncertain as time goes on.

What enables the electric-powered APT to take curves on old lines at

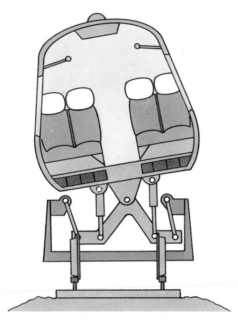

Above: *The Advanced Passenger Train, whose hydraulic tilting mechanism enables it to take sharp bends at high speed.*

'Bullet trains'

It was Japan that pioneered high-speed rail travel. There the first *Shinkansen* ('bullet') trains started to operate in 1964 between Tokyo and Osaka. They were an immediate success. On the old line, which like all Japanese railways had been built to the 1.067 metre gauge, trains had not been able to travel at more than 100 kph (62 mph). On the new standard-gauge line, built as straight as possible, they reach 210 kph (130 mph) bringing Tokyo within little more than three hours of Osaka.

No other train is allowed to use the *Shinkansen* line and the entire line is controlled from one central control-point in Tokyo. There are no signals on the line, however. Instead, the driver receives a signal in the cab indicating the speed the train should travel. The trains do not operate automatically, although should the driver fail to obey a signal the brakes are applied automatically.

A separate electric locomotive would not be powerful enough to haul the 16-coach *Shinkansen* trains. Instead, every axle of each car is powered.

The *Shinkansen* line was an immediate success and has already been extended south from Osaka to Hiroshima and on to Hakata on Kyushu island. There are also plans to extend the *Shinkansen* network north of Tokyo, in a long undersea tunnel on to Hokkaido, the most northerly island in Japan.

Below: *The Japanese 'bullet train'. Like the French high-speed train (TGV), it has a specially built track.*

higher speeds than a normal train is its hydraulic tilting mechanism. This tilts each carriage by up to 9° in the direction of the curve. (The effect is the same as when you take a bend very fast on your bike and lean your body into the bend to help keep your balance.) Although the body of each carriage tilts, the bogie does not. Nor does the pantograph, which an anti-tilt linkage enables to stay upright.

It is this tilting device that enables the APT to take sharp bends at such a high speed. The APT will be able to run through one typical curve at Berkhamsted in Hertfordshire at 193 kph (120 mph), whereas conventional locomotive-hauled trains have to slow down to 145 kph (90 mph).

In the meantime, however, British Rail decided to introduce high-speed diesel operations on some of their other lines. The first of these HSTs (High-Speed Trains) came into operation between London and Bristol, and London and Swansea in 1976; since then they have also been introduced on the east-coast route to Newcastle and Scotland. The HSTs are powered by two units, one at each end of the train, and can run at up to 200 kph (125 mph).

Elsewhere, the Soviet Union has built a new high-speed line between Leningrad and Moscow and is currently testing locomotives for use on it. In Italy a similar line between Florence and Rome is under construction – no less than one third of it will be in tunnels – and in Germany one is being built between Mannheim and Stuttgart in the south.

Levitation trains

These are trains without wheels, that will float above the track rather than run along it. There are two main kinds of levitation train. One is supported by an air cushion, rather like a hovercraft (*see page 58*). The other, which is known as a *maglev* (for magnetic levitation), uses a magnetic field maintained by electricity.

In the early 1970s several countries built experimental hover trains, but the idea now seems to have been abandoned. Maglevs seem to be a much more likely possibility. There are at least two different ways of creating and maintaining the magnetic field that holds the train above the track. One of the most practicable seems to be that which uses electromagnetic suspension. In this system electromagnets in the train are attracted to permanent magnets installed in the track, although instead of touching each other they are held a few millimetres apart. Power is provided by the electromagnets as they switch on and off.

The advantage of maglevs is that they can travel at up to 500 kph (312 mph), but no one has yet been able to devise an efficient system of points for maglevs, for switching the vehicle from one line to another. The other great disadvantage is cost: maglevs will undoubtedly be expensive to develop and expensive to operate, and it may be that no one will be willing to pay the high fares that may have to be charged.

Below: *The Aerotrain, an experimental project by Bertin and Cie in France. The train ran on a cushion of air on its own track, but was technically a non-starter and was superseded by the French TGV.*

THE PETROL ENGINE

With a few exceptions road vehicles of all kinds obtain the power that drives them from an internal combustion engine. These engines are so-called because they create power within their cylinders, in contrast with the steam locomotive (*see pages 66–7*), in which power is created outside the cylinders.

Most cars have petrol engines, and only a very few run on other fuels. In contrast, most trucks and buses have diesel engines. The petrol engine used in cars works on a four-stroke cycle. On the first stroke, called the *induction stroke*, the piston descends in the cylinder. As it does so, it draws a mixture of fuel vapour and air into the cylinder through the inlet valve. This mixture is highly combustible and only needs an electric spark to be ignited. On the second stroke (the *compression stroke*), the piston ascends, compressing the fuel mixture. Towards the end of this stroke, an electric spark produced by the sparking plug ignites the mixture. As it burns, the mixture expands, pushing the piston down the cylinder again. This is the *power stroke* of the cycle. On the *exhaust stroke*, the exhaust gases from the fuel and air mixture are expelled from the cylinder through the exhaust valve.

Thus power is only produced on the third stroke of the cycle. In consequence, an engine with only one cylinder would run very unevenly. Four, six or eight is the usual number, although some cars have as many as twelve cylinders. The four-stroke cycle of each cylinder is so timed that the cylinders fire one after the other; sometimes their power strokes overlap. The cylinders may be positioned in a single row (this is called in-line), in two rows with the crankshaft between them (horizontally opposed), or in various different V shapes.

A connecting rod links each piston with the crankshaft. The connecting rods convert the reciprocating (up and

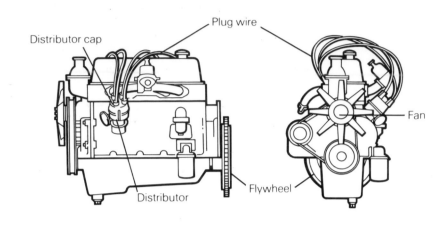

Side, front and cut-away views of a four-cylinder in-line petrol engine. The four cylinders fire in sequence so that an even amount of power is produced. The four-stroke engine is the most common type in use today.

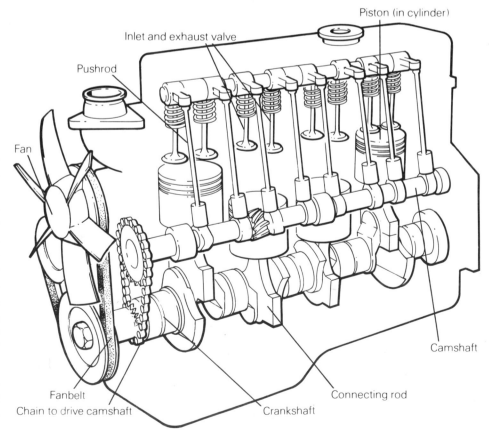

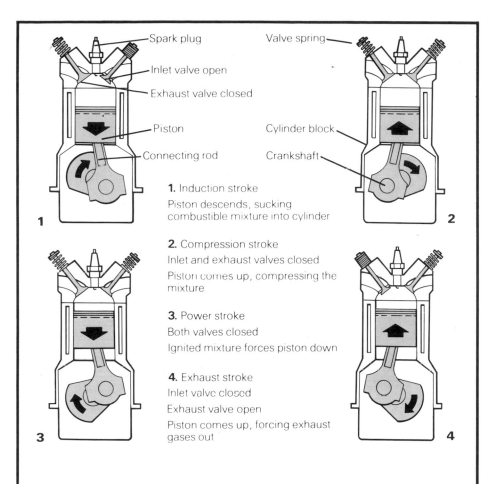

Spark plug
Inlet valve open
Exhaust valve closed
Piston
Connecting rod

Valve spring
Cylinder block
Crankshaft

1. Induction stroke
Piston descends, sucking combustible mixture into cylinder

2. Compression stroke
Inlet and exhaust valves closed
Piston comes up, compressing the mixture

3. Power stroke
Both valves closed
Ignited mixture forces piston down

4. Exhaust stroke
Inlet valve closed
Exhaust valve open
Piston comes up, forcing exhaust gases out

Above: The four-stroke cycle of the petrol engine. A mixture of fuel vapour and air is ignited, and the burning mixture produces the power that drives the car.

Below: The exhaust system, used to expel the hot poisonous gases from the car.

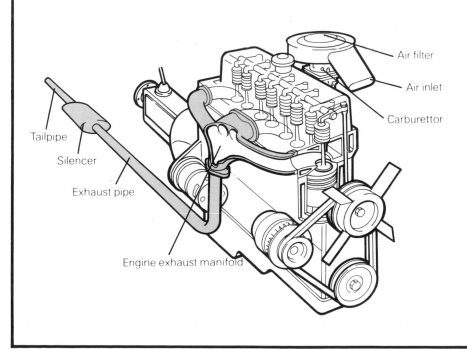

Air filter
Air inlet
Carburettor
Tailpipe
Silencer
Exhaust pipe
Engine exhaust manifold

down) movement of the pistons into a circular movement which drives the crankshaft. The crankshaft drives the flywheel and also, by means of a belt or chain, the camshaft. The flywheel helps to keep the engine running smoothly. The camshaft drives the distributor. It also indirectly controls the opening and closing of the inlet and exhaust valves. This is very important, as these valves must open and close at exactly the right moment in each cycle.

Running the engine

The *ignition system* provides the spark that ignites the fuel and air mixture in the cylinders. The electric current for the spark originates in the battery. The current is boosted to the right voltage by being passed through the coil. From the coil it goes to the distributor which distributes the current to each of the spark plugs. In addition, the act of turning the ignition key also sends current to the starter motor which turns the crankshaft. This starts the engine running, and once it is, it provides its own power for these operations.

The carburettor is the central part of the car's *fuel system*. It is here that the fuel, which is stored in the petrol tank and pumped to the carburettor, is mixed with air and vaporized. The resulting mixture of fuel vapour and air passes along the inlet manifold and enters the cylinders through the inlet valve.

The throttle controls the flow of the fuel vapour and air mixture towards the cylinders. The throttle is operated by the accelerator pedal (itself sometimes called the throttle). When the motorist presses down on the accelerator, the throttle opens and the flow of the mixture increases, so increasing the power of the engine. When the pedal is released, the throttle closes, and in consequence the flow of the mixture, and therefore the car's speed, decreases.

So much friction is created as the moving parts of an internal combustion engine come into contact with each other that some form of *lubrication* is

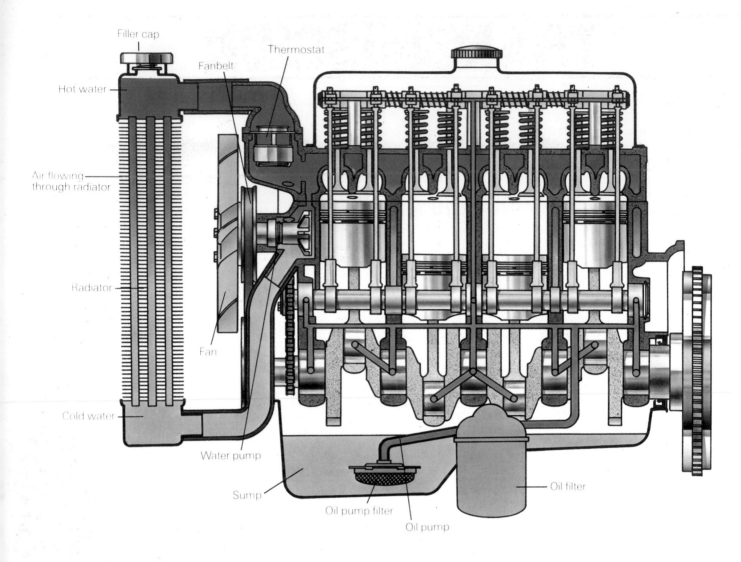

Filler cap

Thermostat

Fanbelt

Hot water

Air flowing through radiator

Radiator

Fan

Cold water

Water pump

Sump

Oil pump filter

Oil pump

Oil filter

essential. Without it the engine would seize up and be completely unusable. The lubricant used is engine oil, which also helps to cool the engine and deaden the noise it makes.

The system works quite simply. An oil pump driven by the crankshaft, or the camshaft, pumps oil from the sump, which holds the oil supply, through passages to all the moving parts of the engine.

The constant burning of the fuel vapour and air mixture in the cylinder means that an engine is an extremely hot place. Less than a quarter of the heat created actually goes towards driving the car, however. It is the job of the *cooling system* and the *exhaust system* together to get rid of most of the unused heat and thus prevent the engine overheating. In most cars water is used to cool the engine, although in some, air is used.

The hot poisonous gases expelled from the cylinders on the fourth (exhaust) stroke of the cycle leave the car by way of the exhaust system. This consists of the exhaust port, the exhaust manifold, exhaust pipe, silencer, and a tail pipe protruding from the back of the car. By the time they have passed through the system, the gases are sufficiently harmless to be released into the open air. The silencer reduces the noise the gases make as they leave the cylinder.

As already explained, the ignition system provides the spark that ignites the fuel and air mixture in the cylinders. The other *electrical systems* contained in a car – lights, indicators, horn, wind-

Above: *The cooling system circulates water through the engine to keep it cool and prevent it overheating.*

screen wipers and washer, rear window heater, warning lights, radio and so on – all receive their power from a dynamo or from an alternator. These are driven by a belt from the crankshaft, which, as we have seen, is itself driven by the engine. Often, when the car is running at speed, the dynamo or alternator produce more electric current than is needed to operate the car's various electrical systems. When this happens, the excess current is stored in the battery. The battery in turn supplies additional current if the dynamo is not generating enough, as often happens in slow-moving, heavy traffic.

TRANSMISSION

The power produced by the car engine must be passed, or transmitted, to the driving wheels to make the car move. This is the job of the transmission system. (The driving wheels actually move the car. They may be either the front wheels or the rear wheels, hence the terms 'front-wheel drive' and 'rear-wheel drive'.)

The transmission system consists of the flywheel, clutch, gearbox and final drive. In some cars, there may also be a propeller shaft. The clutch is attached to the flywheel, which is driven by the crankshaft. The gearbox contains three shafts, the input shaft, the layshaft and the output shaft. Each shaft carries a number of gearwheels. The input shaft links the clutch and the gearbox; the output shaft connects the final drive with the gearbox; and the layshaft runs between the input and output shafts. The final drive connects the output

shaft and the driving wheels. If the car's driving wheels are at the rear and the engine is at the front, a propeller shaft links the output shaft to the final drive. If the car has front-wheel drive and the engine is at the front, the final drive forms part of the gearbox and there is no propeller shaft.

When a driver wants to change gear, or to move into first gear if the car is stationary, the clutch pedal is pushed down. This separates the clutch from the flywheel so that the engine and the driving wheels are disconnected while the gear is being changed. The gear lever is then moved into the correct position for the required gear. The selector rods attached to the lever engage the appropriate gear wheels for that gear so that power can be transmitted through them. The driver releases the clutch pedal, so engaging the clutch and the flywheel again, and the

gear change is complete.

The gearbox

Power is transmitted from one shaft to the next by the act of two gear wheels engaging, or meshing. Each gear wheel consists of a number of teeth, and when they mesh, a tooth on one gear meets a tooth on the other gear. Gears of the same size have the same number of teeth, and in consequence each moves at the same speed. As a result, the shafts to which they are attached also turn at the same speed. If a gear wheel meets a

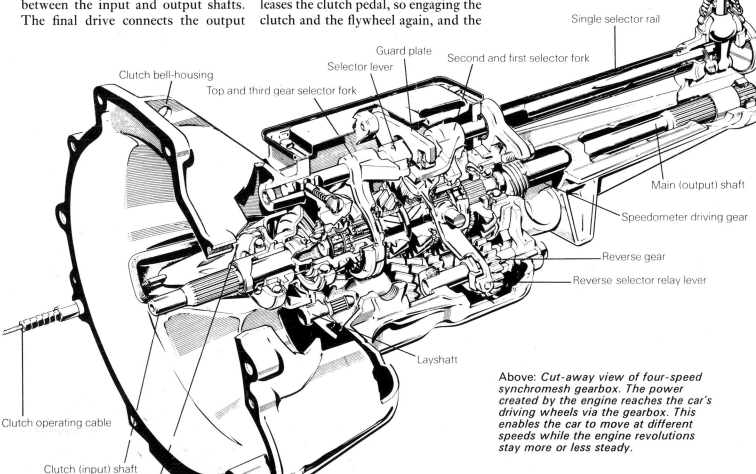

Above: *Cut-away view of four-speed synchromesh gearbox. The power created by the engine reaches the car's driving wheels via the gearbox. This enables the car to move at different speeds while the engine revolutions stay more or less steady.*

second, larger, gear wheel, the second gear wheel will move more slowly, as will the shaft to which it is attached. If, by contrast, a gear wheel meets a smaller gear wheel, the smaller gear wheel and the shaft to which it is attached will move more quickly.

Power is transmitted through the gearbox in the following way. The gear wheel at the end of the input shaft rotates at the same speed as the crankshaft. This is because, as we have seen, the input shaft is indirectly driven by the crankshaft. The gear wheel on the input shaft engages with another, slightly larger, wheel on the layshaft. Because this gear wheel is larger, the layshaft turns at a slightly slower rate than the input shaft.

The layshaft and the output shaft both have three separate gear wheels, one each for first, second and third gear, which engage in pairs to produce the appropriate speed. In first gear, the car wheels turn slowly because the force is being used to start the weight of the car moving. In fourth, or top, gear, the input and output shafts are directly connected, and neither the layshaft nor any of the gear wheels are used, and the car moves at high speeds. This is called direct drive. When reverse gear is selected, a system reverses the direction in which the output shaft, and in consequence the car's

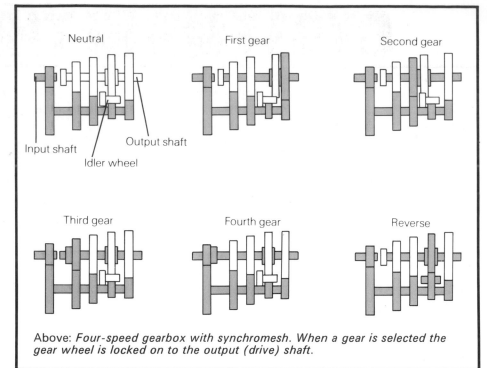

Above: *Four-speed gearbox with synchromesh. When a gear is selected the gear wheel is locked on to the output (drive) shaft.*

wheels, rotate.

The final drive is the last stage of the transmission system. From here the engine's power is passed to the driving wheels. Part of the final drive consists of yet another set of gear wheels which reduce the engine's speed. The final drive also includes the differential. The differential allows the driving wheels to move at different speeds from each other as the car goes round corners.

This is necessary because the outside wheel (the right-hand wheel if the car is turning left) has to travel further than the inside one. Half-shafts transmit power from the final drive to the wheels.

To move a car, a large force is needed by the driving wheel, which turns quite slowly. The engine produces a small force at a very high turning speed. Gears are necessary to reduce the turning speed (revolutions per minute) between the engine and driving wheels, so increasing the force. It is as if more force is concentrated into fewer revolutions.

The gearing system thus produces greater powers of acceleration (*not* greater actual speed) in lower gears, making cars agile in heavy town traffic.

Nowadays, almost all American cars and many large European ones have automatic transmission. An automatic transmission system changes gears automatically according to the speed at which the car is travelling. The clutch pedal is replaced by a fluid clutch. This involves no physical contact between the flywheel and the input shaft, and the force is transmitted instead by the movement of the fluid (oil) within the clutch.

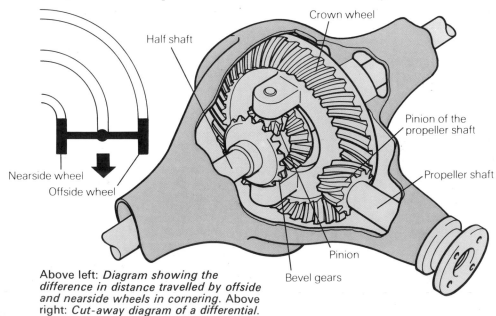

Above left: *Diagram showing the difference in distance travelled by offside and nearside wheels in cornering.* Above right: *Cut-away diagram of a differential.*

SYSTEMS IN THE CAR

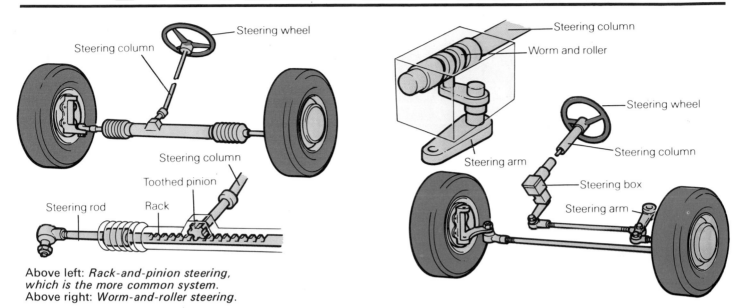

Above left: *Rack-and-pinion steering, which is the more common system.*
Above right: *Worm-and-roller steering.*

The driver controls the way the power from the engine is used by means of the *steering system* and the *brakes*. No matter whether the car has front-wheel or rear-wheel drive, it is always the front wheels that steer the car.

The steering system consists of the steering wheel, the steering box or rack-and-pinion, and track rods linking the steering box and each of the front wheels. When the driver turns the steering wheel, the shaft connecting the steering wheel with the steering box also rotates. Gears in the steering box convert this rotary movement into a lateral (push and pull) movement by which the track rods turn the front wheels. The more common rack-and-pinion system has a toothed pinion wheel at the end of the steering column which engages with a rack, moving it from side to side. Again, track rods at the ends turn the wheels. Each system is so designed that when the car corners, the inside front wheel turns more sharply than the outside one. As large cars are very heavy to steer most models are equipped with power-assisted steering.

There are two main types of brake, drum brakes and disc brakes. Drum brakes consist of the brake pedal, which drivers work with their feet; a series of hydraulically operated brake cylinders; and a pair of brake shoes and a brake drum on each wheel.

The action of the driver pressing the brake pedal down operates the main brake cylinder. The main brake cylinder operates in turn at least one slave brake cylinder on each wheel. The pistons in the slave cylinders press the brake shoes against the brake drum. The brake drum in turn presses against the wheel, so reducing the speed at which it is rotating.

Disc brakes work in a similar way. When the brake pedal is depressed, the same system of cylinders presses a pair of metal brake pads against a cast-iron disc, which stops the wheel rotating. Disc brakes are more powerful and more efficient than drum brakes and enable a car to stop more rapidly.

Below: *Disc and drum brakes. Most vehicles nowadays have disc brakes on the front wheels and drum brakes on the rear.*

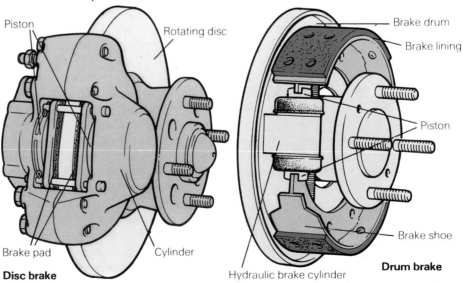

Suspension

Even the smoothest-looking road surface contains bumps and uneven patches. It is the job of the car's suspension system, and to a lesser extent of its tyres as well, to absorb and deaden the shocks created by the impact of the wheels on the road surface and to provide as smooth and comfortable a ride as possible for the driver and passengers. Uneven road surfaces can also be dangerous, and even a small hole in the road can cause a driver to lose control of the car. The suspension ensures that the tyres never leave the ground.

There are a number of different types of suspension system. Most of them consist of springs and dampers. When the car hits a bump, the springs bend or twist so as to absorb the energy created by the impact. Once a spring has absorbed energy, however, it must release it again by expanding. The dampers absorb the energy which is released by the expanding springs. A car without dampers would give its passengers a very bouncy ride indeed, as the springs would be contracting and expanding most of the time. Most dampers work hydraulically.

Below: *Independently sprung wheels: if one wheel meets a bump, the wheel on the other side is not affected.*

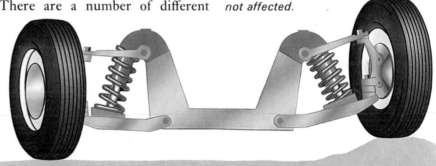

Above: *Cut-away view of a damper, a shock absorber which is fitted to give passengers a smooth, comfortable ride.*

Tyres

Tyres are the points at which the car and the road meet. They grip the surface of the road, thus providing the traction that enables the car to be braked and accelerated, and also help to absorb the vibrations set up by the surface.

Modern tyres are almost all made of a variety of synthetic rubbers. Most cars have tubeless tyres. In contrast with tubed tyres, in which an inner tube holds the air, tubeless tyres retain the air themselves.

There are two main types of tyre. The one most commonly used nowadays is radial-ply. These hold the road well when the car corners and have a very long life, between 40 000 and 48 000 kilometres. The casing cords run radially, and additional plies strengthen the tread. The other type is the cross-ply tyre, in which the fabric cords are stretched diagonally to brace the tread.

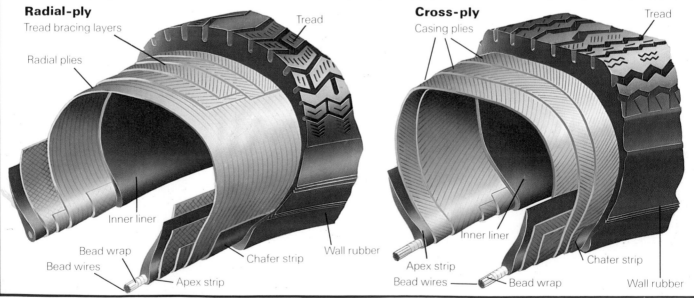

Radial-ply
Tread bracing layers
Radial plies
Tread
Inner liner
Bead wrap
Bead wires
Chafer strip
Wall rubber
Apex strip

Cross-ply
Casing plies
Tread
Inner liner
Apex strip
Bead wires
Bead wrap
Chafer strip
Wall rubber

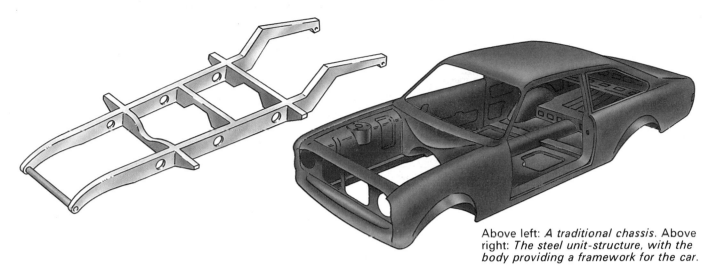

Above left: *A traditional chassis*. Above right: *The steel unit-structure, with the body providing a framework for the car*.

Bodywork

Something has to contain all the various parts of a car, and this is usually the job of the bodywork. Until fairly recently, the bodywork's only function was to enclose the passengers. The car itself rested on a steel frame known as a chassis. There were various designs of chassis: a typical one consisted of a rectangular frame strengthened by an X-shaped brace.

Although the majority of American cars and a few European ones – chiefly sports cars – still have a chassis, in most others the body itself now provides the framework for the car. This is called a *unit-structure*. Although the body is made of thin steel, it is so strong and rigid that in some designs no other support is needed. Some parts of the body are reinforced to give them extra strength, however, and sometimes the engine, suspension systems and final drive are mounted on sub-frames.

A large number of different factors have to be taken into account when the bodywork is designed. It must be strong enough to carry the weight of the engine and all the other systems as well as the passengers and their luggage. It must also protect the passengers in an accident: too weak a body will crumple, too strong a body will not absorb the impact of a collision. The car must also perform as well as possible, which means that the body must be so designed as to minimize wind resistance not just from the front but also from the sides. The moving parts must also be accessible for repairs and cleaning.

Below: *A controlled crash to test how a new car behaves on impact*.

THE MOTOR INDUSTRY

The motor industry is one of the largest in the world and employs countless millions of people. The number whose living depends on cars is of course far greater: not only the families of those who work in the factories but also all the workers in companies supplying car parts and other materials to those factories, and their families, and the people who supply them with services (shopkeepers, for instance), and so on.

Until about the early 1970s, most cars (and motorcycles and lorries as well) were made in western Europe (including Britain) or the USA – in fact in the very countries that had always built cars ever since they were invented.

During the 1970s, however, more and more cars were built elsewhere. Japan, for instance, which built less than 80 000 in 1959, produced over 2 600 000 in 1969 and nearly 6 200 000 in 1979. Korea is another country in which the industry is expanding rapidly, and experts think that as time goes on large numbers of cars will also be built in Brazil and Malaysia.

Planning a new car

Building a car is a complicated process. Thousands of different components (parts) have to be brought together and assembled in the right order. Moreover, the job has to be done as quickly and as accurately as possible. It has to be quick, because the longer it takes, the more the car will cost. And it must be accurate both for reasons of safety and because a customer buying a new car expects it to work perfectly.

If building a car is a complicated process, deciding to build one is just as complex, if not more so. It takes years of work and a great deal of money to develop a new car to the point at which it is put on sale. Development work (designing the car and preparing the factories and machines to build it) on the British Mini Metro, launched in

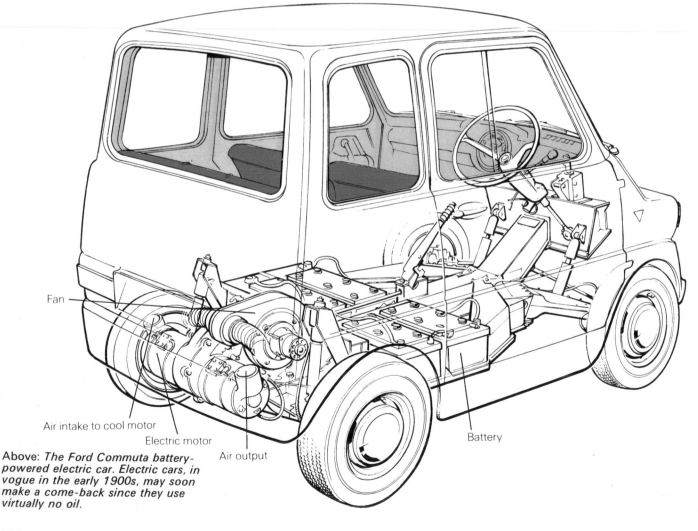

Fan

Air intake to cool motor

Electric motor

Air output

Battery

Above: *The Ford Commuta battery-powered electric car. Electric cars, in vogue in the early 1900s, may soon make a come-back since they use virtually no oil.*

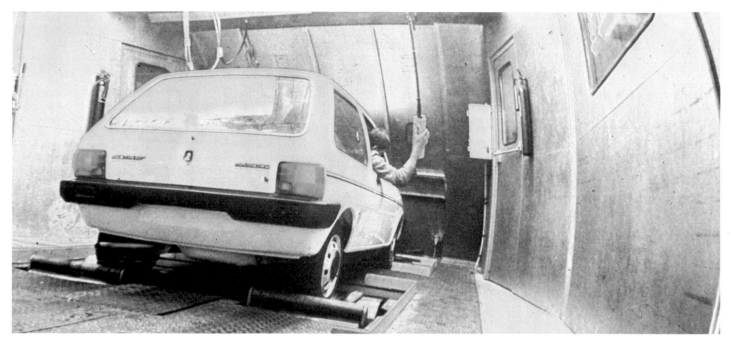

autumn 1980, took about five years, and development costs were as much as £275 million.

Once the type of car has been decided, development work by designers and engineers over the next few years can – and probably will – change the original idea for the car a great deal.

The first stage of development work is product planning. Major decisions have to be taken about the car: will it have front-wheel or rear-wheel drive; what sort of suspension system is best? These and many more questions have to be answered. Drawings are made of all the different versions that could be built, and costs are worked out. This involves estimating both the cost of each car – that is, the cost of the materials that will be used and of overhead costs such as wages – and the cost of developing new machinery or adapting old equipment to build the cars. Once all this has been done, a decision is made about which design to build.

Although there will be at least two years to go before the first cars roll off the assembly line, this decision is an extremely important one, for the next planning stage involves much more work and far greater expenditure. If a new factory will be required to house the production line, construction of the building has to start now so that it will be finished in time. A large amount of extremely sophisticated and highly automated machinery is used to build cars. Engineers must now start to plan these machines in detail specifically for the new car and then get them built by machine-tool manufacturers so that everything is ready in time.

Design

Meanwhile work is proceeding on the car itself. This is the stage at which its detailed design begins to be settled. Many different requirements have to be taken into account. The car must meet government safety standards, not just in the country in which it is being built but also in all the other countries where it will be sold. It must be convenient to use – the controls, for instance, must all be easy to reach and operate – and easy to maintain; all the parts of the engine that have to be checked or repaired frequently must be as accessible as possible. It must be comfortable to ride in, with as much space as possible for passengers and their luggage. And, as always, the cost of everything has to be watched.

Gradually the car takes shape in detail. Scale and full-size models are built and thoroughly tested. Every kind

Above: *Testing a Mini Metro before it leaves the factory.*

of road and weather condition is simulated (reproduced) so that engineers can see how the car behaves in different conditions and how long each individual part takes to break or wear out. Testing almost always results in a number of detailed changes, either to the parts or manufacturing techniques. When an actual assembly-line car is ready, it is tested on the company's private road track and given the equivalent of several years' use.

In the final few months before production is due to start, prototype cars are built by hand and then a few cars, known as pilot cars, are built by the machine tools ordered for the assembly line. At the same time, full-scale production is being organized. This involves compiling both the detailed schedules necessary to make all the different parts of the car arrive at the right spot on the various assembly lines at the right moment, and detailed instructions for the workers on the assembly line.

The last stage is the production on the assembly line of a couple of hundred cars for a final check. These are often shown to the press and used in the publicity campaign for the new car.

HOW CARS ARE BUILT

Car production is organized on an assembly-line basis. An assembly line is exactly what it sounds as if it is: a long line along which cars are gradually put together. The point to remember, however, is that an assembly line is not a production line: although a complete car does indeed roll off the end of the line, it has only been assembled there. The thousands of parts from which it is made have not themselves been manufactured there.

Rather less than half the cars' parts are actually produced by the car manufacturer. The rest are bought in from other specialist manufacturers. Exactly which components are not 'home made' varies from company to company, but usually tyres, wheels and at least some of the electrical equipment are bought from outside, and often the steering column, radiator and gearbox as well. In addition, raw materials for the parts that are made by each manufacturer have to be purchased. These include iron ore for the engine parts, steel for the body, glass, paint, foam rubber for the seats and so on.

Nowadays, almost all the work of ordering parts and materials from out-

Robot workers

Some car factories have automated machinery which can achieve far more accurate and rapid results than any human being. The most modern factories (such as those of the Ford and Fiat companies) have computer-controlled robots. The body frame of British Leyland's Mini Metro, for example, is

Sparks fly as robots work on a car.

made on an automated line containing 14 robot welders which at one point perform 250 welds in 23 seconds.

side is done by computer. Orders are often sent out to suppliers every day so that stocks never run low.

To make things yet more complicated, many large international automobile manufacturers assemble the same car in several different factories and build parts in yet more. For instance, the Ford Fiesta is assembled in factories in Dagenham, Britain; Saarlouis, Federal Republic of Germany; and Valencia, Spain. Parts are also manufactured in these factories and in no less than 10 others in Britain,

Above: *Body shell of a Fiat moving down the assembly line to receive its engine, transmission system and parts.*

France, Germany and Belgium. Ford's entire European operations are yet more complex: the company owns 25 factories in all the countries

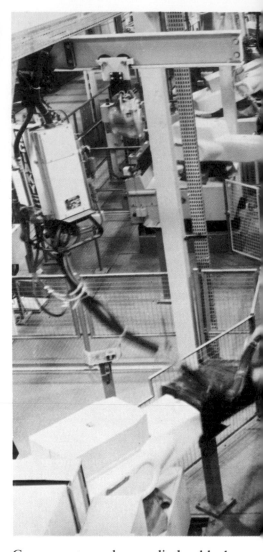

Above: *An automated welding line for side body panels.*

Right: *The 14 robots on this welding line do about 250 welds on the body shell of each car.*

mentioned above and also in the Netherlands, Portugal and Ireland as well. (In the USA, where the company's international headquarters are situated, there are a large number of assembly and manufacturing plants.) In consequence, the flow of parts from the company's own factories to the factories in which final assembly takes place must be carefully controlled.

The complexity of all these arrangements means that it is impractical to manufacture components for immediate use on the assembly line. Instead, parts – which may include engine castings and all the metal and plastic parts of the car, from body panels to arm-rests – are stockpiled in warehouses and are only delivered to the assembly line when they are needed for immediate use.

The assembly line

Before they reach the final assembly line, the various different sections of the car – body, engine and so on – are themselves assembled on sub-assembly lines.

In the body division, sheets of pressed steel are welded to form different parts of the car's body, including the sides, roof, back and floor. These sections are then welded to form the shell of the car. Once the shell is complete, it is immersed in a tank of rust-proofing paint and then, when that has dried, it is spray-painted, often with as many as three undercoats and three final coats.

Meanwhile, work on the different parts of the engine is proceeding.

Components such as cylinder blocks are cast (a process in which molten metal is poured into a shaped mould and allowed to cool and set) and then machined to exactly the right dimensions. Other parts are forged (hammered and pressed) and then machined.

On the final assembly line, which may be over a kilometre long, recognizable cars are created from the products of the various sub-assembly lines. First of all, the trim – chrome strips, seats, carpets, padding, door handles, window glass and so on – is added to the body. Then come items such as the steering column, lights, the radiator, the gearbox and the wiring system. Workers standing in pits beneath the car install the exhaust system and silencer, and many other parts. Finally comes the moment when the engine is

Above: *Electrostatic spraying booth, in which two coats of sealer paint are applied to the car body.*

Below: *A trimmed car body being lowered on to a waiting engine and suspension unit.*

installed, and the car is virtually complete.

At the end of the line, the car is thoroughly checked – lights, brakes, steering, engine – and if all is well it is driven off to await delivery to a dealer. The final check is extremely important, as the company's reputation will suffer if faulty cars are put on sale.

Working on an assembly line can be extremely boring if you have to do the same small task tens or hundreds of times a day. In consequence, some car manufacturers, most notably Volvo in Sweden, have rebuilt the assembly lines in their factories so that a team of workers moves along the line with one particular car. This means that they are responsible for building a complete vehicle rather than for just one tiny part of it.

ROAD BUILDING

Roads are built in much the same way as railways. A firm base has to be provided for the vehicles that will use the road, and construction work only starts after a route has been selected and the people living near it have been consulted.

The first job is to survey all the possible routes so that the best one can be chosen. Gradients are one of the main problems. The steeper the gradient, the more traffic speed will be reduced. Consequently, gradients are made as long and as gentle as possible. Traffic must also be able to reach a new road quickly and easily. Routing the new road straight through a town centre, or even through suburbs, however, creates far more problems than it

solves. Therefore, new roads frequently run on the edge of town, and special feeder roads are built, or existing ones improved, to carry traffic out to them.

Keeping all these factors in mind, road planners select the best approximate route for the new road. Then they make an aerial survey of the route. They also take samples of the land along the route and study local weather patterns. The engineers need all this information for a number of reasons. Cuttings, embankments and so on must be sited as safely as possible. In addition, to keep costs down, as little earth as possible must be moved.

All roads, whatever their size and however busy they will be, are built in much the same way. To give them

strength to withstand being pounded by traffic, they are all made up of several different layers. The number of layers and the material of which they consist may vary, however.

To begin with, bulldozers are used to clear the site of the road. Roots are dug up, and occasionally a path may have to be blasted through rockface with explosives. If bridges or tunnels are necessary, work on them must start straightaway or they will not be ready at the same time as the rest of the road. Next, a start is made on the earthworks. The topsoil is removed and set aside, ready to be used on embankments, grass verges and so on when the road is complete. Then the entire area that the road will take up – if it is a motorway, the grass verges, hard shoulders (emergency stopping lanes), both carriageways and the central reservation – is levelled and shaped.

Drains are installed during the earthworks. Good drainage is a vital part of road construction, since a road on which water collects can be extremely dangerous. Once the earthworks and drainage system have been completed, work on the *pavement* (road surface) can begin. First of all, however, the sub-grade, the bottommost of all the various layers of the pavement, has to be prepared. The sub-grade is simply a layer of compacted earth, often pressed down firmly with a heavy roller. The next layer, the sub-base, consists of aggregate (crushed rock or gravel) and may be up to 60 centimetres thick.

In some cases, the sub-base is omitted, and instead dry cement is injected into the top 15 to 30 centimetres of the sub-grade. Water is then poured on to the earth and cement mixture to harden it, making the base of the road stable.

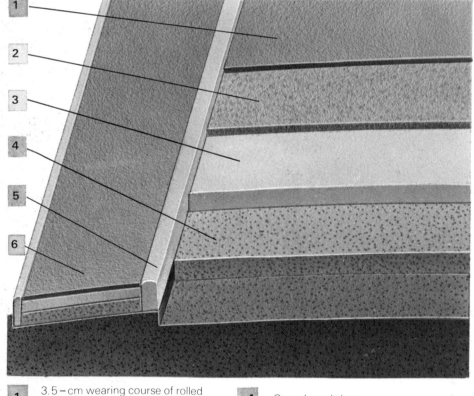

1	3.5 – cm wearing course of rolled asphalt
2	6.5 – cm layer of tar or rolled asphalt
3	25 – cm base layer of lean concrete
4	Granular sub-base
5	Concrete haunch
6	Hard shoulder

Left: *The make-up of a road surface.*

Right: *This motorway flyover is almost ready and the basic structure of the elevated sections is complete.*

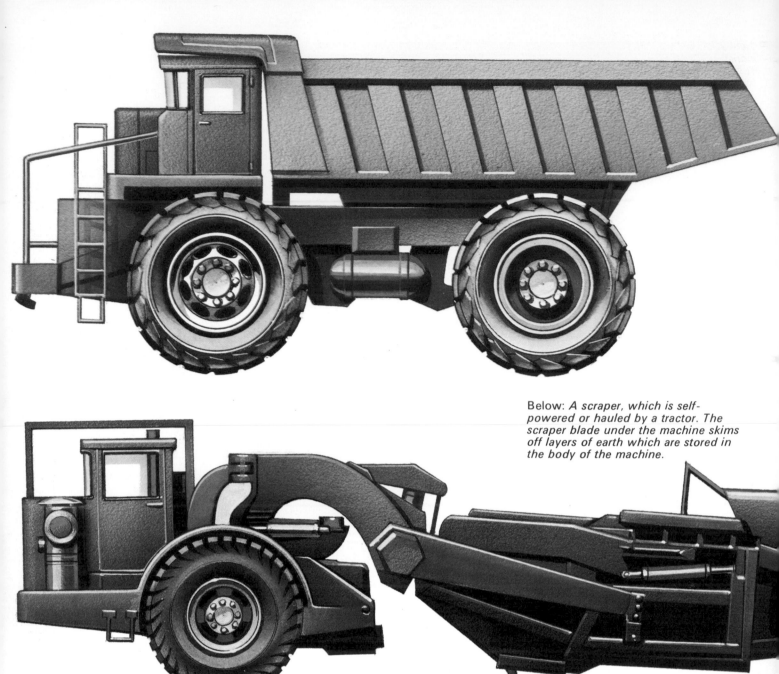

Below: *A scraper, which is self-powered or hauled by a tractor. The scraper blade under the machine skims off layers of earth which are stored in the body of the machine.*

The next stage depends on the type of pavement. The two types are concrete or black top, the latter (used most often) consisting of a mixture of aggregate and bitumen or tar. To make a black-top pavement, successive layers of *macadam* (aggregate mixed with tar, bitumen or both) and *asphalt* (a mixture of aggregate and cement) are laid. First comes the macadam roadbase, which may be up to 25 centimetres thick, then the asphalt basecourse (6 to 7.5 centimetres), and finally the macadam top layer, the wearing course, which is usually about 4 centimetres thick. If the road is to have a concrete pavement, concrete slabs between 15 and 30 centimetres thick are laid directly on to the sub-base.

Although the pavement itself is now ready for traffic, much more work remains to be done before the new road can be opened. Signposts, traffic warning signs and safety barriers have to be erected; overhead lighting must be installed, cats'-eyes laid down, white lines marked out (the lines consist of glass beads embedded in white paint). In addition, the road has to be landscaped: verges and embankments are grassed, and bushes and shrubs are planted.

The road network

In most countries throughout the world, there are five main types of road: cross-country long-distance motor-

Left: *A dump truck, used on most construction sites for carrying earth and rubble. Note the protective headboard covering the top of the cab.*

Right: *A bulldozer, used for digging and excavating.*

Facts and figures about roads and their use

country	kilometres paved road	square kilometres land/ kilometre road	vehicles/1000 inhabitants
Brazil	1 344 374	6.33	41
Federal Republic of Germany	169 146	1.47	360
France	1 520 805	2.79	399
Great Britain	331 483	0.69	329
Mali	7500	160	0.3
Norway	36 976	8.75	350
Switzerland	18 515	2.22	340
USA	4 961 126	1.84	654
USSR	689 700	32.47	figures unavailable

ways; urban motorways; main roads designed for fast speeds, but not of motorway standard; small rural roads; and small urban roads. The number of roads of each type and their length varies a great deal from nation to nation and depends on a considerable number of different factors: how rich the country is; the extent to which road travel is preferred to rail or air for both people and freight; and the importance the government attaches to spending money on roads.

On the whole, it is the richer nations, which have a lot of industry and in which people and goods move about a good deal, that have the most roads. In industrialized countries, where commercial traffic is heavy, motorways are an extremely important part of the road network because they are designed for long-distance high-speed travel. They also take traffic off other roads, leaving them clear. In western Europe, for instance, a dense network of motorways usually with three (sometimes

with two or four) lanes on each carriageway links all the major towns, and quite small communities can be reached by a well-made main road. Even the majority of country roads are paved. Elsewhere, as in Greece for example, there may only be a few motorways, with perhaps two lanes in each direction; there the main roads are fewer in number and smaller, and many rural roads are unpaved. In the poorest countries few roads – if any at all – outside the towns and cities are paved.

TRAFFIC MANAGEMENT

Once the decision to build a road has been made, the civil engineers and contractors employed to construct it are not simply told to get on with the job. Before they can start work, a detailed design specification for the road has to be worked out. This is the task of the traffic engineer.

In essence, traffic engineers plan both individual roads and the entire road network in an area in such a way that the traffic can move as fast and as safely as possible. They achieve this in two main ways: by the design of the roads themselves and by controlling the traffic as it travels along the roads.

Good sight lines are an important part of road design. If the road twists and turns a great deal, the opportunities for overtaking safely are reduced, since motorists cannot see round corners! This is dangerous and also leads to lower speeds.

Contrary to what might be expected, however, the ideal motorway or main road is not dead straight. Experience on the first motorways, which were straight, showed that on a straight road more than a few kilometres long, drivers lose attention and even doze off for a few seconds. In consequence, motorways nowadays are designed to curve gently whenever possible – but not so much that drivers have to slow down to take the bend. As a result, the view in front of drivers changes frequently, and this helps to keep them alert.

Everything on a motorway is designed to enable traffic to travel as fast as possible. Therefore, in contrast with other roads, there are no traffic lights, roundabouts or junctions. Traffic may only leave or enter the motorway at specially built intersections with other motorways or main roads; there is usually no access from the motorway to minor country roads. There are various different designs of intersection: the one used depends on the size and number of roads the intersection has to link.

In all cases, however, intersections are so designed that traffic remaining on the motorway need not slow down.

Whenever possible, slip roads (the roads that carry traffic on to or off the motorway at intersections) slope downhill when leading on to the motorway and uphill when they lead away from it. This gives traffic entering the motorway the chance to accelerate to the higher speed at which motorway traffic travels, while departing traffic can decelerate to the lower speeds on other roads. Exits from the motorway to an intersection are always placed before entrances on to the motorway from the intersection. If they were the other way round, traffic slowing down to leave would get mixed up with traffic increasing speed to enter; this could cause accidents and would mean that through traffic would have to reduce speed.

Traffic control

No matter which type of road it is using, traffic is controlled in four different ways: by road signs of various kinds; by traffic lights; by traffic law; and by the police.

Traffic signs (which by and large follow an international code so that a particular symbol means the same thing throughout the world) have three different functions: they can guide motorists, or warn them, or inform them of regulations. Clear signposting is vital. Motorists have to be able to take in the information they want very quickly, while continuing to concentrate on driving safely. On motorways and main roads, where traffic is travelling very fast, signs are very large and are also repeated several times.

Traffic lights are used at junctions and other busy spots to regulate the flow of traffic. On some stretches of town roads where there are many sets of traffic lights, the lights are computer controlled so that traffic travelling at the regulation speed will always reach traffic lights when they are green and so need not stop. Sometimes traffic lights are controlled by the traffic itself and change according to the number of vehicles travelling in different directions. Traffic lights are also sometimes used on motorways to show motorists which lane they should enter.

Other means of controlling traffic flow in towns include *one-way systems*, in which traffic may only drive in one direction, and *tidal flow systems*. These are designed to cope with rush-hour traffic. On a four-lane main road leading, say, north into a city centre, there may be three lanes taking northbound traffic and one southbound in the morning rush hour; two lanes in each direction in the middle of the day and during the night; and three lanes with southbound vehicles, one with northbound, during the evening rush hour. Drivers are informed of which lanes they can use by means of traffic lights over each lane.

Motorists have to obey a large number of regulations and laws when they are on the road. These are designed to keep traffic flowing efficiently and safely. Some of the most common regulations are parking restrictions in towns and cities; priority rules at junctions and roundabouts; and speed limits. It is the job of the traffic police (which in some countries is organized separately from the rest of the police force) to ensure that motorists obey the traffic regulations. In addition they often have to take emergency action, redirecting traffic after a serious accident has blocked the road, perhaps, or trying to sort out unusually heavy traffic congestion.

Right: *Heavy traffic on an eight-lane freeway in Los Angeles, California. In road conditions like this, it is essential that motorists obey traffic regulations.*

MOTORCYCLES

Like cars, motorcycles are powered by petrol-driven internal combustion engines. Although many of the more powerful models have four-stroke engines like those used in cars, lightweight motorcycles frequently have two-stroke engines.

The principle of a two-stroke engine is the same as that of a four-stroke: a spark ignites a mixture of fuel vapour and air in the cylinder, and the power this creates drives the piston down the cylinder. This happens every second stroke, however, rather than every fourth.

As the piston descends in the cylinder on the first stroke, it opens first the exhaust port and then the transfer port. Exhaust gases escape through the exhaust port. The fuel and air mixture passes from the crankcase (the area below the piston) through the transfer port to the top of the cylinder.

On the second stroke the piston ascends, compressing the mixture at the top of the cylinder so that it is ready

for ignition. It also closes the transfer and exhaust ports and opens the inlet port. This admits more of the fuel and air mixture into the crankcase from the carburettor. At the end of the second stroke, when the piston reaches the top of the cylinder, the mixture is ignited and the cycle begins once again. As in a car engine, the movement of the piston causes the crankshaft to rotate.

Other systems

Most motorcycles have two cylinders. Some have three, a few four, and the cheapest models have only one. The *lubrication system* in four-stroke motorcycle engines works in the same way as a car's. In two-stroke engines lubrication is achieved by mixing a small amount of oil with the fuel. Motorcycle engines are almost always air-cooled.

As on cars, a coil increases the voltage of the current supplied by the battery to that required for *ignition*. On small

machines (mostly those with a single-cylinder two-stroke engine), however, a magneto driven by the crankshaft replaces the battery. Most motorcycles are started by means of a kickstarter which rotates the engine, although some models have electric starters.

Transmission of the power created by the engine from the gearbox to the rear wheel is either through a drive shaft, as in a car, or, more frequently, by means of a chain. Most motorcycles have four gears, some as many as five or six. Quite a number of mopeds have automatic transmission, and a few scooters have direct drive (*see page 100*) to the rear wheel, without a gearbox but with a clutch and an accelerator (throttle).

A foot-operated pedal on the left side of the motorcycle is used to change gear. The clutch is operated by a lever on the left handlebar, and a grip on the right handlebar operates the throttle.

An efficient *suspension system* is extremely important, since motorcycles

Below: *The two-stroke engine, which works on the same principle as the four-stroke engine, except one piston stroke out of every two is a power stroke.*

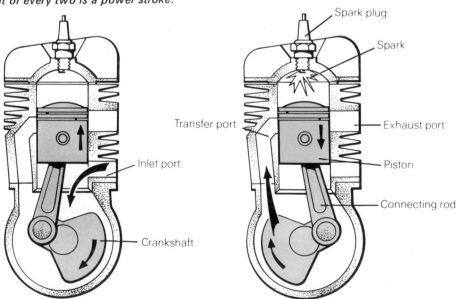
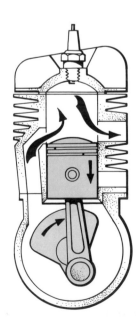

Spark plug
Spark
Transfer port
Exhaust port
Piston
Inlet port
Connecting rod
Crankshaft

Right: *The Yamaha XS750, rapidly becoming a classic. It has a double overhead camshaft three-cylinder engine and shaft drive.*
Below: *The touring Triumph 199 cc Tiger Cub of 1956.*

are far less stable than cars and far more vulnerable to the shocks caused by uneven or bad road surfaces. Each wheel has a separate suspension system, consisting of springs and hydraulic dampers.

Most motorcycles have drum *brakes*. Some recent models have disc brakes, sometimes on both wheels, sometimes on the front wheel only. The front brake is operated by a lever on the right handlebar, the rear brake by a foot pedal on the right side of the machine.

Tubeless *tyres* only began to be used on motorcycles in the second half of the 1970s. Many models are still equipped with tubed tyres, in which an inner tube retains the air.

Motorcycling used to be a specialist interest, and only real enthusiasts would buy a motor bike. The production in the early 1960s first of mopeds and scooters and later of a whole range of lightweight bikes changed all that, and now motorcycles are an extremely popular form of transport throughout the world. Although powerful 'super-bikes' are as expensive to buy, run and maintain as many cars, for economy and speed the lightweight models have no rivals. They are especially useful in congested urban areas, where they can reduce travelling time considerably.

BICYCLES

Bicycles are one of the most efficient forms of transport. They are cheap to buy and maintain, and cost virtually nothing to run. In busy urban areas, they are as fast as cars, buses or underground railways. Like a car, bicycles are available whenever and wherever needed. However, they use none of the earth's valuable resources of oil; nor do they cause any pollution. Furthermore, cycling is good, healthy exercise.

There are two main designs of bicycle: the traditional diamond frame, which has changed very little since the end of the 19th century, and the cross frame, introduced during the 1960s.

This has much smaller wheels than conventional models and often rubber suspension on the front wheel for a smoother ride.

Various types of bicycle are built nowadays. Roadsters are sturdy, reliable and suitable for everyday use; they are especially popular in the Third World where roads are poor. The small-wheelers are best used for occasional local rides, and are not designed for long journeys. Sporting bikes are made of lightweight materials and can cover long distances at high speeds; they are good for both day-to-day use and cycling holidays. Racing bikes are

stripped of all inessentials.

Gears are usually either derailleur or epicyclic. Derailleur are most common on racing bicycles and can provide up to eighteen different ratios. Sports bicycles and roadsters normally have epicyclic, or hub, gears, the most famous of which is the Sturmey-Archer, with which up to five speeds are possible.

Despite all the advantages of cycling, it became less popular in prosperous Western nations after the Second World War, mainly for economic reasons. Earlier, most people could not afford a car, and the only available means of

personal transport was a bicycle. Increased prosperity meant that more people bought cars, and as traffic increased, cycling became less enjoyable and more dangerous.

In the last ten years, however, this trend has begun to change. Sales of bicycles in Great Britain, for instance, increased from 580 000 in 1969 to 1 460 000 in 1979; and between 1977 and 1979 the number of journeys made by bicycle in central London went up by 42%.

In many countries, bicycle paths separated from the rest of the traffic are provided, and sometimes bicycle-only routes through city centres, or avoiding dangerous roundabouts or junctions, are laid out.

For many parts of the Third World, bicycles remain the only form of private transport that many people can afford. In China, for instance, over 12 million cycles were manufactured in 1980, and Peking in the rush hour is as jammed with bicycles as London, Paris or New York are with cars.

Above: *Cycling can be a pleasure as well as a means of transport.*

Below: *Cyclists in Peking, where only senior officials have cars. In the Third World, bicycles are the only means of transport for many people; in the West, more people are choosing to cycle.*

COMMERCIAL VEHICLES

Goods as well as people travel by road, in an equally large variety of vehicles. Small loads are often carried in transporter vans weighing two or three tonnes, such as the Ford Transit or the British Leyland Sherpa. Heavier loads are carried by heavy goods vehicles, often also known as lorries, or, in the USA, as trucks.

There are two main types of lorry – articulated and rigid (called straight in the USA). Articulated lorries consist of two separate parts: the cab in which the driver sits, known as the tractor unit; and the semi-trailer, on to which the goods are loaded. The tractor unit usually has two axles, sometimes three (an axle links a pair of wheels, one on each side of the vehicle); the semi-trailer has one or two axles. The tractor unit and the semi-trailer can either be coupled automatically or by means of a fifth wheel. The fifth wheel consists of a pivoting mechanism on the tractor unit and a kingpin on the semi-trailer.

Articulated lorries have two advantages. The fifth wheel makes them very manoeuvrable, because as the lorry negotiates a corner or a sharp bend, the tractor unit and the semi-trailer turn independently. In addition, because it only takes a few minutes to uncouple one semi-trailer and replace it with another, the tractor unit can be kept in use almost all the time.

In rigid lorries, which can have two, three or four axles, the driver's cab and the area occupied by his load are all part of the same structure. Some rigid lorries have 'demountable' bodies. These are containers which are lifted on and off a flat platform behind the cab. Because it only takes a few minutes to demount one container and put on another, the time wasted between lorry journeys is greatly reduced. Other rigid lorries have a flat platform on to which goods are loaded and covered with sheets and secured with ropes. Yet others have fixed sides that completely enclose the load, or drop-down sides, which make loading and unloading easy.

Both rigid and articulated lorries can also haul separate trailers behind them. (In some countries, however, Britain among them, articulated lorries with trailers are forbidden.) The trailer and the main truck are linked by a drawbar.

In most countries there are laws restricting the weight and length of heavy goods vehicles. In Britain, 32 tonnes is the maximum weight allowed; rigid vehicles may be no more than 11 metres long, articulated vehicles 15 metres and a rigid vehicle and trailer 18 metres. Many other countries per-

Below: *Some of the many types of truck on the road today – from the British Leyland Sherpa to heavy goods vehicles.*

Different articulated lorries. (A) United States FWD 6 × 4 'cabover'. (B) GMC 6 × 4 'cabover'. (C) German Faun drawbar trailer, for heavy or bulky loads.

Below: *A demonstration of the versatility of both rigid and articulated trucks. They can be adapted for many different purposes.*

mit greater weights: in most of western Europe, for instance, 40 tonnes are allowed, and even greater weights are under discussion.

Even the smallest factories own one or two vans or lorries, which they use to collect raw materials and deliver finished goods, among many other things. Bigger companies have much larger fleets of lorries. In addition to the lorries operated by companies such as these, you can also see on the roads a large number of vehicles owned by specialist road haulage firms. These companies do not manufacture anything. Their business is carrying other companies' goods, of whatever shape or size, to wherever they need to be sent.

Most large road haulage companies own a number of depots in different parts of the country which they use as collection and distribution points. Regular services, often one lorry a day, link each depot with all the others. Loads are collected from each customer and assembled in the depots to await

the next lorry going to the depot nearest their destination. Once that stage of the journey is over, the different loads are taken off the lorry and delivered individually.

Lorry operation

Petrol engines have not been used in lorries since the 1950s, and almost all lorries now have diesel engines. Many are turbo-charged to improve economy and efficiency. Experiments with gas-turbine engines have also been carried out.

Most lorries have a large number of gears, sometimes as many as 16 and certainly more than the usual four on a car. Power-assisted steering is almost universal. Most lorries have air brakes, but some are equipped with vacuum or electrical braking systems. There is usually an additional emergency braking system. Many lorries also have anti-skid equipment.

Because of the maximum weight limit, lorry designers are always looking for new ways to reduce the weight of their lorries so that more goods can be carried without infringing the regulations. Aluminium has been used in the USA instead of the traditional steel, and recently new metal alloys that are stronger, lighter and cheaper than aluminium have been employed. Attempts have also been made to reduce fuel consumption by streamlining cab fronts.

Lorry drivers are in control of heavy, awkward vehicles for up to 8 hours a day, often driving in heavy traffic, through bad weather and on poor roads. On a transcontinental trip they may be away from home for a week, sometimes even more, often sleeping in the cab. In consequence, lorry designers do everything they can to make the vehicle as easy to drive and as comfortable as possible. The controls are all within easy reach, and on many lorries the cab has its own independent suspension system. Some of the latest models have air-conditioning. The sleeping compartment, which is usually directly behind the front seats, is made as comfortable as possible. The most modern lorries may have a bunk bed, with a plug-in electric blanket, a reading lamp, blinds, perhaps even a wash-basin, a micro-wave oven and a refrigerator.

Right: *Customized truck en route across the United States.*

Below: *Titan tipper being loaded with rubble.*

PUBLIC TRANSPORT

Above: *Trams used to be a popular form of transport in London, but the last one ran in the early 1950s.*

Below: *Most other European cities have a large fleet of modern trams. This one is from Innsbruck, Austria.*

Nowadays, buses operate a large proportion of public road transport services. But trams are still used in a considerable number of cities, especially in eastern and western Europe, and in some, trolleybuses are still in operation or have been brought back.

For many years trams (known as streetcars in the USA) could be seen in the streets of practically every major city. In Britain, the USA and in many other countries, however, most tram tracks were ripped out during the 1950s and 1960s, and the familiar clanking noise of the old-fashioned trams was heard no more. Those cities which kept their trams, however, developed modern, efficient designs.

Like trains, trams run on rails. Because the rails are usually laid on city streets used by other traffic, the rails are embedded in a conduit in the pavement (surface) of the road.

Trams are powered by electricity, which they take from the national grid. As in an electric locomotive or an emu (*see page 70*), the electricity drives a traction motor. The current is supplied either from overhead wires or from supply rails sunk in the conduit. From the overhead wires, current is transmitted to the traction motors either by means of a pantograph held against the underside of the wire or through a swivel trolley pole which runs along the underside of the wire. Trams running on a system equipped with supply rails are fitted with a plough which travels along the conduit. Two contact shoes, one at each side of the plough, pick up the current from the supply rails.

The main advantages of trams are that they use very little energy in comparison with buses and they produce little pollution. Because, like electric locomotives, they can take additional power from the grid, they also have good acceleration, which helps to make an efficient service possible.

Their chief disadvantage is their in-

flexibility. Trams can only run where rails have been laid, and so altering a tram route takes a lot of time, work and money. In addition, because they cannot draw up to the kerb or the pavement when they stop, traffic has to halt while passengers cross the road to get on or off. Some cities get round this problem by building low platforms in the roadway on which passengers can wait.

Like city buses, modern trams, which are usually single-deckers, have a large amount of standing room and only a few seats. Many different designs are available. Some are articulated; some consist of two cars and others of two articulated cars. They may be manned solely by a driver or by a driver and one or two conductors. Trams operating on separate rapid-transit lines are almost indistinguishable from light rapid-transit vehicles (*see page 93*).

Trolleybuses

Trolleybuses combine features of both buses and trams. Their bodies are like bus bodies, and like buses they run on conventional rubber tyres. Unlike buses, however, their power source is not an internal combustion engine but the national grid, which supplies electricity through overhead cables. Two collector arms transmit the power from the cables to the traction motor.

The advantages and disadvantages of trolleybuses are much the same as those of trams: low energy consumption, quiet, rapid acceleration and lack of pollution, versus inflexibility.

The heyday of the trolleybus was during the middle decades of the 20th century. Although trolleybuses are still running in a number of cities throughout the world, many of the larger systems have been replaced by bus services. The energy crises of the 1970s, when oil prices increased enormously, brought renewed interest, however, and a number of plans for extending or re-starting trolleybus services were put forward. In Helsinki, for instance, where trolleybus services ended in 1974, they began to run again in the 1980s, with sophisticated modern trolleybuses.

Above: *The SWS trolleybus in Helsinki. It has electrical traction-motor drive, auxiliary drives and a diesel-generator.*

One interesting development that might point to a future for trolleybuses was a prototype vehicle built by a British company in 1980 for a South African customer. This double-decker has two power sources. It takes electricity from the national grid through overhead cables and collector arms, just like a conventional trolleybus. It is also equipped with an auxiliary diesel engine which drives the traction motor, as in a diesel-electric locomotive (*see page 70*). This enables it to travel for 50 kilometres independent of overhead cables.

Equipped with a fleet of vehicles of this kind, a transport authority would only need to install overhead cables in the city centre, where a number of different routes would use the cables. In the suburbs, where the cost of erecting the cables for a number of separate routes would be unjustified, the trolleybuses would be powered by their diesel engines.

BUSES

In towns and cities throughout the world, buses are the most common form of public transport, particularly for short journeys.

There are many reasons for this. First, it costs less to establish a bus service than an equivalent train service. Besides the locomotives and passenger rolling-stock, a train service requires track and a signalling and safety system which cannot be used by any other form of transport. Stations (large and small) also have to be built, as well as repair and maintenance depots and so on.

All that a bus service requires, by contrast, is the vehicles themselves, bus stops and shelters (which are much cheaper than even the smallest station), a few bus stations, and repair facilities. The 'track' that the buses use is the ordinary public road, which has in any case to be provided for cars and commercial vehicles (although it should not be forgotten that roads used by buses will probably need more frequent maintenance). The 'signals' they use are traffic lights and road signs. All this means that a bus service needs far fewer passengers to make a profit than a train service.

Therefore, bus companies can operate far denser services than a railway can provide. In most cities there are bus routes from the centre to every suburb; from one suburb to another; and routes that criss-cross the city centre itself. The cost of their infrastructure (track, signals etc) makes it impossible for railways to cover the ground so comprehensively.

Buses are also far more versatile than trains. It is quite easy to extend or alter a bus route, to serve a new housing estate, for example. Trains, however, have to go where their tracks are.

Buses do not have all the advantages, however. Because they stop more frequently, they are usually slower than trains. More important, they are also held up because they have to share road space with other vehicles. Buses also carry fewer passengers than trains.

In consequence, many city authorities have established rapid-transit networks. These set out to utilize the advantages of each form of transport: buses bring commuters from different parts of a suburb to an underground station; the underground carries them to city-centre stations from which they can either walk or take another short bus ride to their places of work. Bus lanes may be provided in the city-centre to prevent buses being held up by other traffic, or people may be encouraged to use buses rather than cars by low fares or free bus services.

At Runcorn, in the north-west of England, where a completely new town was built during the 1960s and 1970s, public transport was given priority from the start. The entire town is served by a Busway, a network of roads on which only buses may run. About 90% of the homes in the town are less than 500 metres away from a bus stop. At the local factories, the car parks are further away from the entrance than the bus stops, and cars also have to be parked a short distance from private houses. Because the buses run very frequently (usually every five, seven and a half or 15 minutes), most people find it quicker to go to work by bus than by car.

Below: *The Runcorn Busway, England, is a network of roads used only by buses. Most shops, homes and factories are very near at least one route.*

Types of vehicle

Most modern buses have a two-stroke diesel engine, power-assisted steering and automatic transmission. The position of the engine varies: it may be at the front (in which case the bus will be rather high off the ground), under the floor halfway along the bus, or at the rear. Many buses used on long-distance inter-city services have air suspension, which gives a comfortable and stable ride.

There are three main types of bus: those used for mass-transit services in and around city centres; suburban buses; and inter-city buses, run on long-distance services.

In most countries, single-decker buses are used for mass-transit services. Like light and heavy mass-transit rail vehicles, single-decker buses have a large amount of standing room (sometimes enough for about 90 people) and

relatively few seats, perhaps no more than 20. There are usually two doors; often one is used by passengers getting on, the other by those getting off, which reduces waiting time at bus stops. The seats have low backs, and there is little or no space for luggage.

In a few countries, notably Britain, double-decker buses are used for city services. These usually have 55 to 60 seats but very little standing room, maybe only sufficient for eight people. Double-decker buses are almost always operated by a crew of two (a driver and a conductor), whereas single-deckers may have a crew of one or two.

In some parts of the world *artic* (short for articulated) buses are in service. These can accommodate up to 180 passengers. They function in the same way as articulated lorries, with a 'trailer' behind the main bus.

Buses used on suburban journeys, and also on short inter-city runs of up to about 50 kilometres, usually have one

entrance at the front and some luggage space. High-back seats provide greater comfort for passengers.

Long distance bus transport

In many parts of the world, where most of the passenger rail network has been closed (as in the USA), or where only a few lines have ever been built (as in most of Africa, Asia and Latin America), buses are the most important form of long-distance public transport. Indeed, for all except those prosperous enough to afford air travel or a private car, they are the only means of moving from one place to another. Even in countries where passenger rail services are still extensive, there are many long-distance bus services. These attract a large number of passengers. This is because they are often not much slower than trains, they serve more places, on

Below: *Different types of modern bus.*

127

the whole they are just as comfortable, and they are much cheaper.

Modern inter-city buses are carefully designed to make what may be at least a day's journey, sometimes two or three, as comfortable as possible. There is usually a lavatory at the rear of the bus; the high-back seats recline, making it easier to sleep; there are individual reading lights, overhead luggage racks for hand baggage and ample room for heavy baggage in compartments under the floor of the bus. Single-decker inter-city buses have seats for 45 to 50 people and can cruise quietly at speeds of 110 kph (68 mph) and more.

Right: *Greyhound buses operate a network of long-distance services throughout the United States.*

Rural bus services

Although in rural areas, buses are often the only form of public transport, there may still only be a few passengers to use each service. This puts up the cost. One solution to this problem is to use smaller buses than normal, perhaps mini-buses seating 10 or 12 people. In many parts of the world such vehicles operate postbus services, collecting and delivering mail as well as carrying people to and from the nearest town. Similar vehicles are used to run community buses in remote parts of Britain; some of these services are organized not by a bus company but by groups of volunteers.

Below: *A country bus in Tanzania. In the Third World buses provide a vital lifeline in rural areas.*

AIR

BALLOONS

Travel by air began as long ago as 1783 when two Frenchmen made a voyage across Paris in a large, highly decorated balloon filled with hot air. The idea of filling a balloon with hot air – which is much lighter than cold air – was developed by two brothers, Joseph and Etienne Montgolfier. They did not wish to fly, so the honour of the first aerial voyage went to Pilâtre de Rozier and the Marquis d'Arlandes. The Montgolfiers' balloon was open at the bottom and in this opening there was a fire carried in a brazier. On 21 November 1783 everything was ready and slowly the balloon filled with hot air: then majestically it lifted off the ground carrying the first balloonists on a historic 9-kilometre flight lasting about 25 minutes.

Two weeks later another balloon flight took place in France but this time the balloon was not filled with hot air.

It was designed by Professor Jacques Charles, who was a scientist at the Paris Academy and therefore knew about the recently discovered gas – hydrogen – which is very much lighter than air. Professor Charles was assisted by the two Robert brothers and on 1 December 1783 the hydrogen balloon carried Professor Charles and the elder Robert on a 43-kilometre cross-country flight.

Ballooning became a popular sport but as a means of transport these craft had one great disadvantage: they were at the mercy of the wind. A balloon travels in whichever direction the wind happens to be blowing, and winds are notoriously difficult to predict. Nevertheless, some remarkable balloon flights were made. In January 1785, a French balloonist called Jean-Pierre Blanchard and an American scientist Dr John Jeffries took off from Dover, England in a hydrogen balloon. The wind was

Above: *The Montgolfier brothers' hot air balloon.*

blowing towards France but after a good start their balloon sank lower and lower. They threw everything they could spare overboard, even their clothes, and the balloon rose again. Blanchard and Jeffries reached France safely – but very cold! Several scientists followed Dr Jeffries' lead and used balloons to explore the unknown atmosphere. The British pair, Coxwell and Glaisher made many research flights and even tried to take aerial photographs. On one of their ascents during 1862 they reached a height of 7600 metres – though this was more by accident than design, because a control valve stuck.

Balloons had been pressed into military service as tethered look-out posts in 1794, but in 1870 a new military use was introduced during a war between France and Germany. Paris was completely surrounded by German troops and because there were no telephones or radio in 1870, the city was completely isolated. Several balloonists trapped in Paris suggested making flights over the enemy lines to the regions still held by French troops. The daring plan worked: passengers and letters were carried by balloons from the city – often at night. Of course the wind had to be blowing in the right direction and if this direction changed during a flight the balloonist was in trouble. Homing pigeons were carried in the balloons to take communications back to Paris; messages on microfilm (very small photographs) were attached to the pigeons and they flew back to their lofts in Paris. This remarkable operation lasted from September 1870 to January 1871.

Ballooning in the 20th century

During the early years of the present century, ballooning became a popular sport for wealthy amateurs, who indulged in games and competitions. The balloons were usually filled with hydrogen or coal gas (which was much cheaper) and the aeronauts (as balloon travellers were called) were carried in a wicker basket. By 1910 the excitement of ballooning was superseded by the thrill of flying in powered aircraft, with the result that balloons almost vanished from the skies. In the 1930s a small number of research balloons were produced to explore the upper atmosphere. One of the most famous scientists to use a balloon for this work was Professor Auguste Piccard of Switzerland. He made the first flight into the cloud-free, extremely cold, upper layer of the Earth's atmosphere called the *stratosphere* in 1931. He and Paul Kipfer ascended to a height of 15 837 metres.

A revival of ballooning as a sport began in the 1960s with the introduction of cheap and reliable hot-air balloons. These work on the same principle as the Montgolfier hot-air balloon but, instead of using a brazier to heat the air, they have a powerful gas

burner which is supplied with propane gas from pressurized cylinders. The balloon's *envelope* is usually made from special nylon but the *skirt* through which the flame passes has to be fire resistant, so asbestos and glass fibre are often used.

One of the most remarkable balloon flights in recent years took place in 1978 when three balloonists from the United States made the first balloon crossing of the Atlantic Ocean. Their balloon, called *Double Eagle II*, was filled with the lightweight gas *helium* and it ascended from Maine, USA, on 11 August. The westerly wind carried it across the North Atlantic, over Ireland and southern England to land in France – about 100 kilometres short of Paris. The journey lasted six days and the distance travelled was over 3000 kilometres – a far cry from Pilâtre de Rozier's and the Marquis d'Arlandes' 9-kilometre flight across Paris in 1783.

Above: *The first Atlantic balloon crossing, made by* Double Eagle II *in 1978.*

An ill-fated flight

One of the most ambitious balloon flights of the 19th century was the attempt by the Swedish engineer Salomon Andrée to reach the North Pole. In 1897 he set out with two companions from one of the Spitsbergen islands to the north of Norway, and they drifted over the ice towards the Pole. Unfortunately, ice formed on the hydrogen-filled balloon and the crew had to dump overboard all the ballast and everything else which could be spared. Despite their efforts the balloon came down on the ice after being airborne for 65 hours, yet they were still not halfway to the Pole. Andrée and his crew set out on the long trek back to civilization but after two and a half months they perished. Their fate was not known until 1930 when their last camp was discovered. Amongst the remains were diaries, and some undeveloped films taken by the explorers: these were carefully processed and remarkable photographs of the ill-fated expedition emerged.

Below: *This photograph of Andrée's balloon was found 33 years later.*

AIRSHIPS

Soon after balloons were invented, enterprising balloonists attempted to control the direction of their flights by operating large paddles or oars. Unfortunately, these had no effect and the balloons still went wherever the wind took them. To make a dirigible (steerable) balloon or airship some form of lightweight engine, driving a propeller, was needed. But, until the late 19th century, the only type of engine available to airship designers was the steam engine and this was particularly heavy because it needed a boiler to raise steam. Nevertheless a steam-powered airship was built in 1852 by the French engineer, Henri Giffard. It consisted of a sausage-shaped balloon some 44 metres long and suspended beneath this was a steam engine driving a large propeller. A triangular rudder was fitted at the rear to steer the craft like a ship. At full power this primitive airship could reach a speed of about 8 kph (5 mph) – a brisk walking pace – so it could not cope with a strong headwind, but it was a step in the right direction.

During the latter half of the 19th century two new sources of power emerged – the electric motor, running off batteries, and the petrol engine. In 1884 Charles Renard and Arthur Krebs built an airship in France, which they called *La France*, and this was powered by an electric motor. Travelling at over 20 kph (12 mph), *La France* could be controlled reasonably well in flight, and it even completed several round trip flights. However, the weight of its

Above left: *Giffard's steam-powered airship, 1852.*
Above right: *Santos Dumont's airship, 1901.*

batteries proved to be rather a handicap. By 1886 two German engineers, Gottlieb Daimler and Karl Benz had both invented petrol engines, and this gave new hope to airship designers. The first airship with a petrol engine was built in 1888 by another German, Karl Wölfert, but this was not a great success. The man who really captured the imagination of the public with his airships was Alberto Santos Dumont – a Brazilian who lived in Paris. His most notable flight took place in 1901 when he flew from St Cloud to the Eiffel Tower and back in less than half an hour, thereby winning a large cash prize. The total distance was only 22 kilometres, but several other attempts

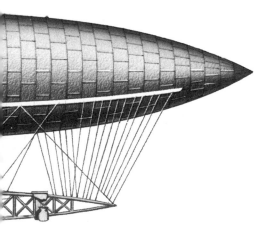

failed because of headwinds.

Most of these early airships consisted of a large sausage-shaped balloon with a *car* suspended below to carry the crew and engine. They were known as *non-rigid* airships because of the flexible nature of the large gas bag. During the First World War, non-rigid airships played an important part by patrolling the seas in search of enemy ships.

Giant airships and blimps

Large, non-rigid airships were very unwieldy and the German airship designer, Count Ferdinand von Zeppelin, designed huge and powerful *rigid* airships. They had a lightweight metal framework and the gas was contained in a large number of separate gas bags fixed inside the fabric-covered framework. After a number of failures, Zeppelin was joined by Dr Hugo Eckener and by 1910 they had regular passenger services operated by airships or *Zeppelins*. During the four years prior to the First World War (1914–1918) these Zeppelins carried a total of 34 000 passengers without loss of life – although there were some narrow escapes.

Throughout the First World War, Zeppelins were in action, patrolling the

seas and bombing targets in Britain. One of them was brought down almost intact in 1916 and British designers set to work designing an airship based on the crashed Zeppelin's design: the previous British airships had not been very successful. Two successful airships – the *R33* and the *R34* – were built to these plans but they were not completed in time to take part in the war. The *R34* made a historic flight in July 1919 when it completed the first nonstop east–west crossing of the Atlantic by air in 4.5 days (the first non-stop flight in the opposite direction took place a few weeks earlier by Alcock and Brown in a Vickers Vimy bomber). Not only did the airship *R34* fly direct from its base in Scotland to New York, but it also made the return journey to England a few days later, in only 3 days, with the help of a following wind.

The *R34* was not able to carry passengers across the Atlantic but within 10 years a passenger-carrying airship was operating a trans-Atlantic service, and once again it was one of German design. The *Graf Zeppelin* first flew in 1928 and made many successful flights. During the following years several giant airships were built – all more than 200 metres long. The British built the *R100* and *R101*, the Americans produced the *Akron* and the *Macon*, and in

Above: *The British airship R34 at Pulham in England after completing a return flight across the Atlantic in 1919.*

1936 the Germans built the largest of them all, the *Hindenburg*. Of these six airships, four were destroyed in dramatic accidents with the loss of many lives: passenger-carrying airships were then abandoned.

Smaller non-rigid airships or *blimps* continued to be built in small numbers and during the Second World War (1939–1945) the United States Navy used blimps from 1941 onwards to escort convoys of ships. These slow-flying airships were ideal for spotting submarines or other enemy warships and it is claimed that no ship was sunk while it had a blimp escort. The Goodyear Tire and Rubber Company built many of the Navy blimps and continued to build airships when peace was restored – as airborne advertisements.

Will large airships return in the future? Predictions that airships will return as the cargo-carriers of the future have been made frequently over the past 20 years or more, yet so far little progress has been made. To attract cargo away from ships or aircraft the airships will have to be not just equal to existing services, they must be better all round.

Above: *As the German airship Hindenburg arrived at New York in 1937 it burst into flames. This was the end of the era of giant airships.*

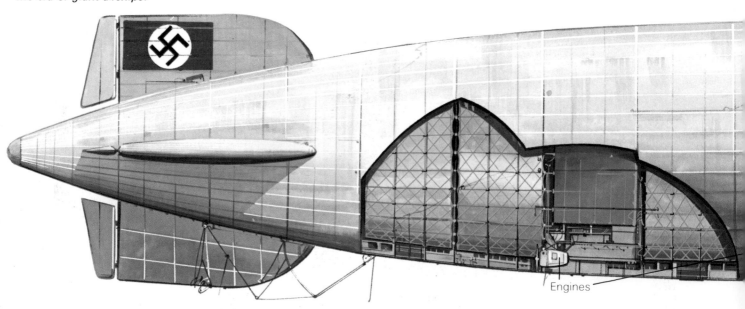

Engines

Above: *A modern non-rigid airship, the Goodyear* Europa *is used for joy-rides, advertising and carrying TV cameras.*

Below: *The gigantic German Zeppelin LZ129* Hindenburg *of 1936 carried 50 passengers in great luxury. They were housed inside the hull where there was even a dance floor. Four large diesel engines propelled the airship at almost 140 kph.*

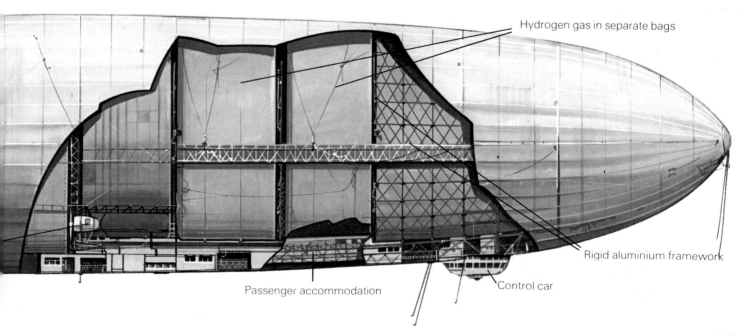

Hydrogen gas in separate bags

Rigid aluminium framework

Passenger accommodation

Control car

BIRTH OF THE AIRLINER

When man first tried to fly with wings it seemed natural to copy the birds and try to recreate their wing-flapping action, yet this was a false trail and no successful wing-flapping flying machine or *ornithopter* has ever been built. That great inventor of the 15th century, Leonardo da Vinci, designed several ornithopters – none of which could ever have worked. The answer was to use fixed wings – like a soaring bird. A British engineer called Sir George Cayley sketched a fixed-wing aircraft in 1799 and half a century later, he built a full-size glider which carried his coachman across a small valley. The coachman was a reluctant pilot and threatened to resign – he did not appreciate the fact that he had made the first gliding flight in history! Although Cayley studied the possibilities of powered flight, he lacked a suitable engine.

In 1842–3 two other British designers made a serious study of powered flight: William Samuel Henson and his friend John Stringfellow designed a magnificent *Aerial Steam Carriage*. Prints of the projected machine were produced, showing it in flight over London and even cruising over the Pyramids in Egypt. Lack of money prevented its construction but Stringfellow did make a steam-powered model which flew across a room.

The invention of the petrol engine in 1886 made powered flight possible, but many of the early attempts were nothing more than uncontrolled hops: real flight required control through the air and, for this, man had to learn the art of gliding. After studying the soaring flight of birds a German engineer called Otto Lilienthal built his first glider in 1891. He controlled it by moving his weight about – modern hang-gliders use the same principle. After making some 2000 flights Lilienthal was killed in a gliding accident but his work was continued by the British pioneer Percy Pilcher who also died as the result of a crash. An American, Octave Chanute, collected together all the available information on gliding and built further gliders – although his most important contribution may have been the encouragement he gave to his fellow countrymen Wilbur and Orville Wright.

Powered flight

The Wright brothers set about solving the problems of flight in their own methodical way. First they developed a means of controlling a glider using movable control surfaces – instead of weight shifting. Then they designed and built their own lightweight petrol engine and on 17 December 1903 they made the world's first genuine flight in their biplane *Flyer*. Because they were worried in case rivals might steal their ideas, the Wrights did most of their flying in secret: in fact the attempts of another American pioneer Samuel Pierpont Langley received much more publicity – despite ending in failure. The original Wright *Flyer* made four flights, the longest lasting just 59 seconds. A new *Flyer* was built in 1904 and this made about 80 flights including

Below: *Otto Lilienthal flying his glider in 1896.*

simple manoeuvres and a complete circuit over the field. The longest flight achieved was 5 minutes 4 seconds. During the following year *Flyer No. 3* made several longer flights – one lasting 38 minutes 3 seconds. In 1908, *Flyer No. 3* was modified to take a passenger and on 14 May, C. W. Furnas became the first passenger on a powered flight. Later in the year Wilbur demonstrated the latest *Flyer* – the model A – in France, and observers were astonished by its performance. After several long flights Wilbur remained airborne for 2 hours 20 minutes on 31 December 1908.

During the period 1903–1914, flying became a popular sport. Some enthusiasts designed, built and flew their own machines as a hobby. Many race-meetings and flying displays were held, and the public flocked to see the weird new machines perform. Records of speed, height and endurance were no sooner established than they were broken a short time later. In 1909 Louis Blériot made history by flying across the English Channel from France to England in less than 24 hours, and in 1911 the first officially sponsored airmail service was introduced, in England, between Hendon and Windsor.

Just when aircraft were emerging as a practical means of transport, the First World War broke out and they were hastily adapted for military purposes. The performance of aircraft and their engines improved rapidly under wartime conditions as each side tried to build better machines than their opponents. A typical flying speed of a scout or fighter in 1914 was 113 kph (70 mph) but by 1918 this speed had been doubled. Bombers too had improved and increased in size: when the war ended, large four-engined *biplanes* (planes having two wings, one above the other) were being produced which were capable of flying from France to bomb Berlin.

With the world at peace again, many pilots were looking for work and un-

Above: *Orville Wright takes off, watched by his brother Wilbur, in 1903.*

wanted military aircraft were available at low prices: the stage was set for air travel to make a promising start. After some pioneering flights during the summer of 1919 the world's first daily commercial scheduled air service opened on 25 August between London and Paris. One aircraft to fly that day was a large converted bomber, the Handley Page 0/400 which could carry up to 11 passengers. A Handley Page Transport leaflet said:

'The seating accommodation is arranged as follows: After-cabin to seat six, forward-cabin to seat two passengers, and for those who prefer to travel in the open, two seats are arranged in front of the pilot. An observation platform with a sliding roof is fitted in the after-cabin.'

– a far cry from the modern jet airliner!

Below: *The Handley Page 0/400 bomber turned airliner.*

TRAIL-BLAZERS

Although the first regular daily airline services started in August 1919 the fares were too high to attract many passengers, consequently there was not enough work for all the qualified pilots. Some of the more adventurous airmen turned their attention to conquering the continents and oceans of the world by air. The Atlantic Ocean was one of the first targets, especially since £10 000 had been offered by a British newspaper as a prize for the first non-stop flight. In May 1919 a United States Navy flying boat, the NC-4, did fly across the Atlantic but it landed at the Azores to refuel and so could not claim the prize. Two attempts to make a direct crossing were made in the same month but both ended in failure. Then on 14 June 1919, a converted Vickers Vimy bomber with a British crew took off from Newfoundland piloted by Captain John Alcock with Lieutenant Arthur Whitten Brown as navigator. Despite fog, rain, high winds and ice, they reached the coast of Ireland after flying for nearly 16 hours. Alcock and Brown crossed the Irish coast near the wireless station at Clifden only a little way off course, a remarkable feat of navigation after covering 3043 kilometres. The first flight in the opposite direction was made a few weeks later by the British airship *R34* which then went on to make the return journey.

Many epic flights were made in these post-war years. The Australian brothers Keith and Ross Smith flew from Britain to Australia in 1919 and a year later Pierre Van Ryneveld and Quintin Brand flew to South Africa, both flights being made in Vickers Vimys. By 1924 the United States Army Air Service was ready to attempt a round-the-world flight, in short stages. Four specially

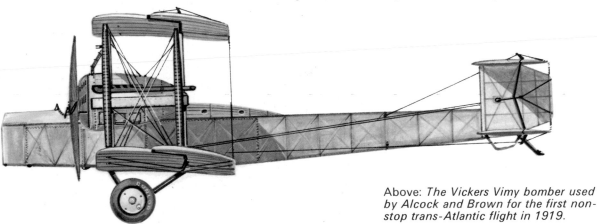

Above: *The Vickers Vimy bomber used by Alcock and Brown for the first non-stop trans-Atlantic flight in 1919.*

Epic flights across the world

Long ocean crossings continued to be a great challenge for the intrepid aviators. The Pacific was conquered in 1928 by the Australian Charles Kingsford-Smith and his crew in a three-engined Fokker F.VII monoplane called *Southern Cross*. In 1927, the American Charles Lindbergh flew solo from New York to Paris in 33.5 hours and became an overnight hero. Women pilots joined the men and keen competition developed to set up the fastest time from place to place. One of the most famous women pilots was Amy Johnson who flew from England to Australia in 1930. Delays on the latter stages of the flight ruled out a record, but she was the first woman to fly solo to Australia.

Right: *Amy Johnson and her Gipsy Moth.*

designed Douglas World Cruisers set out on 6 April and by 28 September two of the aircraft had completed the 42 398-kilometre journey. Another round-the-world flight made headline news in 1931, when an American pilot Wiley Post, and his Australian navigator Harold Gatty, completed the trip in 8 days 16 hours. Two years later, Wiley Post flew round the world again but this time he did it alone and became the first man to make this long journey solo.

Exploring new airways

Not all the pioneering flights were made to break records; some pilots turned their attention towards flights of discovery. A number of these flights were

Left: *Alan Cobham returns from Australia in 1926.*

Below left: *Explorer Roald Amundsen's airship* Norge *before its trans-polar flight in 1926.*

was great rivalry between the American team led by Admiral Richard Byrd and Floyd Bennett, using a three-engined Fokker F.VII equipped with skis, and Amundsen, this time equipped with an airship flown by its Italian designer General Umberto Nobile. Byrd flew from Spitsbergen to the North Pole and back on 9 May 1926. Amundsen was one of the first to congratulate Byrd and, although disappointed, his party set out a day later in the airship. They reached the North Pole and continued to Alaska and so made the first flight across the polar region.

Many flights were made in the northern polar regions during the following years to investigate the possibilities of using this route for airliners. However, a survey of this route in 1933 showed that there were not sufficient airfield sites in these barren lands for the short-range airliners available at that time.

Flying in the Antarctic did not arouse as much interest as the Arctic because it was not on a possible air route, but, after several survey flights, Byrd flew over the South Pole on 28 November 1929.

also notable as first flights, but many were made mainly to survey the unknown areas, sometimes with a view to establishing air routes across them. Suitable sites for airfields or seaplane bases were sought, and observations on the prevailing weather conditions made.

One of the greatest pioneers of the airways was Sir Alan Cobham of Britain who set out to prove that an aircraft could fly long distances but still keep to a time schedule. He also surveyed the most suitable routes and possible airfields along them. Between 1924 and 1928 Cobham made out-and-return flights from Britain to Rangoon in Burma, Cape Town in South Africa, and Sydney in Australia, and also made a 32 200-kilometre flight round Africa. These flights had to be carefully

planned: there were few airfields available, therefore petrol and other supplies had to be transported to the proposed landing sites. Owing to this shortage of airfields, Cobham used a floatplane and a flying boat for his two longest flights because suitable stretches of water could usually be found for landing and taking off.

The vast unknown regions of the Arctic and Antarctic were a great challenge to airmen: the Swedish balloonist Andrée made an unsuccessful attempt to reach the North Pole by air in 1897 (*see page 131*) and in 1925 the great Norwegian explorer Roald Amundsen led an unsuccessful expedition which used two flying boats. Then, in 1926, two expeditions were preparing for an attempt at the same time. There

Above: *American pioneer aviator Richard E. Byrd was the first person to fly over both Poles.*

POWER TO FLY

Once the Wright brothers, Wilbur and Orville, had learned how to fly a glider they had turned their attention to an engine and naturally had looked at the engines powering the recently invented motor car. The early car designers – and the early airship designers – had tried out three sources of mechanical power: the steam engine, the electric motor and the petrol engine. The petrol engine was the most promising because it was lighter than the other two although it needed a fuel tank: the steam engine needed a boiler plus fuel storage, and the electric motor required batteries.

In 1885 a German engineer called Gottlieb Daimler and his friend Wilhelm Maybach built an engine which worked by exploding petrol vapour inside a cylinder (hence the name *internal combustion engine*). The explosion moved a circular piston, which could slide to and fro inside the cylinder: this *reciprocating* movement was converted into rotation by means of

a simple crank. Daimler fitted his engine into a primitive motor cycle. In the same year another German engineer, Karl Benz, working separately from Daimler, produced a three-wheeled car with a petrol engine. The following year Daimler produced a four-wheeled car with a high-speed petrol engine and this engine can be claimed to be the forerunner of modern motor car and aircraft engines.

Daimler's first engine had just one cylinder but most of the successful aero-engines had two or more. Many cylinder arrangements were tried but the one chosen by the Wright brothers had four, one behind the other or *in-line*. The four pistons moved up and down inside the cylinders and were connected to a crankshaft which rotated. The Wrights fitted two propellers to drive their aircraft through the air and these were driven by bicycle chains from the crankshaft. Most designers fitted a propeller to an extension of the crankshaft

and mounted the engine in the nose of the aircraft. In-line engines sometimes had six or even eight cylinders but this arrangement resulted in a very long engine. A more compact engine could be built by arranging the cylinders around a short crankshaft. Since the cylinders radiated from the crankshaft this was called a *radial* engine and once again the propeller rotated with the crankshaft. A very unusual engine was produced in France just before the First World War. It looked like a radial engine but the whole engine rotated around the crankshaft which was fixed to the aircraft: the propeller was attached to the rotating engine. This arrangement created many problems but these were overcome and the *rotary* engine was a great success.

Petrol engines would become too hot if they were not cooled and, like most motor cars, the in-line aero-engines were cooled by water flowing round the cylinders. This heated the water which

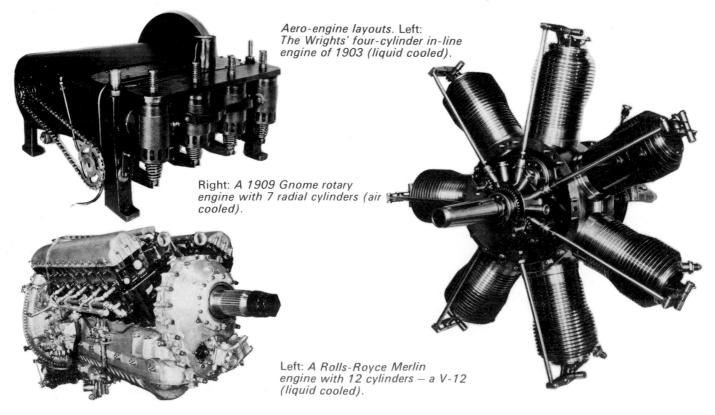

Aero-engine layouts. Left: *The Wrights' four-cylinder in-line engine of 1903 (liquid cooled).*

Right: *A 1909 Gnome rotary engine with 7 radial cylinders (air cooled).*

Left: *A Rolls-Royce Merlin engine with 12 cylinders – a V-12 (liquid cooled).*

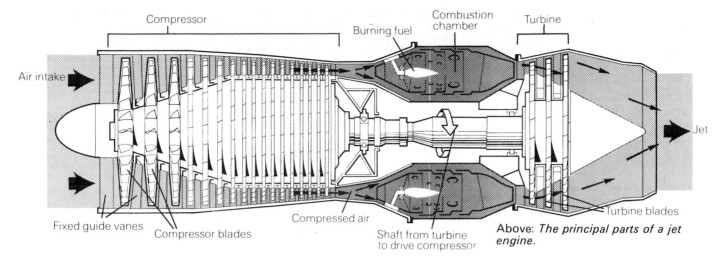

Compressor | Burning fuel | Combustion chamber | Turbine

Air intake

Fixed guide vanes | Compressor blades | Compressed air | Shaft from turbine to drive compressor

Jet

Turbine blades

Above: *The principal parts of a jet engine.*

was then cooled in a radiator. Radial and rotary engines were usually cooled by air flowing over their cylinders and these air-cooled engines can be recognized by the fins on their cylinders which increase the effectiveness of the cooling air.

Between the two World Wars there was great rivalry between the world's leading aero-engine companies. In Britain, Rolls-Royce preferred in-line liquid-cooled engines while the Bristol company favoured air-cooled radial engines. Both companies made some very successful engines, for example the Rolls-Royce Merlin in the Spitfire (introduced in 1936) and the Bristol Hercules which powered the later Wellington bombers (introduced in 1939). Two of the largest engine companies in the United States favoured the radial layout: Wright produced their famous Whirlwind and later Cyclone engines, while Pratt and Whitney built the Wasp, Twin Wasp and Wasp Major. The Allison Division of General Motors concentrated on in-line liquid-cooled engines and these were fitted to several American fighter aircraft of the late 1930s. In Germany, another type of internal combustion engine was developed for aircraft use – the diesel. The Junkers factory built diesel engines for industrial use and they adapted their design for use in aircraft. The Junkers Jumo was probably the most successful diesel aero-engine and was used to power several German bombers and flying boats.

The jet engine

The invention of the jet engine revolutionized aircraft design and performance, yet the significance of the first jet aircraft passed almost unnoticed just before the Second World War. This was the German Heinkel He 178 which flew in August 1939, some two years before the first British jet engine was ready for flight testing. However, the Heinkel's engine was never developed for production, whereas many of the early British and American jet aircraft were powered by engines based on the British design developed by a Flying Instructor in the Royal Air Force called Frank Whittle (later to become Sir Frank Whittle).

Jet engines belong to a whole family of engines called *gas turbines*. In a gas turbine, air is drawn into the engine and compressed by an air compressor, then it passes to a combustion section into which fuel is sprayed and ignited. The fuel burns fiercely and produces hot gases at a high temperature and pressure. These gases expand and rush out from the rear of the engine through a pipe and nozzle as a jet which produces propulsive thrust. However, before emerging they pass through a turbine (a high-speed 'windmill'), and the revolving blades of the turbine turn a shaft which drives the compressor. If a larger turbine is fitted it can be used to drive a propeller in addition to the compressor, and this is called a *turbo-*

prop or *prop-jet* engine.

The power of a jet engine can be increased by burning more fuel in the jet as it emerges from the engine into a special jet pipe, and this is called an after-burner or reheat. Although this is a relatively simple alteration it does use rather a lot of expensive fuel. A more efficient way to produce an engine of increased power is to design one with several compressors and turbines in stages. Each set of compressor-turbine units is called a spool: one of the first twin-spool engines was the Bristol Olympus which was later developed for use in Concorde. The next improvement in jet engine design was to allow some or all of the air from the first compressor to bypass the rest of the engine and emerge in the jet pipe. This *bypass* engine gives more power, yet uses less fuel. Finally a variation of the bypass, called a *turbo-fan* or *ducted-fan*, has been introduced in recent years to power the largest jet aircraft such as the Boeing 747 'Jumbo', the Lockheed TriStar and the Douglas DC-10. Even more air bypasses the engine and this is done by fitting a large compressor at the front of the engine which consists of a fan (a multi-bladed propeller) and is housed in a large tubular fairing (or duct) – hence the name *ducted-fan*. Such fan engines are not only more powerful and efficient but, since the bypass air surrounds and blankets the engine and jet, they are quieter too, which is a very important consideration nowadays.

HOW AIRCRAFT FLY

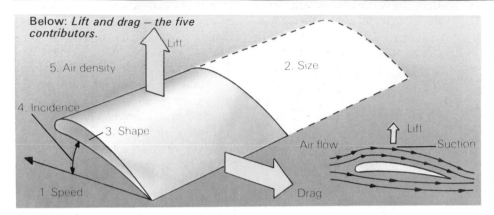

Below: *Lift and drag – the five contributors.*

5. Air density

4. Incidence

3. Shape

2. Size

1 Speed

Lift

Air flow

Lift

Suction

Drag

A balloon lifts into the air because it is lighter than air, but an aircraft, which is heavier than air, must find some other way of producing *lift*. The wing of an aircraft moves quickly through the air and the flow of air over the wing produces an upwards force or lift. The study of air flowing around objects is called aerodynamics and one of the first aerodynamicists was the Ancient Greek philosopher Aristotle. He studied a projectile flying through the air and declared that in the wake of the projectile there was a region without air – in other words a vacuum. In this he was correct, but then his theory went astray for Aristotle suggested that the surrounding air rushing in to fill this vacuum pushed the projectile along. The opposite is in fact true, for this region of vacuum or suction behind the projectile tries to hold it back and this slows it down. The air resistance at the nose of the projectile, caused by a region of pressure, also retards the projectile and the combined effect is known as *drag*. All high-speed vehicles suffer from the effects of drag and these include aircraft, cars, motorcycles and railway trains but streamlining helps to reduce drag and so increase maximum speeds.

An aircraft in steady flight is subjected to a double tug-of-war. Lift from the wing pulls the aircraft upwards and balances the weight which acts downwards. Then in the horizontal direction, the thrust backwards from the engine causes a reaction which pushes the aircraft forwards, while the drag holds it back. Unfortunately the useful lifting force and the retarding drag depend on the same five things:

1. Speed – higher speeds produce more lift (and more drag).
2. Wing size – a larger wing or two wings give more lift (and more drag).
3. Wing shape – a thicker wing section gives more lift (and more drag).
4. Wing inclination or *incidence* – as the wing is inclined to the direction of flight, so it produces more lift (and much more drag).
5. Air density – the thin air at high altitudes results in less lift (and less drag).

Of these five factors, speed has the most marked effect because doubling the speed produces four times the lift and drag. But just when an aircraft needs all the lift it can get – at take-off – it is moving slowly. So can anything else be changed? The air density cannot be altered and it is not easy to increase the size of the wing very much. The angle of incidence can be increased by flying the aircraft in a nose-up attitude, but if this angle is increased too much then the flow of air becomes turbulent and the aircraft drops out of the sky in a stall. So the final item to be considered is the wing shape or *aerofoil section*. A flat wing section gives only a little lift, but a curved or *cambered* section increases the lift considerably. So the *flap* was devised to increase the camber of the lower surface of the wing.

A number of flap designs have been tried out over the years, ranging from a simple hinged flap or the split flap to the more complicated versions such as the slotted flap or the Fowler flap. The Fowler flap had a double advantage – it increased the camber and it moved out to increase the wing area. Lowering the flaps increases not only the lift but also the drag. This is a good thing during a landing when the aircraft is slowing down but not so good for take-off when the aircraft is accelerating. Conse-

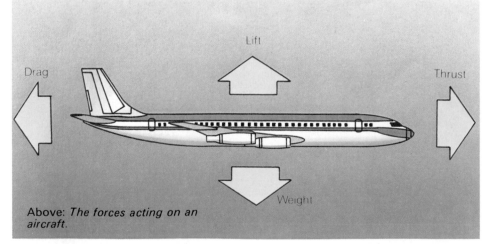

Lift

Drag

Thrust

Weight

Above: *The forces acting on an aircraft.*

quently a pilot lowers the flaps only part of the way for take-off.

In the 1920s, a British aviation pioneer, Frederick Handley Page, developed another device to produce more lift from a wing at low speeds. It was called a *slat* and consisted of a mini-wing mounted along the *leading edge* leaving a *slot* between the slat and the wing. The Handley Page slat enabled a wing to fly at a much greater angle of incidence without stalling. The wings of modern jet airliners usually have flaps along part of the *trailing edge* plus a leading edge slat or drooping leading edge to increase the camber.

Controlling the aircraft's direction

Once it is airborne an aircraft must be under complete control. A ship is controlled by a movable control surface called a *rudder*, and most aircraft also have a rudder hinged to a vertical *fin*. The rudder controls movement to the left or right (*yawing*). But an aircraft has much more freedom of movement than a ship, consequently it needs more control surfaces. The up or down movement (*pitching*) is controlled by an *elevator* hinged to a horizontal *tailplane*. The elevator was sometimes called a horizontal rudder in the past and this was a very descriptive name. If an aircraft attempts to turn using just its rudder, it tends to slew round and slip sideways. To make a smooth turn it has to *bank* round with one wing dropping down and the other moving up (*rolling*). Rolling is controlled by *ailerons* which are hinged control surfaces on the trailing edge of each wing near the tip. When an aileron is moved down it increases the lift on that wing so by moving one side up and the other down the aircraft can be made to bank or roll.

On most modern aircraft the ailerons are controlled by turning a cut-down steering wheel on the *control column* in the cockpit. Turning the wheel clockwise makes the aircraft bank to the right. Some aircraft have a control column which moves sideways to control the ailerons. The elevators are controlled by moving the control column forwards or backwards. Pushing the control column forwards moves the elevator down and the aircraft nose dives. Finally, the rudder is controlled by foot pedals mounted on a hinged *rudder bar*. Moving the left foot forward and the right foot back swings the rudder to the left and the aircraft will yaw to the left but for a smooth banking turn the wheel would be turned anti-clockwise at the same time.

Above left: *An Airbus airliner with its trailing-edge flaps and leading-edge slats extended.* Left: *Shown in the normal flight position.*

143

AIR TRAVEL 1919-1959

Above: *An Armstrong-Whitworth Argosy airliner of Imperial Airways, 1926.* Inset: *The interior of an Argosy.*

When the world's first regular international air service opened in August 1919 between London and Paris the passengers were carried in converted bombers. The journey took anything from 2.5 to 5.5 hours depending on the headwinds, compared with 7 or 8 hours by train and steamer. Fares were very expensive, consequently only the rich could afford to fly. Film stars were frequent passengers; not only did flying save time but also it attracted the press photographers! From November 1919, mail was carried officially on the London to Paris route, and because people were prepared to pay extra for the speed of air-mail, it provided a very useful source of income to struggling airlines.

By the mid 1920s most of the European capitals were linked by air and the first aircraft designed to carry passen-gers were replacing the converted bombers. One of the first true airliners was the Armstrong Whitworth Argosy of 1926, a large biplane with three engines, used by the British airline Imperial Airways on their European routes. The Argosy could carry 20 passengers in reasonable comfort at a steady 150 kph (93 mph). However, its range was only about 500 kilometres so it had to land many times on a long journey: nevertheless the airways expanded and by 1929 Britain was linked with India.

Many famous airlines were flying regular services by 1930 – and most of them are still operating today. Within the United States there were four very large airlines: American, Eastern, United and TWA (now Trans World Airlines), while Pan American concentrated on international services. In Europe a number of airlines had become well established with both inter-city flights and long-distance services: several European countries still had overseas empires. The Netherland's airline KLM (Royal Dutch Airlines) flew to the Dutch East Indies (now Indonesia) and Belgium's Sabena flew to the Belgian Congo (now Zaire). Several small French airlines operated services to French possessions in Africa and the Far East, and these joined forces in 1933 to form Air France. The German airline Deutsche Lufthansa was the largest in Europe: they flew to most European cities and pioneered the use of flying boats to South America. Most of these European airlines used aircraft built in their own country; for example, Deutsche Lufthansa had an all-German fleet of 220 aircraft.

In 1931 a new airliner, capable of carrying 38 passengers, had been introduced by Imperial Airways but its speed and range were little better than the Argosy. However, the new Handley Page HP42 gained a great reputation for comfort, reliability and safety. In the following year a regular service was started between London and Cape Town, South Africa, but a passenger had to be prepared for a long and arduous journey. There were 33 stages and it took 11 days (assuming there were no delays) to cover nearly 13 000 kilometres – an overall average of under 50 kph (30 mph). The fastest alternative was to travel all the way by surface transport and this would have taken 17 days.

Below: Helena, *a Handley Page HP42 airliner.*

The revolutionary flying boats

In 1936, Imperial Airways received the new Short 'Empire' flying boats which revolutionized their long-distance routes. The first of these four-engined mono-planes could carry 17 passengers in luxury, plus two tonnes of mail or freight, and cruise at 260 kph (160 mph). But most important, their increased range reduced the number of re-fuelling stops by half. Consequently, when the Empire flying boats were introduced on the service to Cape Town, in 1937, they cut the time from 11 to 6.5 days. The following year this was further reduced to 4.5 days. Several nations went on to build impressive flying boats, which were used to pioneer Atlantic and Pacific crossings until war in 1939.

Below: *A Short Empire flying boat.*

All-metal airliners

The airlines flying across America needed fast, long-range airliners which could operate from the many airfields which had been built during the 1930s. In 1936 an airliner called the Douglas DC-3 was in service for the first time for American Airlines, on their trans-continental route. It was an all-metal aircraft of advanced design, powered by two powerful engines which enabled it to carry 21 passengers at 275 kph (170 mph) over distances in excess of 800 kilometres.

When the Second World War started in 1939, airline services were severely reduced and many of the factories that had produced airliners turned over to military transport aircraft – especially in the United States. By the end of the war a new generation of four-engined long-range aircraft had emerged. Two of the most successful were the Douglas DC-4 and its rival, the Lockheed Constellation. The Constellation could carry 47 passengers over a distance of 2500 kilometres and cruise at 450 kph (280 mph) – a speed which only ten years earlier would have way outstripped even the fastest fighter planes.

Above: *The Lockheed L-049 Constellation began service in 1946, and was used by the British Overseas Airways Corporation among others.*

Left: *The Douglas DC-3 airliner first flew in 1936, and some are still in service.*

When the war ended, some airlines started operations using surplus military transports converted to carry passengers, but the large national airlines were more interested in the new four-engined airliners which included enlarged or 'stretched' versions of existing aircraft. The most popular trio were the Boeing Stratocruiser, the Douglas DC-6 and a stretched Lockheed Constellation. These each carried 70–80 passengers at about 500 kph (310 mph) over a distance of 5000 kilometres – still using conventional petrol engines.

For a period of 10 years from 1947 the Douglas and the Lockheed companies competed with each other, introducing a new variant of the four-engined airliner every few years. Boeings retired from this competition and concentrated their efforts on designing a jet-engined airliner. By the end of this 10-year period, airliners with the traditional petrol engine, such as the Douglas DC-7C and the Lockheed Starliner, were carrying 100 passengers at 550 kph (340 mph). But this was not good enough, and even their long range of around 10 000 kilometres did not save them when jet-engined airliners made their first appearance in the late 1940s.

Right: *A Boeing 377 Stratocruiser airliner with double-decker fuselage.*

THE JET AGE

Above: *The first Vickers Viscount.*

Jet aircraft were used during the Second World War but in its early days the jet engine was not very suitable for airliners because its fuel consumption was too high. Most of an airliner's load-carrying ability would have been taken up with fuel instead of fare-paying passengers or *payload*. In July 1948, the world's first completely jet-driven commercial aircraft flew from London to Paris in 34 minutes but this new airliner could not carry enough payload to be a financial success. It was an experimental Vickers Viking fitted with two Rolls-Royce Nene jet engines in place of its usual Bristol Hercules piston engines: the Viking was a 27-seater airliner developed from the faithful old Vickers Wellington bomber of the Second World War.

However, in that same month Vickers-Armstrongs produced another new British airliner which was to make a much greater impact on the airways of the world – this was the Viscount. The Nene-Viking and the Viscount were both fitted with gas-turbine engines, but the former used pure-jets in contrast to the Viscount which carried four Rolls-Royce Dart turbo-prop engines. One great advantage of the turbo-prop was that it used much less fuel than the pure-jet. Yet despite its low fuel costs, high cruising speeds and a very quiet passenger cabin, the Viscount did not sell. In fact it was very nearly scrapped. Then British European Airways showed interest, and during the 1950s the Viscount emerged as one of Britain's most successful airliners.

After the Viscount, Vickers-Armstrongs produced the Vanguard. This was another turbo-prop airliner but considerably larger, carrying 139 passengers, yet it was extremely economical to operate. On all but the very short hops it could fly with two-thirds of its seats empty and still make a profit. Despite this advantage only two airlines

Below: *A Sud-Aviation Caravelle.*

bought the Vanguard, for the fare-paying passengers were choosing to fly in a rival pure-jet airliner. The French twin-jet Caravelle needed to fly almost full in order to pay its way because it was powered by pure-jets which had a high fuel consumption. The designers of the Caravelle mounted its engines on the side of the *fuselage* behind the passenger cabin, which resulted in a very low noiselevel in the cabin. During the 1960s the attraction of jet-travel plus the quiet cabin, ensured that the Caravelle was nearly always full – so despite its fuel consumption it was a great success.

Another turbo-prop airliner, the Lockheed L.188 Electra, was built in America but was not successful. The most successful of all the western turbo-prop transports was the Dutch Fokker F.27 Friendship, which first entered service, with West Coast Airlines of America in 1958, accommodating 48 passengers. In Europe, it was used by Aer Lingus, and it is still in production.

The Boeing 707, a new American jet airliner introduced in 1958, followed the layout of the old piston-engined airliners with four engines mounted on the wings in contrast to the Comet which had its four engines buried inside the wing to give a more streamlined shape. A wing free of engines is said to be a 'cleaner' design and of course the Caravelle with its two engines attached to the sides of the fuselage had a clean wing. This arrangement was also used very successfully by the BAC One-Eleven. De Havilland followed the Comet with the Trident, a three-engined airliner which had one engine on each side of the rear fuselage and one in the centre with its intake in the base of the fin. Vickers built the four-engined VC10 with two engines on each side of the rear fuselage. In all these European designs the wings were free of protruding engines, but in America the Boeing 707 was followed by the Douglas DC-8

and Convair's 880 and 990 and these aircraft all had four engines on the wings.

Airliners of the sixties

Boeing and Douglas went on to produce whole families of airliners. Boeings have always favoured wing-mounted engines except for the three-engined 727 which has the same layout as the Hawker Siddeley Trident. The Boeing 727 made history in 1973 when the thousandth model rolled off the production line: no civil aircraft in the world had ever achieved this figure and orders continued to arrive. The Douglas DC-9 with two fuselage-mounted engines also proved to be very popular with sales figures around the 1000 mark. These jet airliners are typical of the 1960s but in the 1970s two new dimensions in airliner design appeared – the 'Jumbo' jet and the supersonic airliner. Supersonic air travel became a possibility in December 1968 when the Russian Tupolev Tu-144 made its first flight, to be followed two months later by the Anglo-French Concorde. However the Concorde won the race to carry passengers on regular services when flights to Rio de Janeiro in Brazil and Bahrain started in January 1976.

The large airliners of the 1960s were designed to carry about 180 passengers and these were later 'stretched' by

lengthening their fuselages. For instance the original Douglas DC-8s carried a maximum of 173 passengers whereas the final version could carry 257 but the seating arrangements remained the same with three seats on either side of a central gangway. The airlines wanted even larger airliners so the designers had to turn their attention to the width of the fuselage and the 'wide-body' jets emerged. The first of these was the Boeing 747 Jumbo which entered airline service in 1970 and could carry up to 490 passengers sitting

Above: *The four jets of a Vickers Super VC10.*

10 abreast. Like the earlier 707, the 747 had four engines mounted on the wings. Rival wide-bodied airliners soon followed but the Douglas DC-10 and the Lockheed TriStar both had three engines, one on each wing and one in the lower part of the fin. In Europe the Airbus Industrie A-300 was produced, by Germany, France, the Netherlands, Spain and Britain in collaboration, for shorter routes and it used just two wing-mounted engines.

First jet passenger service

The world's first regular passenger service to be flown by a jet airliner was the British Overseas Airways Corporation's service to Johannesburg, South Africa. On 2 May 1952 a de Havilland Comet left London with 36 passengers and reached its destination in under 24 hours having flown 10 821 kilometres. The Comet was powered by four de Havilland Ghost jet engines. Unfortunately on two occasions Comets crashed due to a structural weakness and the airliner had to be redesigned. In 1958 the new Comet 4 began services across the Atlantic.

Right: *The first de Havilland Comet.*

A MODERN AIRLINER

One of the most common sights at any large international airport is the original 'Jumbo' jet – the Boeing 747. When it first appeared in the early 1970s it caused quite a sensation because it was so much larger than the previous generation of jet airliners, such as the widely used Boeing 707. The 747's height is perhaps its most noticeably different dimension, for the highest point of its fuselage is almost 11 metres above the ground compared with 6 metres for the 707. An average two-storeyed house stands about 6 metres high, but the 747 has three 'storeys'. At the lowest level there is a freight hold, then comes the main passenger cabin and finally a spiral staircase leads up to a smaller passenger cabin and the cockpit or *flight deck*. The interior of the main passenger cabin, like the rest of the aircraft, is huge, with seats for 10 people side-by-side instead of the usual six across. There are two gangways and the seats are grouped three-four-three. The number of passengers carried varies, depending on the airline's requirements, but two popular layouts are: 66 first-class plus 308 economy-class seats, or 490 economy-class seats. To look after the passengers, about 15 stewards or stewardesses are carried, so, with a flight crew of two pilots and a flight engineer, the total number of people on board could exceed 500. Some layouts include a lounge and bar on the upper deck, and film shows are an optional extra.

Sitting in the comfortable seats, high above the clouds, passengers may not realize that the air outside is so 'thin' that they would not survive for very long if the cabin were not *pressurized*. Mountaineers and the crews of high-flying military aircraft breathe oxygen through a face mask: this would not be a practical or popular solution for airline passengers! An alternative solution is to compress the thin air using air compressors and pump it into the sealed *pressure cabin*, bringing the pressure back to a comfortable level. Airliners fly at these high altitudes to save fuel, because the thin air offers less air resistance or drag. An added advantage is the smoother air, because most of the storms and severe gusts of wind occur at lower altitudes.

The pilots of a 747 are seated some 9 metres above the ground and 30 metres forward of the aircraft's main wheels, and these distances can take some getting used to when manoeuvring along a winding taxi track before take-off. The 747 has an impressive array of wheels – the main landing gear consists of 16 wheels mounted as four-wheel bogies on four separate legs. When the *undercarriage* designers set to work on the 747, they were able to fit a simple twin-wheel nose gear but they could not use the usual eight-wheel main gear (two four-wheel bogies) be-

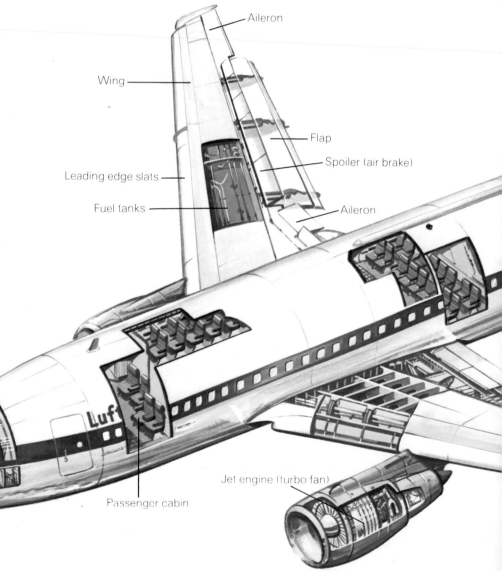

Aileron

Wing

Flap

Spoiler (air brake)

Leading edge slats

Aileron

Fuel tanks

Flight deck

Passenger cabin

Jet engine (turbo fan)

cause the weight of the 747 was more than twice the weight of existing airliners. The runways of the world's airports just could not cope with double the landing impact load under each wheel, so the designers had to double the number of wheels instead.

Flight controls

Once the Jumbo lifts into the air it is no more difficult to fly than any other jet airliner – in fact many pilots claim that it is easier than some smaller aircraft. At first sight the cockpit appears to be a mass of instrument dials, electrical switches and levers. In fact these are highly organized and many are standard for all modern airliners. In front of each pilot are the instruments which give information about the flight of the aircraft – its speed, height, direction and so on. Between the pilots, and positioned so that both have easy access, are the engine controls. There are four levers which are the throttles controlling the power from each of the four engines, and above these are rows of instruments, in fours, giving details of each engine's performance. Above the windscreen are a host of switches controlling the lighting, engine starting and electrical services. The flight engineer's panel gives details of the fuel situation, the cabin pressurization, the movable control surfaces, and the electrical power supply.

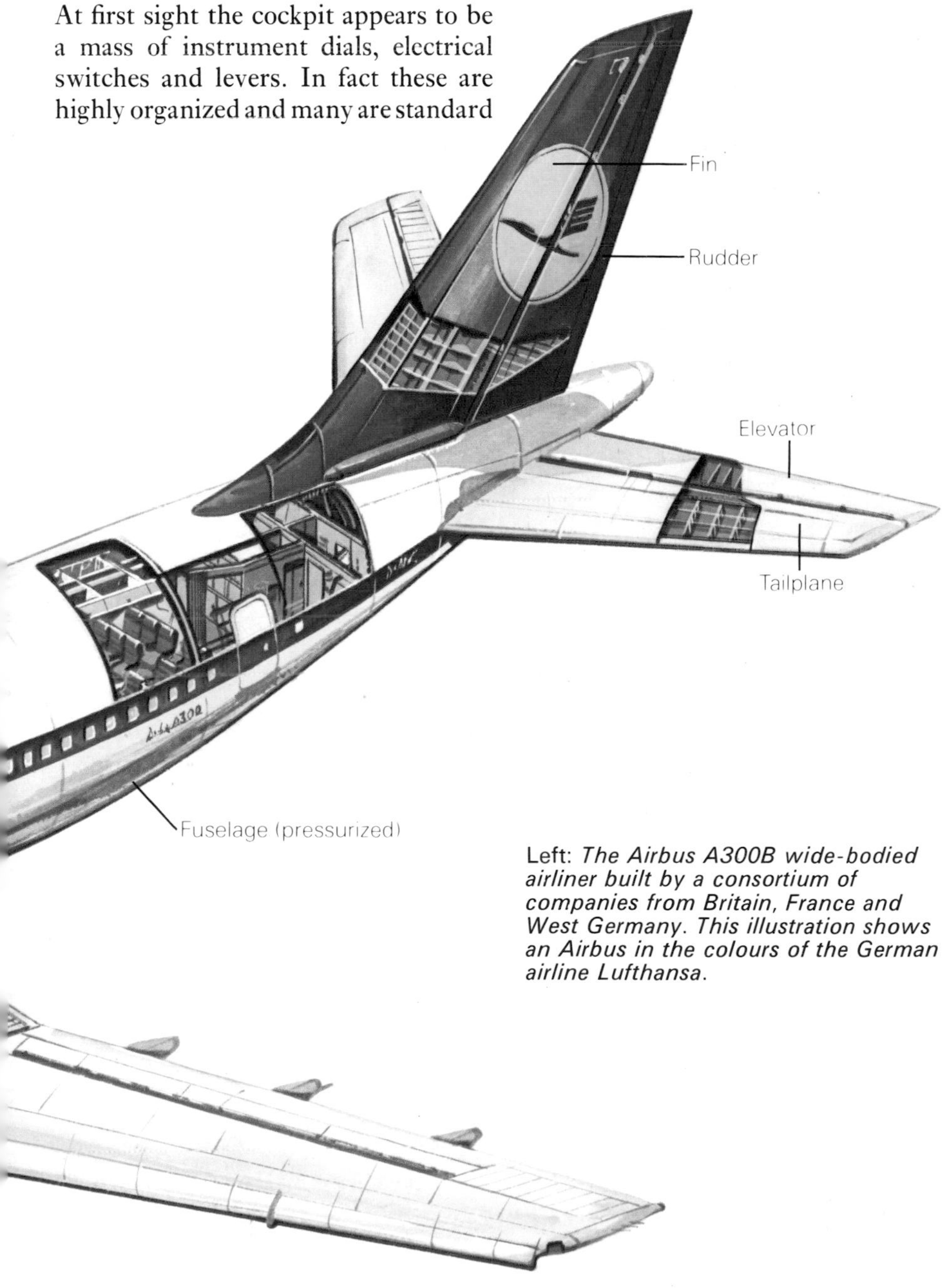

From the cockpit, and hidden away behind the furnishing panels or below the floor, run a multitude of pipes, wires and cables which link the vital systems. The pilot's control column has to be connected to the elevators and ailerons; the rudder pedals to the rudder. In the early days simple cables were used, but the heavily loaded control surfaces need power-assisted systems – just as many cars today have hydraulic brakes and power-assisted steering. A *hydraulic* system works like a bicycle pump in reverse. If air is blown into a bicycle pump, its handle will move out: similarly, if high-pressure hydraulic fluid is pumped into a *jack*, a rod emerges and this can be linked to a moving part. The hydraulic system is used to move control surfaces, retract the undercarriage, open and close doors, steer the aircraft on the ground and work the brakes. The system is triggered by mechanical links to the pilot's controls, but this linkage is progressively becoming electrical rather than mechanical.

All aircraft need electricity and this is supplied from generators driven by the engines. This power is used to supply cockpit instruments, radio sets, radar equipment, navigational aids, lighting and heating to keep the food warm in the galleys. The fuel system also needs electricity to drive its pumps, but it is a complex system in its own right. Fuel has to be pumped to each engine at the correct rate, and this is made more complicated by the fact that any one airliner has many fuel tanks. As the fuel is used, it is important to keep the balance of the aircraft correct; for instance, taking fuel only from the rear of the aircraft would lead to it becoming nose heavy. All these systems are vital to the safety of an airliner so should one fail, a second and even a third has to be available to take over in an emergency. Safety is all important in the design of a modern airliner.

Left: *The Airbus A300B wide-bodied airliner built by a consortium of companies from Britain, France and West Germany. This illustration shows an Airbus in the colours of the German airline Lufthansa.*

Fin
Rudder
Elevator
Tailplane
Fuselage (pressurized)

FASTER THAN SOUND

During the later years of the Second World War, pilots of the new, high speed fighter aircraft ran into trouble when their aircraft went into a dive. The pilots experienced severe buffeting and the trim (or balance) of their aircraft changed suddenly. Sometimes these strange effects were so serious that the aircraft broke up in the air or the pilot completely lost control. When the newspapers heard about these accidents, the reporters blamed the mysterious 'sound barrier', for the aircraft must have been approaching the speed of sound. At lower speeds the disturbances in the air, caused by the aircraft's movement, can escape as waves moving at the speed of sound, but as that speed is approached, the disturbances ahead of the aircraft cannot escape fast enough. The building up of air waves results in a sudden

increase in the drag on the aircraft and the formation of shock waves. Indeed, the complete airflow around the aircraft changes. In the case of the Second World War fighter aircraft, these changes were critical, but specially designed aircraft were able to cope with the problems of supersonic flight. However, one difficulty remained: the shock waves, which could be heard on the ground as a *sonic boom*. This loud boom follows the aircraft all the time it is flying at supersonic speeds and is a serious problem for supersonic aircraft flying over inhabited areas.

The speed of sound varies at different heights, so it is difficult to keep track of what its speed is. Therefore, instead of measuring the aircraft's speed in kilometres per hour, it is measured by comparison with the speed of sound – which is called *Mach 1*. (This name honours

an Austrian scientist Ernst Mach who studied the behaviour of sound waves.) An aircraft flying at twice the speed of sound is said to be flying at Mach 2 and the speed is indicated on a machmeter. Despite the predictions by scientists and aerodynamicists about what could happen when an aircraft reached Mach 1, no one could be really certain. Usually, advanced new designs for aircraft were tried out by making a model which was tested by blowing air over it in a *wind tunnel* but the shock waves produced at Mach 1 made this kind of test unreliable.

Although the first generation of jet airliners such as the de Havilland Comet and the Boeing 707 were subsonic, they flew at speeds approaching

Below: *Air flow shown in a wind tunnel.*

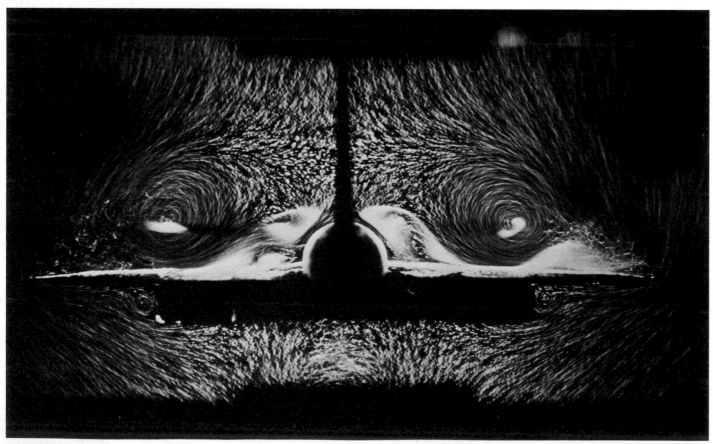

The first supersonic aircraft

The first man to exceed the speed of sound in level flight was Captain Charles ('Chuck') E. Yeager of the United States Air Force. He named his Bell X-1 rocket-powered aircraft 'Glamorous Glennis' after his wife but officially it was number 6062. On 14 October 1947 Chuck Yeager achieved a speed of Mach 1.015 or 1078 kph (670 mph) and proved that there was no sound 'barrier'. The cautious preparations leading up to this flight ensured that Yeager could control the X-1 as it went supersonic. The research programme into supersonic flight continued and improved versions of the X-1 were designed. In June 1954 Yeager reached a speed of Mach 2.42 in the X-1A. But these aircraft were rocket-powered flying laboratories and it was some time before supersonic aircraft were ready for military service. Supersonic airliners were even further away in the future.

A supersonic Bell X-1 research aircraft.

Mach 1 and this presented problems to the designers. For instance, as air flows over a wing the speed of the air increases – an increase which could take it up to the critical Mach 1. It was found that this effect could be reduced by sweeping the wings backwards. The Boeing 747, with a maximum cruising speed equivalent to Mach 0.9, is slightly faster than the 707 – so its wings have just a little more sweep back.

Right: *Swept-back wings reduce air resistance as the speed of sound (Mach 1) is approached. Here, three airliners and their cruising speeds are compared. The smallest is the De Havilland Comet (Mach 0.74). The largest is the Boeing 747 (Mach 0.90), and Concorde (Mach 2.04) is half-way between the other two in size.*

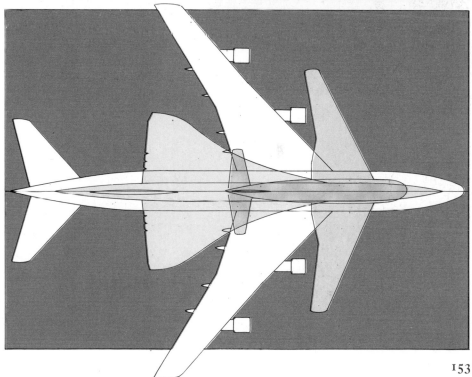

Concorde

Around 1960, several countries which already had supersonic military aircraft were considering designs for a supersonic airliner, including Britain, France, Russia and the United States. In 1962, British and French aviation experts combined to share the design and construction work for a project which was named Concorde. Many shapes were investigated: the wings had to be swept back very sharply and this brought the wing tip very close to the tailplane. The designers decided to combine wing and tail into a large triangular shape. This was called a *delta wing* – named after the Greek letter 'capital delta' which is a triangle. Military aircraft had used this delta shape already but the Concorde designers settled for a very long thin triangle – a *slender delta*. Two research aircraft were built to test this shape – one at low speeds and the other at supersonic speeds. The final Concorde wing had a slightly curved leading edge – a shape known as an *ogee*.

To drive an airliner carrying 100 passengers through the air at supersonic speed requires engines of great power to overcome the immense drag. In the case of Concorde this power is supplied by four Rolls-Royce (Bristol)/Snecma Olympus engines. One of these engines supplies 17 260 kilograms thrust during take-off, which is just about the same power as the four engines mounted in the de Havilland Comet airliner. Keeping the passengers and the aircraft cool is another major problem. At very high speeds the friction between the air and the airliner's skin generates enough heat to raise the temperature of the skin above the boiling point of water. To keep the inside of the passenger cabin at a comfortable temperature, the skin has to be lagged and a refrigerating system installed. However, the effect of this heat on the metal airframe is more serious because the strength of the aluminium alloys used in aircraft construction drops very rapidly as the temperature rises. The designers of Concorde had to allow for this reduced strength and make allowances for the expansion of the various parts as they became hot.

Concorde began to carry fare-paying passengers in January 1976. Timetables become very confusing when travelling at supersonic speeds, because the airliner moves round the Earth faster than the Earth moves round the Sun. New York time is five hours behind London time, so if a supersonic airliner leaves London at 8.00 am and takes four hours for the journey, it arrives in New York at 12.00 noon (London time) which is 7.00 am in New York. Strange though it sounds, the passenger arrives one hour before leaving – just in time for a second breakfast! Of course, flying in the opposite direction adds time to the journey.

Right: *An Avro Vulcan bomber used to test Concorde's Olympus engine.*

Below: *Concorde being serviced at Heathrow airport, London.*

BUILDING AN AIRLINER

Modern airliners such as the Concorde and the Boeing 747 Jumbo look very solid, but their structural shell has to be as light as possible otherwise they would never leave the ground. Weight has been a problem for aircraft designers since the days of the pioneers who ventured into the air in flimsy gliders. Otto Lilienthal and Percy Pilcher based their gliders on soaring birds, so they built bird-like skeletons of willow or bamboo covered with a strong fabric. To make the framework strong enough for flight, an array of external bracing wires had to be added. But some other pioneers decided that the box kite layout could be adapted to make a glider and so a different shape emerged with two wings, one above the other. Octave Chanute and the Wright brothers made such biplane gliders, and of course the Wrights went on to build the first successful powered machine – their 1903 'Flyer'. Although these biplanes were a very different shape from the gliders of Lilienthal and Pilcher, the materials used in their construction were the same – wood, wire and fabric. This kind of structure, nicknamed 'stick and string', remained in use throughout the First World War and even lasted until the Second World War.

Over the years, improvements were made to increase the strength of aircraft structures, while keeping the weight to a minimum. One change was to use thin plywood for the skin instead of fabric. Plywood was glued to the framework, thus increasing the overall strength because the plywood could carry some of the loading whereas fabric could not. Because the plywood skin was carrying some of the stresses and strains, this arrangement was called *stressed-skin* construction. Other designers introduced thin steel tubes in place of the wooden framework, while others used a mixture of wood and metal – but in both cases the fabric and wires remained.

Aluminium is much lighter than steel but it is very weak and consequently not suitable for a highly loaded aircraft structure. However, small quantities of other metals such as copper and magnesium can be added to aluminium to produce an *alloy* which is very much stronger than pure aluminium. During the 1930s a new aluminium alloy called *duralumin* became widely used and this was almost as strong as steel, although much lighter. Some aircraft were built using a duralumin framework covered with fabric, but the great step forward came when stressed-skin structures were designed in this aluminium alloy. One of the first aircraft to use stressed-skin construction was the Douglas DC-3 airliner of 1935. Its smooth lines and robust structure made it one of the most successful aircraft of all times – indeed several examples are still flying. The DC-3 has been called 'the first modern airliner' and the stressed-skin structures of the Douglas DC-10 and the Boeing 747 have many features in common, but of course the fantastic increase in aircraft size has necessitated certain changes to the major structural members.

Supersonic airliners, such as Concorde, need a very special structure because of the problems imposed by flying at very high speeds. The basic shape of the aircraft has to be different, so the designers cannot base the structure on any previous designs. Supersonic speeds result in very high aerodynamic loadings (intense air pressures) which impose high stresses on the structure; the speed also results in an increase in the skin temperature due to the rubbing action which takes place between the skin and the air. The skin becomes so hot that aluminium alloys lose their strength. For the parts which bear the brunt of this heating effect, alternative materials have to be found: the two most widely used are stainless steel and a relatively new material called *titanium* which is lighter than steel but very strong.

Below: *Aircraft structures old and new.*
Left: *A 'stick and string' framework.*
Right: *Modern all-metal stressed-skin construction.*

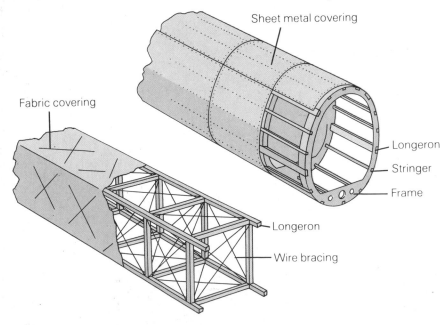

Sheet metal covering

Fabric covering

Longeron

Stringer

Frame

Longeron

Wire bracing

Design and testing

The design of an airliner involves many hundreds of experts: aerodynamicists, draughtsmen, stress engineers, systems experts and weights engineers. Once the drawings have been produced planners decide how the parts are to be made; the special tools and equipment are prepared and then production begins. Until recent years, most aircraft structures consisted of parts cut and shaped from sheets of aluminium alloy and then joined together by rivets or nuts and bolts. Modern structures are often carved in one piece from a large block of metal by machines which appear to work themselves: actually they are controlled by a computer which has been carefully programmed to perform every operation automatically. Once the parts have been manufactured they are assembled and the shell of the airliner takes shape, but there are still many months of work ahead fitting the engines, undercarriage, instruments and lengths of pipes and wires.

Before the airliner is allowed to fly, a long programme of testing has to be carried out. Two complete airframes may be built and tested to find the point of destruction: one is tested under the most severe single loading the aircraft might experience and the other under the repeated loading of a *fatigue* test. For instance, a wing flexes up and down, and this relatively low loading, applied frequently, can start a minute crack which will grow until the wing breaks. This is called a *fatigue failure* and it was this type of structural weakness which caused the early de Havilland Comets to crash. There are many other ground tests designed to check all the moving components and the systems. Hundreds of hours are then spent on test flying: first to ensure that the airliner can fly safely, then to prove that it can carry out all the tasks for which it was designed. If it passes all these tests it will then be allowed to carry passengers – but not before.

Below: *The wing of an Airbus airliner in a test-rig at a German factory.*

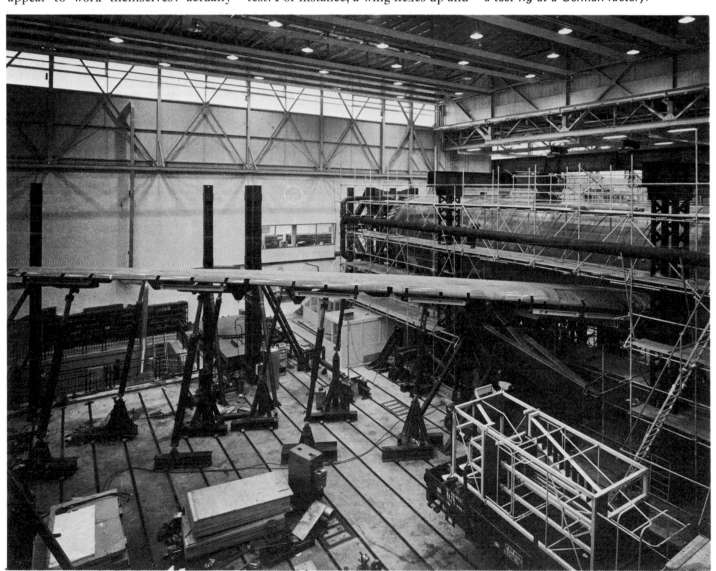

FLYING AN AIRLINER

Airliners have taken over from the grand ocean liners on almost all the passenger routes which link the continents of the world and this take-over includes usage of many of the old nautical traditions and titles. An airliner is commanded by a Captain who is the senior pilot, and the co-pilot is called the First Officer. Their cockpit is referred to as the *flight deck* while the passengers are housed in a *cabin*. Other members of the crew include Stewards and Stewardesses who look after the passengers and serve food from the *galleys*. On long-distance flights the crew may also include an Engineer, a Navigating Officer or a Radio Officer. Because modern radio equipment is extremely reliable and simple to operate, the pilots usually cope without a Radio Officer. Navigating Officers, too,

Above: *Airport marshallers in bright clothing guide each aircraft to its parking place.*

Below: *Air traffic controllers following an aircraft's progress on a radar screen.*

are becoming redundant as electronic equipment and computers take over. The Flight Engineer supervises a large instrument panel and his main responsibility is to ensure that the engines are running smoothly and using the correct amount of fuel. He must also ensure that the fuel is taken from the correct tanks otherwise the balance of the airliner could be upset.

Long before an airliner departs, work begins on the preparations for the flight. The Operations Department of the airline ensures that airliners have a complete crew – a task which needs careful planning, especially on the long distance routes such as Britain to Australia. The airliner and passengers will make the complete journey but the crew will change because the number of hours they spend in the air is strictly limited. A weary pilot might make a mistake and there is no room for any error when lives are at stake. Another section of the Operations Department will probably prepare a *flight plan*. This gives details of the aircraft's weight including passengers, cargo and fuel; it also sets out the route for the flight with all the speeds, heights, estimated arrival times and many other factors which have to be taken into account.

The Captain and his crew report for duty about an hour before the airliner is due to depart. The Captain checks the flight plan and consults the latest weather reports, which may alter it – for instance, strong headwinds may force him to carry more fuel. Once he is satisfied with the flight plan the Captain briefs his crew and the plan is sent to the *Air Traffic Control* centre. If this authority is satisfied with the plan, then details are transmitted by teleprinter to controllers along the route and to the destination airport.

Take-off and landing

The crew board the airliner and, while the cabin staff look after the passengers, the Captain and First Officer (or co-pilot) carry out the pre-flight cockpit checks. A long list of items to be checked is worked through systematically. Once all the passengers are aboard, the doors are closed, then the servicing vehicles are moved safely out of the way and the pilot is given permission to start the engines. This comes by radio from the Ground Controller, at Air Traffic Control, who also gives clearance for the aircraft to taxi out to the runway. After a final check on the engines and flying controls the pilot requests permission from Air Traffic Control to take off. When this permission is received, the engine power is increased and the airliner surges forward. At a pre-determined speed, the pilot eases the control column back and first the nose lifts, then the aircraft becomes airborne.

Once clear of the airport the pilot climbs to his cruising height along one of the *airways*, which are like main roads of the air (*see pages 160–61*). At this point the pilot can switch control to the *automatic pilot* or *autopilot* which does the routine work of flying the airliner along its set course. The autopilot is controlled by *gyroscopes*. (A gyroscope is a rotating wheel so mounted that it is sensitive to any change in the direction of its axis.) Should a gust of wind divert the aircraft from its course these gyroscopes 'feel' this movement and make automatic corrections to the aircraft's control surfaces. The first automatic pilot was built as long ago as 1912 by Lawrence Sperry in the United States and was fitted to a Curtiss floatplane (*see page 172*).

As the airliner flies along the airway its progress is reported to the Air Traffic Controllers on the ground. In busy areas this progress will be followed by ground radar operators. Incidentally, the airliner also carries radar equipment which scans the sky ahead and warns the pilot if the aircraft is flying into a storm or some obstruction.

As the airliner nears its destination airport, the pilot comes under the control of the Airport Control Tower where radar operators follow every aircraft, and control their movements by sending instructions over the radio. Sometimes a queue builds up of aircraft waiting to land, and the Controller has to order the aircraft to fly in circles until their turn comes. Each aircraft is allocated a different height in this *stack* and the Controller tells them when they may descend to a lower level. Once a pilot reaches the bottom of the stack it is his turn to land. He can be guided to the end of the runway either by the well-tried *Instrument Landing System* (ILS) equipment or the Approach Controller can 'talk him down' using radar. In each of these cases the pilot takes over for the actual touch-down, although in recent years some airliners have been equipped for fully automatic landings.

An airliner arriving at a busy airport may have to queue in a stack.

Holding pattern
approach route

One aircraft at each level

Levels separated
by 1000 feet

Control tower

Runway

Radio beacon

AIRWAYS

In the early days of aviation, pilots found their way by observing the land below and map-reading with the help of a compass. Railway lines and rivers were a great help – in fact some railway stations had their names painted on the roof especially to help pilots. When oceans had to be crossed there were no such landmarks, consequently the pilot had to rely on his compass to guide him in the right direction. But a compass course needed to be checked, so the airmen copied the sailors and navigated by the Sun and stars. They used a *sextant* to calculate latitude and longitude, but the calculations took a long time, with the result that a fast aircraft would have moved on by the time they were completed!

Between the two World Wars, radio began to be used to assist the navigator. An aircraft transmitted a radio signal which a ground station picked up on a *direction-finding aerial* – the aerial rotated until it pointed in the direction of the aircraft. If a second station picked up the signal, the bearings of the two stations enabled the aircraft navigator to *fix* his position. During the Second World War, new radio aids to navigation were invented to help bombers find their targets over enemy territory – where there were no helpful direction-finding ground stations. The very successful British systems were called *Gee* and *Loran*. From these the *Decca Navigator* was developed which, using radio signals from the ground, showed an aircraft's position on a moving map in the aircraft. In the United States another system was developed called *VOR/DME* (Very-high-frequency Omni-directional Radio-range/Distance Measuring Equipment). This could be described as a lighthouse sending out radio signals instead of light. An instrument in the aircraft picked up these signals and worked out a fix. Both the Decca system and VOR/DME needed ground stations, so for long distance flights over the sea some other system was needed. First came *Doppler* which used radar mounted in the aircraft to measure its track and speed, then the *Inertial Navigation System* which is also used to navigate in outer space. This very complicated system uses gyroscopes, acceleration-measuring instruments and computers.

All these aids to navigation helped to prevent airliners from getting lost, but on some busy routes there was another hazard – the possibility of a mid-air collision. It became clear that airliners had to be controlled in some way – especially over Europe and the United

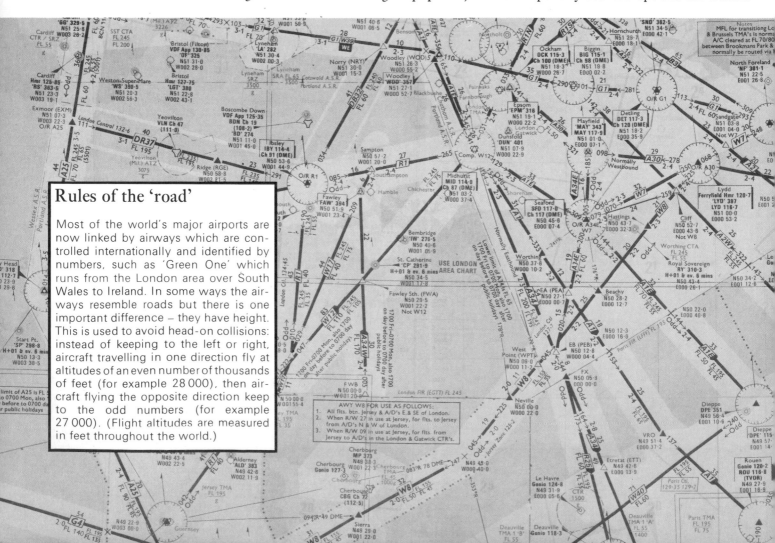

Rules of the 'road'

Most of the world's major airports are now linked by airways which are controlled internationally and identified by numbers, such as 'Green One' which runs from the London area over South Wales to Ireland. In some ways the airways resemble roads but there is one important difference – they have height. This is used to avoid head-on collisions: instead of keeping to the left or right, aircraft travelling in one direction fly at altitudes of an even number of thousands of feet (for example 28 000), then aircraft flying the opposite direction keep to the odd numbers (for example 27 000). (Flight altitudes are measured in feet throughout the world.)

States. *Airways* were introduced as the 'highways of the air' to simplify the problem of navigating and to ensure that airliners did not collide with each other. A radio beam was transmitted from a *radio-range* station and aimed along an airway. Following this beam was so simple that the pilots could navigate without the aid of a navigator. They just listened to the station's signal on their headphones and when they heard a steady note the aircraft was on course. To obtain a fix the pilot tuned in to a *fan-marker* beacon which transmitted a signal upwards. A receiver in the aircraft picked up this signal only when the aircraft was passing over the beacon. The old radio beacons have now been superseded by the modern systems of radio navigation – primarily VOR/DME.

Controlling air traffic

Just as any road system needs traffic police to enforce the safety rules of the Highway Code, so the airway system has to be controlled. This is obviously a problem since traffic lights or a policeman cannot be positioned at the intersection of two airways. All the controlling has to be done from the ground by Air Traffic Controllers using radio and radar. This is organized in stages depending on conditions, for instance the pilot of an airliner on a trans-Atlantic flight finds that mid-Atlantic traffic is very different from that on the approach to London's Heathrow Airport or New York's John F. Kennedy International. Large areas, such as the North Atlantic, are divided up into *Flight Information Regions* and each region has one Control Centre. The controllers tell the pilot at what height and speed he should fly, and then they ensure that no other aircraft fly at that height unless they are a safe distance ahead or behind.

As an airliner crosses the Atlantic and nears Britain, it is picked up by the radar of the London Air Traffic Control Centre at West Drayton, Middlesex.

The controllers of this busy centre use a very advanced computer system called *Mediator* which is linked to three radar sites. The radar scanners track each aircraft in the area and the computer predicts their flight path. To do this the computer has to store a host of information such as details of each aircraft's performance, the weather forecast, and airway rules and regulations. Using Mediator the controllers guide each airliner to within 20 kilometres of Heathrow. At this point the airliner is handed over to the Approach Controllers who are based in a darkened room crowded with radar screens. Their job is to maintain a steady flow of aircraft to or from the runways. The final stages of a landing are controlled from the glass-house on the top of the control tower by the Air Controllers. After landing, the Ground Controllers direct the airliner to its parking area.

Below: *Part of a British Airways Radio Navigation Chart covering from southern England to northern Europe.*

AIRPORTS

In the early days of aviation, aircraft could fly from any large field and these fields became known as flight grounds or flying-grounds. Gradually, aircraft hangars and buildings for the passengers were added and the name aerodrome was used. In the 1920s some of the larger civil aerodromes were called *airports* for the first time.

Today's airports have come a long way from the early days of those at Newark and Croydon when passengers were measured in thousands. John F. Kennedy Airport, New York and London Heathrow handle many millions of passengers every year and the airports never stop expanding. In fact a large modern airport can be compared to a town with a working population of 50 000 or more. There are shops, banks, restaurants, bars, hotels, buses, taxis, cars and car parks. In addition there are all the workers who ensure that everything runs smoothly – telephone operators, receptionists, police, firemen, electricians and cleaners. All these services and people could be found in any town, but at the airport there are also many staff working for the airlines. Some of these look after passengers on the ground and in the air, while others service the aircraft between flights and overhaul them at regular intervals.

When an airliner lands after a flight it is immediately surrounded by a fleet of vehicles of all shapes and sizes. One of the first to arrive is a mobile power unit which supplies electricity to the aircraft, since its own generators do not function when it is stationary. Then there is the air-conditioning truck to keep the passenger cabin at a comfortable temperature. Sometimes fuel is brought to the aircraft in tankers but at many modern airports fuel is piped to the servicing areas and a hose connects the aircraft to a *hydrant*. Fuel is pumped aboard at very high speed – it would fill a motor car's petrol tank in a fraction of a second. Oil and water are both brought to the aircraft in small tankers. Engineers give the aircraft a routine between-flights inspection to make sure that there are no loose parts or fuel leaks. Other vehicles are busy looking after the passengers' requirements – transporting baggage, removing rubbish, bringing fresh food and drink and emptying the toilets.

Every few weeks the aircraft is taken out of service for a minor overhaul, and there are graded checks up to a major overhaul which involves stripping down the aircraft to inspect every component. Naturally this takes a long time but it only has to be done every few years. By careful planning the airlines try to arrange for these overhauls to be carried out in the winter months when they are not so busy with holiday traffic. Before any aircraft in the world can fly, it must have a *Certificate of Airworthiness* ('C of A') and this is issued by a government department. In Britain, inspectors of the Civil Aviation Authority ensure that aircraft meet the very high standards of safety demanded before issuing a 'C of A'.

Below: *The central area of London's Heathrow airport, seen from an airliner's window.*

The first airports

In 1920, London's first real airport was opened at Croydon and like all airports at that time it had grass runways. A great step forward was made in 1928 when New York's first airport was opened at Newark for it had a hard-surfaced runway. Croydon remained a grass airfield until it was closed in 1959. During the Second World War many of the fighter bases were just grass airfields, but the heavy bombers and transport aircraft needed hard-surfaced runways and some of these airfields were converted to airports after the war.

Below: *Croydon Airport in the 1920s.*

Below: *Modern airport layouts ensure that passengers can board aircraft without being exposed to the weather.*

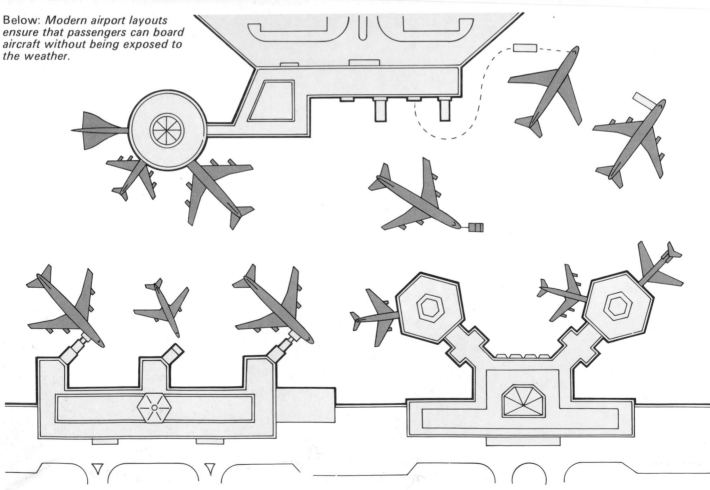

Getting passengers to the aircraft

When passengers arrive at an airport, the first thing they do is *check-in*. This is a simple operation for passengers, consisting of a few formalities such as having their baggage weighed. The airline staff then have to ensure that the luggage is loaded on to the correct flight and that the aircraft is not overloaded. The flight number is called over the loudspeaker and after a short wait, passengers are shepherded through the security search and, on international flights, their passports are checked. Passengers then board the waiting aircraft where a stewardess welcomes them aboard and inspects their tickets. When all the passengers are aboard and the doors closed, the engines are started under the supervision of the ground crew and firemen. The aeroplane is then ready for the flight to begin.

Building a new airport presents many problems for the surveyors, engineers and meteorologists looking for a perfect site. If the airport is to serve a city it must be near the city centre, but on the other hand the noise of its aircraft should not disturb the residents. Runways have to be built on solid ground to withstand the landing impact of large airliners and they also cover a large area; consequently the only available site is usually far from the centre of the city. The ends of the runways must be free of dangerous obstructions such as tall buildings and hills. Weather conditions, too, have to be studied to ensure that the area is not prone to mist and fog, but there should be an alternative airport somewhere near – just in case.

One of the major problems for designers of large airports is how to get the passengers from the terminal building to the parked airliner without making them walk an excessive distance. Many airports have *fingers* radiating from the terminal building and an adjustable covered ramp from the finger to the doorway of the airliner. As more aircraft use the airport so the fingers become longer and longer. One solution is to install moving walk-ways along the fingers, but completely different solutions have also been tried out. At some airports, buses are used to transport passengers from the terminal building to parked airliners, but a Jumbo needs a fleet of buses. This arrangement was taken a stage further at Washington DC's Dulles International Airport where huge mobile lounges were introduced. In contrast Los Angeles International was built with a number of satellite terminals – in other words there are several mini airports on one site.

Above: *Passengers disembarking from a Boeing 707 in southern Peru.*

Below: *One way to save passengers from a long walk – a mobile lounge in Mexico.*

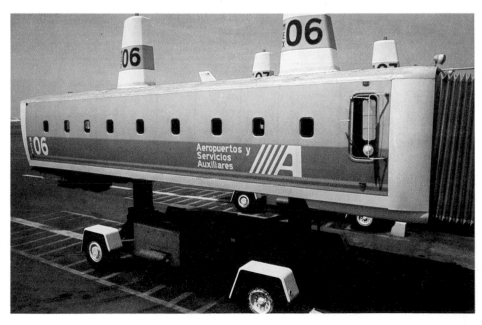

WORLD AIRLINES

There are about 500 airlines in the world and this figure does not include companies which fly only small aircraft. Of course some of the 500 have very small fleets, for example the French airline Air Fret has just one Boeing 707 and a staff of 35 employees – but this small airline has been flying since 1964. At the other extreme is the Russian airline Aeroflot, with about 500 000 workers and an aircraft fleet of thousands. It is a little unfair to compare Aeroflot with other airlines because it is really a government department which is responsible for virtually all civilian aviation in the USSR. Aeroflot carries passengers and cargo like any other airline but it also operates agricultural and ambulance aircraft and carries out fishery, ice and fire patrols.

The largest privately owned airline in the world is United Airlines of the United States, with a fleet of 330 aircraft and a staff of 54 000. The history of United Airlines goes back to 1931 when four pioneer airlines joined together, one of these, Varney Air Lines, having been founded in 1926. Today, United Airlines operates a large network of routes inside the United States and a few overseas services. United's foremost rivals within the United States are Eastern Air Lines, who introduced the *shuttle* service idea (a service where the passengers don't need to book in advance, and may pay for tickets on the aircraft), and American Airlines who, over the years, have sponsored many new designs such as the Douglas DC-3 of 1936. The two major airlines of the United States flying on international routes are Pan American World Airways and Trans World Airlines. 'Pan Am' operates a round-the-world service and flies to most capital cities in the world.

In Europe the largest airlines are British Airways, Air France and Luft-hansa German Airlines. Of these, British Airways was the largest though is now having to reduce its staff and fleet of aircraft. An unusual feature of this fleet was that it consisted of over 20 different types of aircraft ranging from Concorde to small helicopters, due to the merger of the fleets of two national airlines in 1972. British Airways had the largest network of routes in the world covering 800 000 kilometres and serving 77 countries.

Air France also has a world-wide network of routes which includes several supersonic services flown by Concorde. British Airways and Air France started their Concorde operations simultaneously in January 1976, and now these include flights to North America, South America, the Middle East and the Far East. Air France also operates a night airmail service within France which is noted for its very high standard of reliability and regularity. Many of the

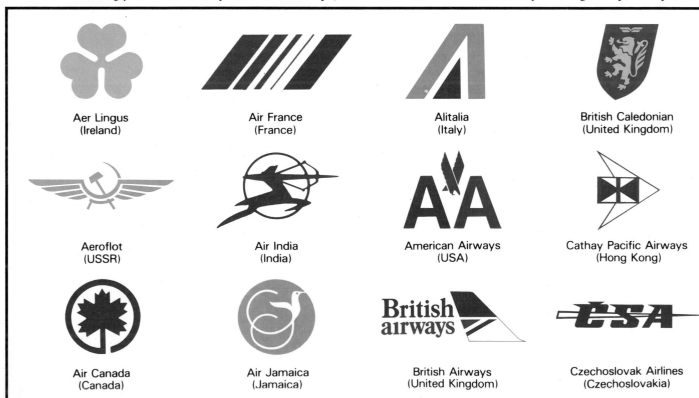

Aer Lingus
(Ireland)

Air France
(France)

Alitalia
(Italy)

British Caledonian
(United Kingdom)

Aeroflot
(USSR)

Air India
(India)

American Airways
(USA)

Cathay Pacific Airways
(Hong Kong)

Air Canada
(Canada)

Air Jamaica
(Jamaica)

British Airways
(United Kingdom)

Czechoslovak Airlines
(Czechoslovakia)

European airlines, founded in the 1920s, are still flying extensive services – often to their former colonies. KLM (Royal Dutch Airlines) began operations in 1919 and claims over 60 years of continuous operation. The Belgian airline Sabena, and Lufthansa German Airlines were founded in the 1920s, but in contrast the Scandinavian Airlines System which pioneered flights to America via the North Pole was founded as recently as 1946.

Although many of the largest airlines are based in Europe and the United States, there are some very important companies in other parts of the world. Air Canada has over 20 000 employees and the Brazilian airline Varig is only a little smaller. QANTAS of Australia claims to be the second oldest existing airline – just a few months younger than KLM. But QANTAS set another record in 1979 when it sold its last Boeing 707, because this meant the airline was flying just one type of airliner – the Boeing 747 Jumbo. Of course a fleet of 20 Jumbos can carry a very large number of passengers and the servicing problems are simplified.

Air India was founded after the Second World War, in 1946, and has a fleet of 19 aircraft with over 12 000 employees. Even more recently, Singapore Airlines started in 1972 and now has a fleet of 38 aircraft.

International organizations

Because there are so many airlines operating world-wide services an international body was set up to ensure that all the airlines and the Air Traffic Controllers have a standard way of working. The International Civil Aviation Organization (ICAO) was founded as an offshoot of the United Nations and today about 150 countries are members. It is vitally important that all aircraft observe the same rules of the air and procedures, especially when approaching an airport. Amongst items covered by ICAO are such things as maps, radio and navigational aids, aircraft inspection and licences for personnel.

There is a second international organization involved in air travel but this one represents the airlines themselves and is called the International Air Transport Association (IATA). The work of IATA which affects the traveller most directly is reflected in the airline ticket, for international fares are agreed between IATA members. Making a reservation seems to be a very simple operation, but behind the scenes there is a large staff using a computer system to check reservations and make sure aircraft are not over-filled. Sometimes a journey may involve two or more flights on different airlines but this is no problem – one ticket is sufficient. This interchangeable ticket is very convenient for the air-traveller but requires much work behind the scenes to ensure that the airlines which carry the passenger get the money. The IATA *clearing house* staff work out how much money is due to each member airline. Many other financial, commercial and technical problems are solved by the joint efforts of the airlines through IATA.

Below: *Airline insignia from around the world.*

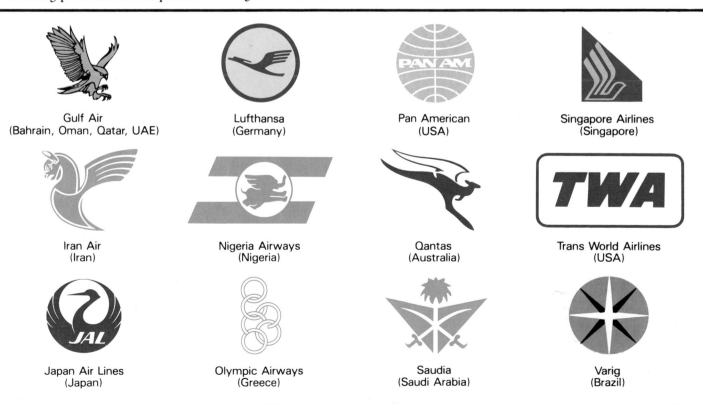

Gulf Air
(Bahrain, Oman, Qatar, UAE)

Lufthansa
(Germany)

Pan American
(USA)

Singapore Airlines
(Singapore)

Iran Air
(Iran)

Nigeria Airways
(Nigeria)

Qantas
(Australia)

Trans World Airlines
(USA)

Japan Air Lines
(Japan)

Olympic Airways
(Greece)

Saudia
(Saudi Arabia)

Varig
(Brazil)

FREIGHT AIRCRAFT

During the years between the two World Wars, a typical load of air freight consisted of passengers' baggage and a few bags of airmail letters. These were usually carried in the small freight compartment of a scheduled passenger airliner. Contracts to carry airmail were very much sought after by the early airlines as they struggled to survive. During the mid 1920s the Post Office in the United States offered lucrative contracts to carry airmail and special mail planes were designed. One of the best of these was the Boeing Model 40 biplane which could also carry two passengers.

Aircraft carrying only freight played a vital part in supplying the armed forces during the Second World War. The majority of these freighters were airliners, such as the Douglas DC-3, modified by fitting a stronger floor and larger doors. After the war many old freighters were bought by airlines and a new industry of air-freighting was born. Sending freight by air is generally more expensive than by rail, road or sea but it does reach its destination more quickly. For instance speed is essential for the transportation of mail, newspapers, perishable items – such as flowers – and urgently needed spare parts for broken machinery. An unusual freight operation started in July 1948 when Silver City Airways opened a car-ferry service between England and France. Instead of a ferry-boat, they used freight aircraft – the specially designed Bristol 170 Freighter. Two cars and their passengers were carried each trip, which lasted less than half an hour.

Cargo aircraft

Today air freight (or air cargo, as it is now often known) has grown into an industry in its own right employing many thousands of people and transporting anything from day-old chicks to space rockets. The aircraft in use can be divided into three groups: old passenger aircraft modified to carry cargo, airliners redesigned as freighters, and specially designed freight aircraft. (Military freighters are usually called transport aircraft.)

The first group contains some straightforward conversions such as the Vickers Vanguard which was fitted with a larger door and a stronger floor to become the Merchantman. Other conversions produced some more unusual aircraft – none more so than the Guppy. In 1963 the United States space programme needed a large aircraft to transport sections of the Apollo-Saturn V moon rocket to Cape Kennedy: no existing transport aircraft could do the job. An old Boeing Stratocruiser airliner was rebuilt with a huge bubble on the upper part of its fuselage, so that, with the nose hinged to open sideways a rocket up to 7.5 metres in diameter could be carried. This aircraft was called a Guppy because of its resemblance to the fish of that name. An improved Super Guppy with turbo-prop engines was also built and this aircraft has been used by the builders of the European Airbus to transport large sections of aircraft to the assembly factory.

Manufacturers of most modern airliners usually offer a choice of layouts for any particular aircraft. For example, Boeings offer three very different layouts for their 747 Jumbo; a conventional airliner carrying passengers, a convertible aircraft which can switch between passengers and cargo, or a specialized cargo aircraft. The cargo version has a nose section which hinges upwards to reveal a large hold capable of carrying an incredible 90 000 kilo-

Below: The bulky shapes of three cargo aircraft from the United States.

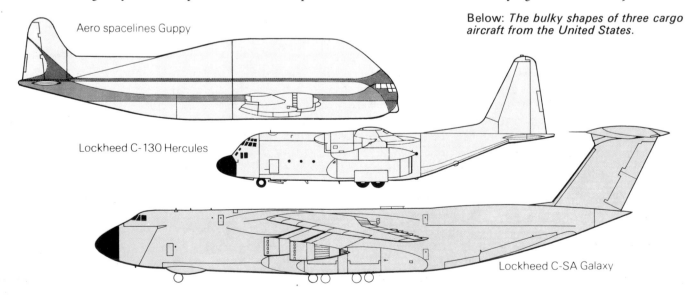

Aero spacelines Guppy

Lockheed C-130 Hercules

Lockheed C-5A Galaxy

The Berlin Air Lift

Freight aircraft can sometimes fly in supplies when no other form of transport is available – such as in the northern areas of Canada where the 'bush' pilot carries vital supplies to isolated communities. In June 1948 a whole city became isolated: the Russians refused to allow supplies for West Berlin to travel by either road or rail through East Germany, thus cutting West Berlin off from the rest of West Germany. Britain and America decided to fly-in the vital supplies and the 'Berlin Air Lift' began. Not only food had to be carried by air, but also bulky items such as coal, industrial materials, petrol – in fact everything a city of two million people required to live and work. It was a mammoth undertaking which called for all available freight-carrying aircraft. At times aircraft were landing at the rate of one every three minutes. After almost a year the Russians relented and re-opened the roads and railways to West Berlin: the Air Lift had beaten the blockade. It was a very expensive operation and in normal circumstances it would not be practicable to fly such a bulky substance as coal, but it did demonstrate the effectiveness of air transport.

Below: *American and British aircraft at Gatow Airport, Berlin, for the Air Lift.*

grams of cargo inside.

Of the specially designed freight aircraft flying today, the Lockheed C-130 Hercules is probably the most widely used, since it is in service with a number of commercial cargo airlines and many air forces. It first entered service in 1956 and by 1978, 1500 had been delivered. The Hercules has four turbo-prop engines and can carry 20 000 kilograms of cargo or 92 fully-equipped soldiers, but it is dwarfed by two later Lockheed military transports – the C-141 StarLifter and the C-5A Galaxy. The Galaxy can carry 345 soldiers or a load of tanks and lorries.

During recent years new systems of loading cargo into an aircraft have been introduced to reduce the amount of time an aircraft wastes on the ground. Instead of loading individual items into the aircraft, one at a time, they are packed on to a movable platform (or *pallet*) or loaded into a *container*. This loading is carried out in a special cargo shed, which means it can be done before the aircraft arrives. A loaded pallet is usually covered with a net to secure the cargo. The pallets and containers are then weighed and moved on to a lorry which takes them to the waiting aircraft. They are lifted aboard by a fork-lift truck, loaded into position and locked to the floor of the aircraft. Pallets and containers are made to international standard dimensions so they can be carried by any aircraft, or transferred to land or sea transport.

An important aspect of air cargo which does not lend itself to containerization is the transportation of live animals. Race horses are frequently flown to distant race courses: sheep and cattle are also frequent travellers by air. Most airports have special facilities for dealing with this rather unusual cargo – which needs regular food and water. Some 'passengers' need more attention than others, for instance when dolphins are carried they have to be carried in special foam-lined slings and sprayed with water at regular intervals! It has been claimed by one airline that every fourth 'passenger' carried is an animal.

FLYING BOATS

Once an aircraft is in the air, its wheels or other type of undercarriage are just dead weight and a source of drag, but during take-off and landing the undercarriage is vital. The Wright brothers devised an unusual undercarriage: their 'Flyers' did not have wheels – they had two skids. European aviators preferred wheels, for example the monoplane designed and flown by Louis Blériot on the first cross-Channel flight in 1909 had two wheels at the front and one at the rear. During the 1930s, undercarriages were greatly improved, first by the introduction of more efficient springing, then by making the wheels fold up inside the wing or fuselage. These *retractable* undercarriages reduced the drag during flight, but in general were heavier than fixed wheels.

As airliners grew in size and weight they needed longer runways to become airborne. They also needed firmer runways to withstand the impact of landings. Finding suitable airfields was a problem, but there was an alternative and this was first demonstrated in 1910 when a French aircraft with a very different kind of undercarriage made its first flight. Henri Fabre's peculiar looking flying machine was fitted with floats and took off from water. Many seaplanes followed and perhaps the most spectacular were the racing *float-planes* flown in the famous Schneider Trophy races in the late 1920s. In 1931 Britain took the Trophy outright having won it three times in succession, and the winning Supermarine S.6B went on to break the world air-speed record at 655 kph (407 mph). Larger seaplanes were often designed as *flying boats*. In these, the fuselage or *hull* floated on the water and small, steadying floats were fitted at the wing tips. In the early days of long-distance flying, seaplanes were very convenient because a suitable stretch of water could usually be found for landing or taking-off, whereas aerodromes were few and far between.

The first aircraft to fly across the Atlantic Ocean was a flying boat, which had to stop and refuel during the journey. The United States Navy Curtiss NC-4 flying boat alighted on the sea at the Azores Islands which are about two-thirds of the way between Newfoundland, Canada, and Lisbon, Portugal. The idea of alighting on the sea to refuel during long flights was used by the German airline Deutsche Lufthansa in the 1930s. Their Dornier Wal (Whale) flying boats operated a mail service to South America. They could not reach their destination non-stop, so they alighted on the sea near an anchored depot ship which lifted them aboard with a crane. After being refuelled, the flying boat was catapulted into the air to continue its flight. This catapult launch saved a considerable amount of fuel, because a take-off from the sea required a long run to become airborne.

Long-distance flying boats

During the 1930s, flying boats reigned supreme on the long-distance air routes of the world. Imperial Airways started many of its services with biplane flying boats such as the Short Calcutta and later introduced the very popular Short 'C' class Empire flying boat which was a four-engined monoplane. In 1931 the United States airline Pan American Airways introduced the Sikorsky S-40 *amphibian* which could operate from land or water. Then, in the mid 1930s, Pan American extended its services with the larger Sikorsky S-42, the Martin 130 and the Boeing 314. These four-engined flying boats were christened 'Clippers' and they pioneered routes across the Pacific and Atlantic Oceans.

Many other countries built flying boats and seaplanes, but the Second World War ended most passenger

Below and right: *The largest aircraft ever constructed, the Hercules flying boat, which had a wing span of almost 100 metres and was intended to carry 700 passengers. It was built by American millionaire industrialist, aviator and film producer Howard Hughes, and made its only flight in 1947.*

Above: *Howard Hughes built his gigantic Hercules with a wooden framework, which resulted in its nickname the* Spruce Goose.

Below: *The United States Navy Curtiss NC-4 seaplane at Lisbon, Portugal after flying from Newfoundland via the Azores. This was the first aircraft to cross the Atlantic, taking off from Canada on 16 May and landing 11 days later.*

services, and flying boats became widely used for patrolling the seas in search of enemy shipping. Aircraft such as the Short Sunderland of Britain and the Consolidated PBY-5 Catalina of the United States were outstanding at this.

When peace returned flying boats were superseded by the new land-based airliners, but many smaller flying boats, floatplanes and amphibians were built for island services and for use in the Canadian bush where lakes are plenti-

ful. Will the large flying boat return? Supporters of the flying boat have always maintained that very large aircraft should operate from water, and not from long and expensive runways. In 1929 the Germans built the Dornier Do.X with a wing span of 48 metres; in 1935 the French built the Latécoère 521 with a wing span of 49.27 metres, then in 1947 an American millionaire, Howard Hughes, built his Hercules with a span of 97.54 metres. The whole air-

craft was built of wood and was intended to carry 700 passengers. This still holds the record as the largest aircraft ever built, but it made just one flight. None of these extra-large flying boats, nor the British Saunders-Roe Princess, with a span of 66.9 metres, were produced in large numbers. In the post-war years there were plenty of runways and it became increasingly difficult to keep long stretches of water clear of ships, boats and floating debris – a log floating just below the surface is a major hazard for a flying boat. Flying boats in the future would also need bases and few of the pre-war bases survive – consequently the future of the flying boat does not look promising.

Right: *A British Supermarine S.6B floatplane in 1931.*

Pickaback aircraft

One solution to the problem of getting a very heavily loaded aircraft into the air was tried out in Britain during 1938. Major R. H. Mayo suggested a pickaback arrangement with a large aircraft lifting a smaller one into the air. The two aircraft were built by Short Brothers of Rochester: the lower one was a large flying boat called 'Maia' while the upper one was a floatplane called 'Mercury'. The composite aircraft took off, and when a suitable height had been reached, Mercury was released to fly its heavy load of mail to a distant destination while Maia returned to base. Promising trials came to an end with the outbreak of the Second World War.

Below: *The Short-Mayo composite aircraft.*

HELICOPTERS

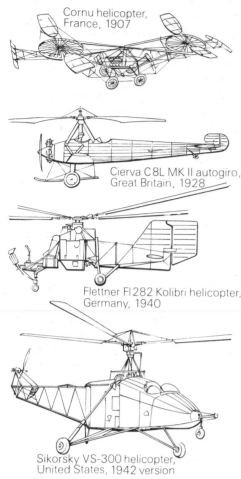

Cornu helicopter,
France, 1907

Cierva C8L MK II autogiro,
Great Britain, 1928

Flettner Fl 282 Kolibri helicopter,
Germany, 1940

Sikorsky VS-300 helicopter,
United States, 1942 version

Above: *Early helicopters and autogiros.*

Below: *Rescue at sea – a Sea King helicopter and the lifeboat from Cromer, England.*

Not very many years ago the sight of a helicopter flying overhead was a rare event, but today these *rotary-wing* aircraft hardly rate a second glance. The development of the helicopter has really taken place since the end of the Second World War, although its actual history goes back much further. In the 15th century Leonardo da Vinci sketched a helicopter which had a large spiral 'screw' to lift it vertically into the air. Indeed the name helicopter comes from the Greek words *helix* (a screw) and *pteron* (a wing). Like so many of Leonardo da Vinci's inventions this one was never built – it was just an idea. Another idea for a helicopter was published in 1843 by the British inventor Sir George Cayley and this had four lifting *rotors* (large propellers) but again it was never constructed. Many weird and wonderful designs followed during the 19th century, but none of these made even a short flight – some merely shook themselves to pieces!

In 1907 two French helicopters did actually leave the ground. One designed by Louis Breguet and Professor Richet reached a height of 1.5 metres but had to be steadied by men holding on to it. The second, built by Paul Cornu, made a free flight lasting just 20 seconds and reached a height of about 0.3 metres – later it rose to nearly 2 metres!

In the 1920s a great step forward was made when the Spanish engineer, Juan de la Cierva, invented the *autogiro*. Both the autogiro and the helicopter obtain their lifting power from a large, horizontal rotor with two or more blades, each acting as a rotating wing. The basic difference between the two flying machines lies in the method of driving this rotor. It is driven by an engine in a helicopter, but rotates freely in an autogiro. In flight, the rotor of an autogiro is blown round due to the forward speed of the aircraft. A piston engine and propeller are usually fitted to provide this forward speed. When an autogiro takes off it requires a short run to start the large rotor turning, and of course a head wind helps. It can climb almost vertically, fly very slowly and land vertically.

The success of the autogiro encouraged helicopter designers and by 1937 the Germans had produced an experimental helicopter. It could not lift a heavy load, but could remain in the air for over an hour and it was reasonably controllable. Controlling a helicopter in flight was a major problem for the early designers. A few years later in America, the first usable helicopter was designed and flown by the Russian-born Igor Sikorsky. His VS-300 set the pattern for the majority of helicopters built since that date.

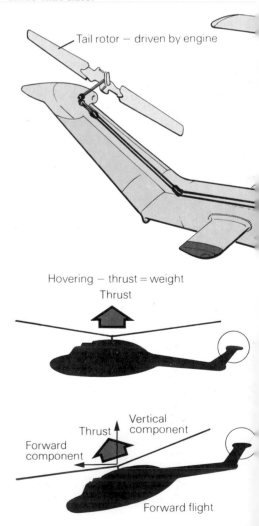

Tail rotor – driven by engine

Hovering – thrust = weight
Thrust

Thrust
Vertical component
Forward component
Forward flight

Controlling a helicopter

Sikorsky's helicopter had a large lifting rotor and a propeller at the tail facing sideways: both were driven by the same piston engine. Without the propeller (or a small rotor) the fuselage would have rotated in the opposite direction to the main rotor. Several Sikorsky designs were hurried into production and over 400 had been built by the end of the war. The Sikorsky layout of rotors has remained popular since those early days but several other layouts have emerged. For example, two main rotors rotating in opposite directions eliminate the need for a tail rotor.

When a helicopter is hovering, the upward thrust from the rotating rotor blades just balances the weight of the machine. If the pilot wants the helicopter to move upwards, this thrust must be increased. The pilot operates a lever in the cockpit which is called the *collective pitch lever* and this increases the pitch (angle of twist) of all the rotor blades. If each rotating blade is compared with an aircraft wing, then this operation increases the angle of incidence of each 'wing' and hence the lift (*see page 142*). More lift requires more power from the engine, so the collective pitch lever incorporates a twist grip throttle control (like that of a motor cycle) which means the pilot can control the two operations with one hand.

The pilot also needs to control his direction of flight – forwards, backwards or even sideways – and once again the pitch of the rotor blades is used. The blades trace out a large disc as they rotate, so if the pitch angle is increased in the rear half of this disc and decreased in the forward half, more lift will be produced over the rear half than the front half. This results in the disc (and the helicopter) tilting into a nose-down attitude. The thrust from the rotor is thus divided into an upwards component and a component pulling the machine forwards. The pilot controls the direction of the rotor's thrust by means of a control lever called the *cyclic pitch control* which is usually mounted between his legs – like the control column of a light aircraft. To control the direction in which he is heading, the pilot operates rudder pedals which are linked to the sideways-facing tail rotor.

Almost every day helicopters are in the news, usually because they have rescued someone in distress. But in addition to their rescue missions helicopters are used as a means of transport, as lifeboats, cranes, observation posts, ambulances, lorries, agricultural implements and as weapons of war. The secret of the helicopter's success lies in its ability to hover and operate from any small open space. But helicopters do have some disadvantages, such as their noise. They are also expensive, both to buy and to operate, a fact which is largely due to their rotors and the complicated mechanism controlling them.

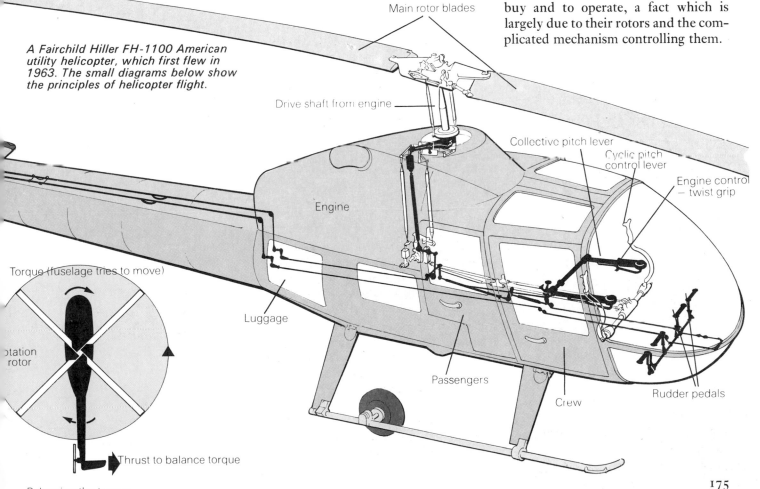

A Fairchild Hiller FH-1100 American utility helicopter, which first flew in 1963. The small diagrams below show the principles of helicopter flight.

Main rotor blades

Drive shaft from engine

Collective pitch lever

Cyclic pitch control lever

Engine control – twist grip

Engine

Luggage

Passengers

Crew

Rudder pedals

Torque (fuselage tries to move)

Rotation of rotor

Thrust to balance torque

Balancing the torque

HELP FROM THE AIR

During the 1920s, farmers in the United States took to the air to wage war on insects which were eating their crops. Old biplanes flew low over the fields, dropping a stream of powder which fell on the crops and killed the insects. *Dusting* crops from an aircraft had two advantages over the more conventional tractor: it was faster and it did not damage the crops with its wheels. The dropping of fertilizer or *top dressing* was developed in New Zealand where barren hills were converted to grass pastures for grazing sheep by dropping the much needed phosphate fertilizer from the air. In the United States, farmers pioneered the dropping of seeds from the air and large areas were sown with wheat and rice: in fact almost all the North American rice crop is now seeded from the air. Liquid pesticides could also be sprayed on to the crops very easily by air.

The early agricultural aircraft were all second-hand machines converted for their new work. This involved fitting a large tank or *hopper* into the fuselage and mounting the spraying or dusting gear along the wings. The aircraft converted in this way ranged from small de Havilland Tiger Moths to Boeing B-17 Flying Fortress bombers. Helicopters were also used and they had two advantages over other aircraft: they could operate in confined spaces such as narrow valleys, and the 'downwash' from their rotor blades helped to blow the chemical right into the heart of the crop. During the 1960s, farming by air became a very successful business and aircraft were specially produced for such hard work. The resulting aircraft were not very elegant because they had to carry all the external spraying gear

Above: *A Fletcher FU-24, built by New Zealand Aerospace Industries Ltd, spreading phosphate fertilizer on barren hills in New Zealand.*

and be strong enough to stand up to frequent landings on rough ground in order to recharge the hopper. The cockpits were carefully designed to keep out the chemicals and to withstand a crash – accidents do happen, especially when the spraying 'runs' are made a metre or so above the ground. Many of the successful agricultural aircraft have been built in the United States where they are widely used. The New Zealand inspired American Fletcher FU-24 was one of the first to sell in large numbers but there were a number of American rivals such as the Piper Pawnee, the Cessna Agwagon and the Grumman Ag-Cat biplane.

176

Surveying from the air

An observer in an aircraft obtains a 'bird's eye view' of the Earth which can be very useful, and, in addition, it can if necessary be recorded with a camera. Balloons and military aircraft have been used for observation purposes since their early days, and in the 1920s aerial map-making of the Earth's surface started. With a camera pointing downwards from the aircraft, photographs were taken at regular intervals along a straight line. By timing the camera carefully the photographs were taken so that they overlapped slightly. Having completed one run, the aircraft returned alongside the original line, and by flying to and fro in this way the required area was covered by a chequered pattern. Modern map-makers still operate in the same way but their equipment has improved tremendously.

Maps usually show what is visible on the surface of the Earth, but geologists are interested in the materials beneath the surface. Aircraft are equipped as flying laboratories, carrying delicate instruments which record information continuously during a survey flight. From these records the geologists can find out if there are any valuable minerals such as oil, uranium or iron ore beneath the Earth's crust.

Even historians have taken to the air to study archaeological remains. Patterns of buildings, long since demolished, can often be seen from the air. Fields of oats reveal remains of old buildings particularly clearly. Because the soil in the region of the building is often poorer than the surrounding area, the oats grow less well and so reveal the shape of the building. The Royal Air Force photographed Hadrian's Wall in the north of England as a training exercise and archaeologists discovered remains of several Roman camps which were previously unknown.

Below: *Archaeological remains seen from the air. Crops grow less well over buried foundations, revealing the shape of buildings.*

Farming from the air

Aircraft can be used in countless ways by an enterprising farmer – especially if he has a very large farm or ranch. Sometimes he flies around in his aircraft instead of driving a motor car or riding a horse. For example, a boundary fence can very easily be checked from the air to ensure that it has not been damaged. A modern cowboy might round-up his cattle by helicopter and fruit-growers find the downwash from a helicopter's rotor very useful for drying wet fruit. In the United States, the Fish and Wildlife Service has used aircraft to hunt wolves and to drop baby trout into lakes. But one of the most unusual jobs carried out by aircraft is to make it rain. In areas suffering from a long drought, clouds have been 'seeded' with chemicals and this has brought on the much-needed rain.

Right: *'Rain maker' aircraft in Australia*.

STOL AND VTOL AIRCRAFT

All aircraft have to fly slowly some of the time, especially during take-off and landing, but some aircraft are designed to fly slowly for long periods. This creates a problem because one of the most important factors in producing lift from a wing is speed. Reducing the speed reduces the lift, yet the wing still has to support the weight of the aircraft. To compensate, extra lift is needed, and the designers have to study the other factors affecting lift (*see page 142*). The two high-lift devices most widely used are: large extending flaps from the trailing edge of the wing; and slats along the leading edge which produce slots. Flaps increase the lift by changing the shape or camber of the wing, and they can increase its area. Slats and slots allow the aircraft to fly with a greater angle of incidence (nose up) without stalling.

Short take-off and landing aircraft

Special aircraft have been designed to operate from short landing strips in jungles or remote regions and these are usually referred to as *STOL* aircraft (Short Take-Off and Landing). One of the first such aircraft was the Handley Page Gugnunc of 1929 which had large

flaps and movable slats. The Handley Page Company had introduced a fixed slat and slot design in 1920, but the movable slats on the Gugnunc retracted on to the leading edge thereby closing the slot when the aircraft was flying quickly. The inboard slats were connected to the flaps and moved out from the wing to prevent stalling as the flaps were lowered to increase lift. The outboard slat sections moved automatically when the speed of the aircraft dropped and therefore delayed the stall.

During the Second World War, STOL aircraft were widely used for communications duties, and these included the German Fieseler Storch and the British Westland Lysander. Both could land almost anywhere with vital messages or important passengers. The Lysander was also widely used for landing spies, and supplies for resistance fighters, behind the enemy lines.

After the war several companies produced STOL aircraft for both civil and military use. For example, Scottish Aviation built their Pioneer and followed it with the larger twin-engined Twin-Pioneer. Both these aircraft made their mark flying from short airstrips hacked out of the jungle in the Far East.

Canadian 'bush' pilots also have to operate from short, rough airstrips, consequently the Canadian company de Havilland Canada have concentrated on STOL designs. Their Otter was followed by the turbo-prop Twin Otter and more recently they have built the four-engined Dash 7 which can carry 50 passengers. The Dash 7 is described as a 'quiet STOL' airliner and it is designed to operate from small airports near city centres – so low engine noise is an important feature.

Below: *Britain's VTOL aircraft, the Harrier – a two-seat trainer version.*

Vertical take-off and landing aircraft

It took many years for aircraft designers to produce a really effective Vertical Take-Off and Landing, or *VTOL*, aircraft in order to dispense with large and costly airports. The helicopter fulfils some of the requirements: it can certainly take off vertically but the large rotor makes it difficult to produce a helicopter capable of high speeds; also helicopters are expensive and noisy. A number of strange-looking VTOL aircraft appeared, often using several small rotors (or large propellers) to lift the machine off the ground. Sometimes two or four engines were mounted on a tilting wing: for take-off the wing and engines pointed upwards so the propellers lifted the aircraft off the ground, then the wing was tilted into the usual horizontal position with the engines pointing forwards and the *convertiplane* flew as a conventional aircraft. None of these aircraft progressed beyond the experimental stage.

The invention of the jet engine with its powerful thrust made VTOL aircraft a distinct possibility. In 1953 the Rolls-Royce 'Flying Bedstead' lifted into the air, powered by two Nene engines with their jets directed downwards. The Short SC-1 followed, using four *lifting* engines and one more engine for forward propulsion, but this aircraft was only experimental – although its layout is favoured by some people for the airliner of the future. Another variation is to change the direction of a jet between take-off and flight – either by tilting the engine or by deflecting the jet as it emerges from the engine. The most successful aircraft with this *vectored thrust* is the British Hawker-Siddeley Harrier fighter flown by the Royal Air Force and other airforces and also the US Marine Corps. The Harrier has a single engine but its jet emerges from four movable nozzles, which point downwards for take-off or to the rear in flight.

VTOL aircraft which are designed to carry passengers have one great advantage, in theory, for they should be able to operate from small areas of ground near a city centre. In practice there are many problems: VTOL aircraft are very expensive to operate because hovering burns up large quantities of fuel, they are extremely noisy and the jet itself can cause havoc on the ground. The VTOL aircraft has so far failed to supersede the helicopter and future designs may produce a cross between the two to give an improved all-round performance. The Bell Helicopter Company of the United States has been experimenting with *tilt-rotor* machines since the late 1950s. By the

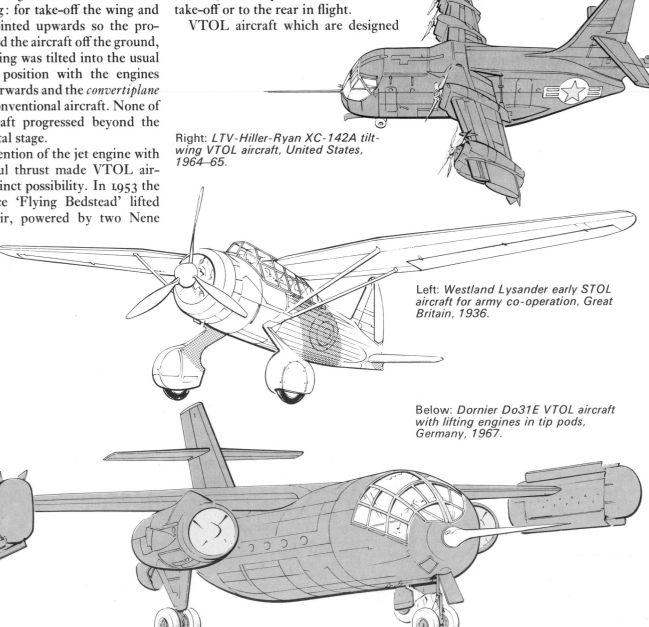

Right: *LTV-Hiller-Ryan XC-142A tilt-wing VTOL aircraft, United States, 1964–65.*

Left: *Westland Lysander early STOL aircraft for army co-operation, Great Britain, 1936.*

Below: *Dornier Do31E VTOL aircraft with lifting engines in tip pods, Germany, 1967.*

early 1980s their XV-15 was still experimental. In normal flight it looks like a conventional twin-engined aircraft but its turbo-prop engines are mounted at the wing tips. For take-off these engines and their rotors pivot to point upwards. Bells claim that the XV-15 can travel twice as fast as a helicopter, yet its noise level is about the same as an average helicopter.

There have been some weird and wonderful designs for VTOL aircraft produced over the years but it may be many more years before they carry passengers and freight.

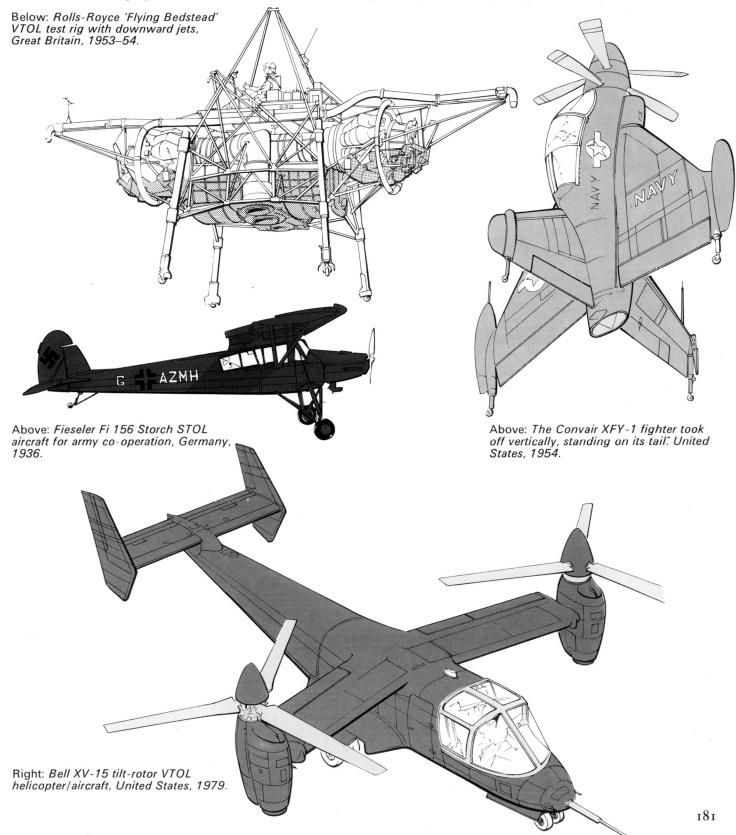

Below: *Rolls-Royce 'Flying Bedstead' VTOL test rig with downward jets, Great Britain, 1953–54.*

Above: *Fieseler Fi 156 Storch STOL aircraft for army co-operation, Germany, 1936.*

Above: *The Convair XFY-1 fighter took off vertically, standing on its tail. United States, 1954.*

Right: *Bell XV-15 tilt-rotor VTOL helicopter/aircraft, United States, 1979.*

A Junkers F13 airliner helping in the dramatic rescue of the survivors from the Soviet ship Chelyuskin *in 1934.*

AIR RESCUE

In an emergency, speed of action can make the difference between life and death, so, if long distances have to be covered, high speed aircraft are of great importance. Within the relatively short history of aviation there have been many examples of dramatic rescues and emergency relief. An early rescue took place in 1934 when the Russian steamer *Chelyuskin* sank in the Arctic. Despite many difficulties, aircraft landed on the ice and many people were flown to safety.

When natural disasters such as floods, earthquakes, hurricanes, or famines occur, aircraft are almost always on hand to rescue stranded people and fly-in food supplies. For example, farms and villages in mountainous areas can easily be isolated by a heavy snowfall and if food supplies run low, lives could be in danger. Aircraft can drop supplies of food for both people and animals.

When someone is seriously ill they need attention quickly which usually means getting a doctor to the patient or transferring the patient to hospital. In a village, town or city this is not normally a problem but in a very remote area, fast travel becomes vital. In some parts of Australia, Africa and South America there are settlements where the only means of reaching civilization used to be a long ride on horseback. Aviation has provided the answer to this problem and they now have flying doctor services.

Australia has one of the best schemes, called the Flying Doctor Service when it was founded in 1927 (becoming the Royal Flying Doctor Service in 1955). The problem it had to solve was twofold – poor surface transport and no telephone system. To improve communications, isolated farms were equipped with radio transmitter-receivers, but many of them did not have any electricity either so they had to make their own by driving a generator fitted with bicycle pedals. Once the farmers could radio for help, aircraft were hired from the local airlines to fly out a doctor or transport the patient to hospital. Aerial ambulances are also used in Britain to rescue patients in the 'highlands and islands' of Scotland. A normal airline service can easily be diverted to pick up a patient in an emergency or a special helicopter flight might be ordered if the patient is

Above: *A United States Air Force pararescueman with his equipment prepares to jump.*

stranded on a mountain or at sea.

In the United States a new rescue service has been introduced in recent years using 'para-rescuemen'. These highly trained men drop by parachute to help anyone in trouble, but one of their most important tasks has been to recover space capsules and the astronauts after their journeys into Space. The para-rescuemen have to be trained in many skills including parachuting, first aid, mountaineering, arctic survival and skin diving.

Below: *A DHA Drover ambulance aircraft brings in a patient from the outback in New South Wales, Australia.*

Fire-fighting by air

Aircraft can be used as mobile viewpoints, which makes them ideal for spotting forest fires. Trees are a valuable crop, grown to produce timber and wood pulp for paper-making, and a forest fire can destroy them only too quickly. A fire which gets out of hand can also endanger human and animal life, so the effects of a forgotten camp fire or of lightning can be devastating.

In 1919 the United States Army Air Corps began to patrol some forests in California and from this small beginning, world-wide fire-spotting operations have grown. Pilots soon learned to spot fires, almost before they happened, by keeping an eye on campers and following in the path of any dangerous-looking thunderstorm. In the 1930s fire-fighting equipment was first dropped from the air to firemen on the ground. Then in the 1940s firemen were dropped by parachute in the region of a fire. This was rather dangerous but the 'smoke-jumpers' got to the fire very quickly and, with luck, they could bring it under control before it had time to spread and become really dangerous. Since the Second World War helicopters have been introduced to carry firemen and their equipment to forest fires – or any other fire in a remote area.

Water-bombing

A new method of fighting forest fires has been widely used in recent years and this is called water-bombing. Each aircraft is fitted with a large water tank and a release valve so the pilot can drop the water on a fire. One load is not usually sufficient, so the pilot has to fill up his tank and return to the fire. Seaplanes are frequently used because there are usually lakes to be found in forest country – but no airfields. With a seaplane the pilot can alight on the lake and fill the tanks by scooping up water as the aircraft taxies into position for a quick take-off.

The Canadian company Canadair designed an aircraft specifically for water-bombing. Their CL-215 is a twin-engined, amphibious flying-boat which has very large tanks, mounted in its fuselage, capable of carrying 5455 litres of water – which is 10 times as much as earlier water-bombers. What is even more remarkable is the fact that these tanks can be filled, as the CL-215 skims across the water, in under 20 seconds.

PEOPLE AT WORK

Around the world there are hundreds of thousands of people whose work depends upon aviation. Many work directly for an aircraft manufacturing company, for an airline or at an airport, and some of these jobs have been mentioned in earlier sections. But there are many other people, in a wide variety of industries, who are less obviously dependent upon aviation for a livelihood.

Before an aircraft can be built, the manufacturer needs the basic materials. Wood has been replaced by metals, and in particular aluminium and its alloys (aluminium with a small amount of copper, zinc or magnesium added). Even after the discovery of these alloys, the metal companies had to develop methods to produce them at reasonable prices. Steelworkers are also involved in the aviation industry, for steel is used where its high strength is required on such items as engines and under-carriages. Tyres are also needed and they are supplied by the rubber manu-

facturers. Instruments are supplied by specialist firms, while furnishing manu-facturers, glass makers and many others all contribute to the success of an aircraft.

The aero-engine companies have built up a whole industry to design, develop and manufacture engines for a wide range of aircraft: they have even adapted their engines for other uses. For example, a modern frigate in the British navy is powered by two Rolls-Royce Olympus together with two Rolls-Royce Tyne gas turbine engines. These are marine versions of the aero-engines used in Concorde and the Vickers Vanguard. Another use for modified aero-engines is to pump North Sea gas along the long pipe-lines to the areas where it is needed.

Engines need fuel and oil, so most of the large international oil companies have specialist sections which produce and distribute aviation fuel to the four corners of the world. At major airports each company has its own staff to refuel

aircraft – either by tanker vehicles or a piped-hydrant system. In contrast to these operations, fuel has also to be available in remote areas such as the Australian 'outback' or the Canadian 'bush'. The owner of a local garage or a general store may sell aviation fuel as part of his business.

Research and development in the oil industry are vital; fuel technologists are constantly striving to improve their products, and maintain the quality of existing supplies. Should any impuri-ties such as water or dirt find their way into aviation fuel, the result could be an engine failure and a major catastrophe. The oil companies are not only sup-pliers to the aviation industry – they are also good customers. Oil wells and pipe-lines are usually situated in re-mote areas where surface travel is difficult, consequently air transport is used. For example, most of the oil rigs in the North Sea have a regular heli-copter service linking them to the mainland.

Below: *Tyres are a vital component which have to be checked regularly for damage.*

Right: *Height-measuring altimeters are tested and inspected at each stage of manufacture.*

Servicing and research

Keeping a single aircraft in the air can involve hundreds of workers on the ground, particularly if it is a large airliner or a powerful military aircraft. Routine servicing is usually carried out on the spot, but major overhauls or modifications are often handled by specialist companies. Modifications may involve converting an old airliner into a freighter, or converting a military aircraft to take new equipment.

When an aircraft is serviced at an airport it is surrounded by a host of specialized vehicles and equipment. For companies who manufacture tanker vehicles, tractors, trailers, fork-lift trucks, runway sweepers, special buses and other mechanical equipment, the aviation industry is a large and lucrative customer.

Few industries move forward faster than the aviation industry and many people are engaged in research. This ranges from developing new materials to the theory of flight, particularly supersonic flight. Work is carried out by government-sponsored establishments, universities and manufacturers. Sometimes military aircraft are used to assist with research projects. For example, in the USA a considerable amount of research into supersonic flight was carried out by the United States Air Force in conjunction with the National Aeronautics and Space Administration. Britain's Royal Air Force carried out a series of flights in the region of the north magnetic pole which assisted in the solving of the navigational problems in that area.

In addition to research projects, government establishments employ many scientific, technical and legal experts to maintain the safety standards of aircraft based in their country. The electronics industry also works very closely with the aircraft designers to supply radio, radar, navigational aids and other equipment.

Below: *A Boeing 707 being serviced.*

187

LIGHT AIRCRAFT

For business people 'time is money' and this includes travelling time which, as far as the company is concerned, is wasted time. After the Second World War, the use of business aircraft grew, steadily at first, but then quite rapidly.

In the United States, where long distances are a problem, business aircraft are widely used. Many senior executives have a jet aircraft converted for business use, complete with desk, telephone, typewriter, conference table and even a bar. Some extremely wealthy executives and oil millionaires own jet airliners converted for their personal use with luxurious fittings including a bed and even a bathroom. Most executive aircraft, however, are more modest, carrying from four to twelve passengers.

In Britain, de Havilland's Dove and Heron of the late 1940s were widely used as executive aircraft and they were succeeded by the small twin-jet Hawker Siddeley HS-125 (de Havilland being incorporated in Hawker Siddeley by

then). The HS-125 can cruise at 800 kph (500 mph) and it has even sold in America – the home of the business aircraft! The choice of aircraft in America is very wide and competition for sales is fierce. For example, one company, Cessna, offers over 30 different models ranging from the two-seater Model 152 to the luxurious Citation powered by two jet engines. Their great rivals, Beechcraft and Piper, also offer a similar selection, and a number of other American companies offer executive jets. Although the sales of executive aircraft are dominated by the American manufacturers, there are manufacturers in many parts of the world. From Canada comes the Canadair Challenger, while in France Dassault-Breguet produce the Falcon, and Aérospatiale the Corvette. Mitsubishi of Japan build the Diamond, and Embraer of Brazil manufacture the Xingu.

Below: *Cessna Model 172 four-seat light aircraft – one of the most popular aircraft of all time; United States, 1955.*

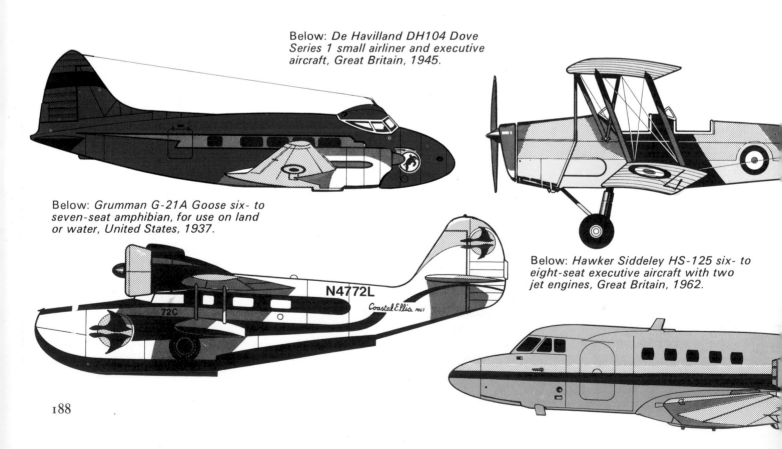

Below: *De Havilland DH104 Dove Series 1 small airliner and executive aircraft, Great Britain, 1945.*

Below: *Grumman G-21A Goose six- to seven-seat amphibian, for use on land or water, United States, 1937.*

Below: *Hawker Siddeley HS-125 six- to eight-seat executive aircraft with two jet engines, Great Britain, 1962.*

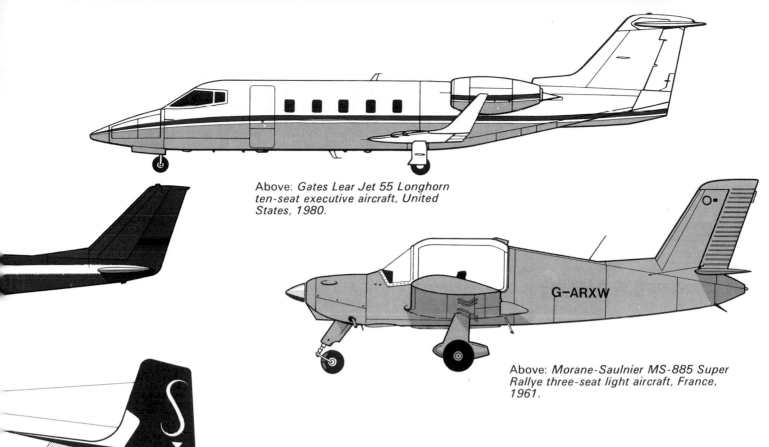

Above: *Gates Lear Jet 55 Longhorn ten-seat executive aircraft, United States, 1980.*

Above: *Morane-Saulnier MS-885 Super Rallye three-seat light aircraft, France, 1961.*

Above: *Cessna Model 310B five-seat twin-engined private or light business aircraft, United States, 1953.*

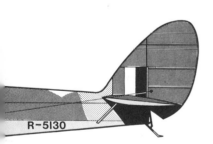

Above: *De Havilland DH82 Tiger Moth biplane trainer in wartime markings, Great Britain, 1931.*

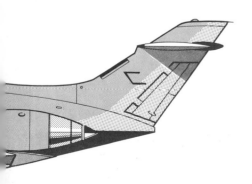

Private aircraft

In the years before the First World War, flying as a hobby was only for people with plenty of money, and the average member of the public just went along to watch. Things changed after this war when there was a determined effort to get more people into the air: joy rides, flying clubs and home-built aircraft were all available at modest prices. Flying clubs were founded near most large towns and many light aircraft were built for amateur pilots: these could be bought for little more than the price of a motor car. One of the most popular light aircraft of this period was the de Havilland Moth biplane which was followed by the Gipsy Moth and the Tiger Moth.

The Second World War brought private flying in Europe to a halt. When peace returned in 1945 some of the clubs re-emerged but the cost of flying in Britain has never decreased to the level of the 1930s. In the United States, the story is very different, for private aircraft are extremely popular and flying is relatively inexpensive. The term

General Aviation (G.A.) is used to cover private, business, air-taxi and all other branches of aviation other than military and airline operations. There are over 200 000 G.A. aircraft in the United States and the figure continues to rise. The modern equivalent of the de Havilland Moth is the American Cessna Model 150 and its successor, the Model 152. The two-seater Model 150 first flew in 1957 and by the time it was phased out in 1977, a total of almost 24 000 had been built. Even this success was surpassed by the larger, four-seater Model 172 Skyhawk for which the production figure passed 30 000. All three of these Cessnas are single-engined high-wing monoplanes which can cruise at about 200 kph (125 mph). They are widely used by private owners and flying clubs in many parts of the world.

Some private owners use their aircraft instead of a car – especially in the United States – but others fly as a hobby. For those who enjoy competitions there are air rallies, races and aerobatic competitions. The latter two sports can be very competitive and specially designed aircraft are produced for these events.

THE FUTURE

In Jules Verne's famous story *Around the World in Eighty Days* written in 1873, the only air travel mentioned was a short trip in a balloon; the rest of this eventful journey made use of practically every other form of transport from elephants to steamers. Today it is possible to sit in the comfort of an airliner and fly round the world in a few days.

Jules Verne would not have been surprised by this – indeed, many of the predictions made by writers of fiction, such as Jules Verne and H. G. Wells, have proved to be more accurate than the forecasts of acknowledged experts.

Over the years, experts have placed limits on almost every aspect of aircraft design and performance – only to be proved wrong a few years later. The maximum possible speed for an aircraft was once thought to be about 240 kph (150 mph), and in the 1920s a United States Navy committee decided that the largest possible aircraft would weigh about 20 000 kilograms – a Jumbo weighs 350 000 kilograms. So the designers of aircraft have often proved the predictions wrong, but sometimes the designers have been wrong too. Some of their major mistakes have been with large aircraft which were ahead of their time. Back in 1921 the Italian designer Count Gianni Caproni built a flying boat which had nine wings (three sets of three) and eight engines. It was in-

Left: *One of the most unusual aircraft ever built – Count Caproni's flying boat with nine wings, 1921.*

tended to carry 100 passengers but after two short hops the unwieldy machine was abandoned. History repeated itself several times over and one of the most spectacular repeats was Howard Hughes' giant Hercules (*see pages 172–3*).

Will the airliners of the future continue to increase in size or is the Boeing 747 Jumbo, with its 490 seats, the end of the line? Larger aircraft result in cheaper air fares so there is a great temptation to increase the size of airliners. On the other hand, the existing runways of the world's airports cannot cope with ever-increasing aircraft weights and these runways may prove

to be the brake on progress. A group of some 500 passengers can present a problem when they have to be checked through passport control or moved to a distant loading gate. Consequently, larger groups would need improved passenger-handling arrangements – perhaps conventional passports will be replaced by plastic cards which could be checked by a computer.

Some routes just do not have enough passengers for the largest airliners so there will continue to be a use for the smaller airliner. For example, 500 passengers per day may wish to travel on one particular route. It would be economical for an airline to operate one

flight per day using a 500-seat airliner, but this might not suit the passengers and five flights during the day, each carrying 100 passengers, might be more acceptable. There will certainly be a considerable effort to make all airliners, large or small, quieter, safer and less expensive to operate. Because fuel is so expensive, engines must be designed to use less fuel. On many of the shorter routes, helicopters, STOL and VTOL aircraft will probably dominate the scene for some years to come, but the future of the flying boat is doubtful.

Below: *Artist's impression of a future airliner powered by hydrogen and capable of 6500 kph.*

Faster or slower?

Will airliners of the future fly faster or slower than those of today? People are always looking for ways of saving time – the faster we travel, the more time we save. But there are problems. Conventional subsonic airliners cannot fly any faster without running into the high drag of the 'sound barrier'. Supersonic airliners, such as Concorde, are expensive to operate – although they may become cheaper in the future. But an airliner designed to fly much faster than Concorde would be very expensive to produce because it would have to be built from stainless steel and titanium to withstand the high temperatures generated at Mach 3 and above. It has even been suggested that passenger-carrying space rockets might be built to transport passengers between Britain and Australia in only an hour or so.

Of course, speeds may change in the other direction, with slow-flying air travel gaining popularity. The airship might return, perhaps with nuclear-powered engines. These engines could run for years on just a drop of fuel, but the protective shield around the reactor would need to be so heavy that, at present, the prospects do not look too promising. A new development in nuclear science could change this state – or an exciting new source of power might be invented which would reduce the cost of air travel to a fraction of its present figure.

For most passengers, hopes for the future are largely directed towards reliable, safe and cheap air travel.

The airliner of today – but what does the future hold in store?

SPACE

It is astonishing to think that at the turn of this century nobody had flown in an aeroplane. And when they first did, in 1903, they could only average less than 60 kph (40 mph). Yet today people fly in orbit around the Earth at speeds of 28 000 kph (17 500 mph). They can venture forth at still higher speeds into deep Space to visit another world – the Moon. Plans have also been advanced for manned trips to the planets. Suggestions have been made for space colonies and for converting the planet Venus into a twin of the Earth. And scientists are scanning the heavens for signals that might herald the presence of other intelligent creatures on other planets in other solar systems, somewhere among the stars.

But people have been dreaming of travelling in Space for centuries and written stories about it. One of the earliest, written by the Greek author Lucian (2nd century AD) with tongue in cheek, called *True History*, describes the adventures of a band of sailors plucked from Earth by a whirlwind and set down on the Moon.

Most early science fiction writers – for that is what they were – regarded the Moon as being inhabited. They numbered among their ranks Johannes Kepler, the astronomer whose laws of motion correctly described how the planets move around the Sun. Kepler's book, *Somnium*, also described a trip to the Moon, as did that of English bishop Francis Godwin, *The Man in the Moone*. Both were published in the 1630s. Later, Jules Verne also sent his heroes to the Moon in such books as *From the Earth to the Moon* (1865), and so did H. G. Wells in *The First Men in the Moon* (1901).

Above: *By the mid-1800s several European armies had rocket squadrons. Here is the British Army practising.*

Rocket power

The means employed by the writers to dispatch craft to the Moon ranged from evaporating dewdrops and flying swans to anti-gravity material and space trains. Needless to say, none was feasible. But all the authors overlooked a method of propulsion that could work, using a device well-known since the Middle Ages. This was the rocket.

As early as 1232 rockets were being used intermittently as projectiles in warfare. But they did not begin to be developed intensively until the early 1800s. The first great rocket designer was the English colonel, William Congreve. Congreve's rockets saw service at the Battle of Waterloo, and in battle in America. They carried either incendiary material or shot, which exploded like shrapnel to kill and maim.

In 1855 Edward Boxer in England built the first successful two-stage rocket, for carrying lifelines to stricken vessels at sea. This two-stage rocket pioneered the principle that would ultimately lead to the launching of Sputnik 1, the first artificial satellite, in 1957.

Exactly a century earlier, a man was born in Russia whose ideas on space flight were to come true in the future. He was named Konstantin Tsiolkovsky. He became a noted mathematician and teacher, but his ideas on travelling in Space made him seem a crank to most people. Yet he is now regarded as the father of astronautics – space flight.

Tsiolkovsky delivered his first important paper on astronautics in 1903, and in this and later papers he outlined

Above: *Tsiolkovsky was a man of vision who laid the foundations for astronautics.*

Below: *Rocket pioneer Robert Hutchings Goddard in his workshop in 1935.*

many of the principles of modern space flight. He saw that only a reaction engine – that is, a rocket – could work in Space; that to achieve sufficient power, *multi-stage rockets* must be used; and that these rockets should be propelled by liquid fuels, not gunpowder.

Tsiolkovsky only worked on theories of space flight and never built any rockets, and his work was virtually unknown outside Russia. His ideas were unwittingly taken up in Germany by Hermann Oberth, who published in 1923 the first classic book on space flight, entitled *The Rocket into Interplanetary Space*. Again, he never built any successful rockets. It was left to the American Robert Hutchings Goddard to pioneer the development of the modern rocket, which uses liquid fuel.

Goddard first successfully tested such a rocket in 1926. By 1935, the year Tsiolkovsky died, Goddard's rockets could travel at 1100 kph (700 mph) and reach an altitude of 2.5 kilometres.

Society for Space Travel

In Germany, Oberth's book inspired a group of enthusiasts to form, in 1927, a Society for Space Travel. The society designed, built and tested rockets, but without much success. By 1933 it had disbanded. But its work did not go unnoticed. In that same year, the British Interplanetary Society was formed, which has been in the forefront of astronautical development ever since. In the United States, the American Interplanetary Society – later the Rocket Society – had been formed three years earlier.

An ex-member of the Society for Space Travel, Wernher von Braun, soon found himself conducting rocket research for the German army. In 1937, as Europe edged closer to war, the research group transferred to a secret test base at Peenemünde on the Baltic coast. There, von Braun and his team developed the rocket that was the direct ancestor of the modern space launching vehicle. It was the notorious V-2.

ROCKET PROPULSION

If you fire a rifle, you must hold on to it tightly because as the bullet shoots out forwards, the rifle is thrust backwards against your shoulder. The *action* of the bullet travelling forward is accompanied by a *reaction* that forces the rifle back. This same law of reaction, originally put forward in the 1600s by Isaac Newton, also explains the principle of the rocket and of the jet engine.

Though jet engines and rocket motors work on the same principle, they differ in one important respect. A jet engine draws in oxygen from the atmosphere to burn its fuel. A rocket, however, carries its own supply of oxygen to burn its fuel. This is why a rocket can operate in Space, whereas a jet engine cannot.

Rockets can be built to have very much greater thrust than jet engines. The fuels and the oxidizers – the substances that provide oxygen – burn to release much greater energy.

The fuel and oxidizer that are burned to propel a rocket are known as *propellants*. The original rocket propellant was gunpowder – a mixture of powdered charcoal, sulphur and saltpetre (potassium nitrate). This mixture is still used in firework rockets even today. Gunpowder is a solid propellant. But it is not powerful enough for use in space travel. Today a kind of synthetic rubber is used as a solid propellant.

Right: *The launch vehicle for Russia's Soyuz spacecraft. It has four liquid-fuelled 'strap-on' boosters around a two-stage rocket core.*

Power from gases

Rocket motors and jet engines both work in similar ways. Fuel is burned in a combustion chamber to produce hot gases. The hot gases expand through a nozzle to form a high-speed jet, which shoots backwards out of the engine. The *action* of the jet shooting backwards results in a *reaction* that thrusts the engine, and what it is attached to, forwards.

It is a commonly held, but wrong, belief that jet engines work by pushing against the air. Nothing could be further from the truth. If this were so, rockets, which work in the same way as jet engines, would not operate in Space where there is no air to push against! In fact rockets work better in Space than they do in the atmosphere.

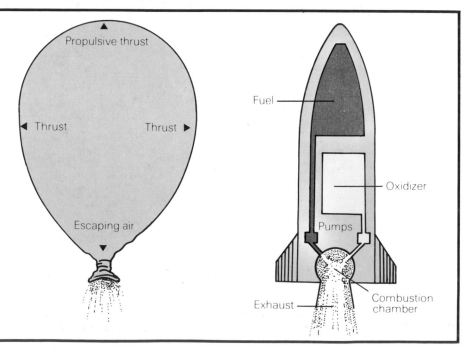

Solid-propellant rockets are widely
... launching vehicles as
... lift-off. The Space Shuttle,
..., uses twin solid boosters
...26). Smaller solid boosters
... used to jettison stages of
... rockets once a stage's fuel is
...id rockets are very simple in
...ion, being essentially tubes
...ld the propellant and double
...bustion chambers. The only
...an space launching vehicle that
...-solid rockets is the Scout, but
...ly suitable for launching rela-
...small payloads.

...e main rockets of most space
...hers use liquid propellants. The
...st obtained from liquid propellants
...ery much greater than that from
...id propellants. Also, by varying the
...ow of propellants to the combustion
...hamber, the thrust can be varied, or
cut off, at will.

The commonest liquid oxidizer used
is liquid oxygen. This is oxygen gas
that has been cooled to $-183°C$, at
which temperature it turns into liquid.
The most powerful rocket motors burn
the even colder liquid hydrogen as fuel,
with liquid oxygen. Other rockets burn
kerosene (paraffin) with liquid oxygen.
Another common propellant combination is UDMH (Unsymmetrical Di-
Methyl Hydrazine) as fuel, and nitrogen tetroxide as oxidizer. Whereas most
fuels must be ignited before they burn,
UDMH and nitrogen tetroxide ignite
spontaneously when they are mixed.

The multi-stage rocket

Even using liquid propellants, a single
rocket cannot be built with a sufficient
power-to-weight ratio (the ratio of the
power which will be produced by the
propellants compared with the weight of
the rocket plus propellants which has to
be moved) to lift itself into Space.

Right: *The European Space Agency's
heavy launcher Ariane stands on the
launch pad at Kourou in French
Guiana. This conventional three-stage
rocket is 47 metres in overall length.*

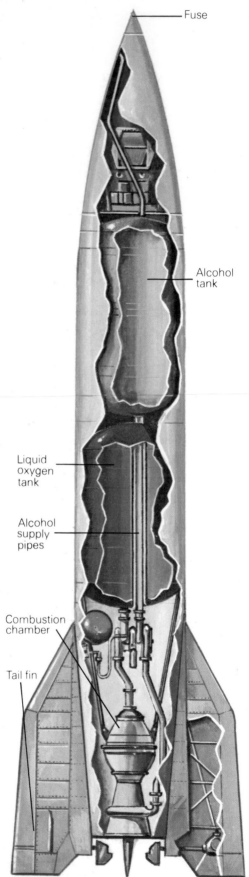

Fuse

Alcohol tank

Liquid oxygen tank

Alcohol supply pipes

Combustion chamber

Tail fin

Rockets burn several tonnes of propellants every second, and the bulk of a rocket is occupied by the propellants. A favourable overall power-to-weight ratio can be obtained, however, by linking a number of rockets together end to end. Each rocket fires in turn and then falls away. The progressively lighter vehicle can then readily be boosted to the speed necessary to achieve orbit, which is a staggering 28 000 kph (17 500 mph).

Linking rockets together in this way produces a multi-stage or step rocket. Most launching vehicles have three stages. This arrangement may comprise three rockets placed end to end, or a two-stage rocket core, to which are attached a number of first-stage boosters. For example, the massive Saturn V Moon rocket, which stood no less than 111 metres high, was a three-stage rocket. The Delta, one of NASA's long-standing workhorses, has a two-stage core with a cluster of nine solid fuel boosters strapped to the first stage.

The multi-stage launching vehicle must accurately follow a pre-arranged path, or trajectory, if it is to reach orbit successfully. This requires that the vehicle be constantly guided. This is done by means of an *inertial guidance system*. In this system sensitive instruments sense every movement of the rocket and feed the information to a computer. The computer compares the path the vehicle is following with what course it should be on. If there is any discrepancy, it orders the rocket engines, which are mounted so that they can swing in any direction, to move this way or that to counter the error.

Left: *Cut-away diagram of a V-2 rocket, developed by Germany in the Second World War, which carried 750 kg of high explosive in the nose cone. This deadly weapon provided the impetus for American and Russian Space rocket development after the war (see p. 200).*

Right: *Cut-away diagram of the American Saturn V Moon rocket, 111 m long and weighing 3 000 000 kg. It was a three-stage vehicle fuelled by kerosene (first stage) and liquid hydrogen. Three astronauts rode in the conical capsule at the top.*

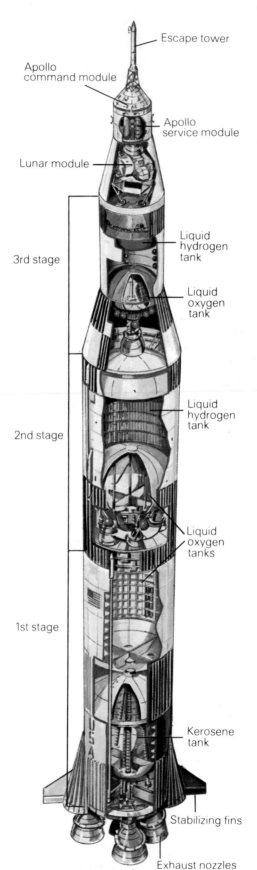

Escape tower

Apollo command module

Apollo service module

Lunar module

3rd stage

Liquid hydrogen tank

Liquid oxygen tank

2nd stage

Liquid hydrogen tank

Liquid oxygen tanks

1st stage

Kerosene tank

Stabilizing fins

Exhaust nozzles

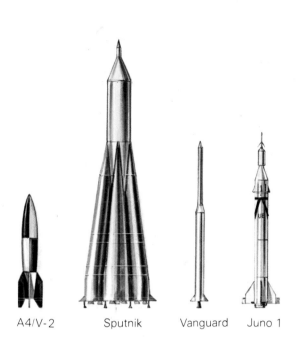

A4/V-2   Sputnik   Vanguard   Juno 1

Some of the most important Space launching vehicles used since the dawn of the Space age, drawn approximately to scale. Dwarfing them all is Saturn V, the biggest rocket yet developed, which was over three times the size of the rocket that launched the first Sputnik in 1957. The design of Russian rockets (to launch Sputnik, Vostok and Soyuz) has changed little over the years, being distinguished by the cluster of boosters around the base. Of the rockets depicted, only the Soyuz launcher and Ariane are still in service. Ariane is now competing with the Shuttle for international satellite launches.

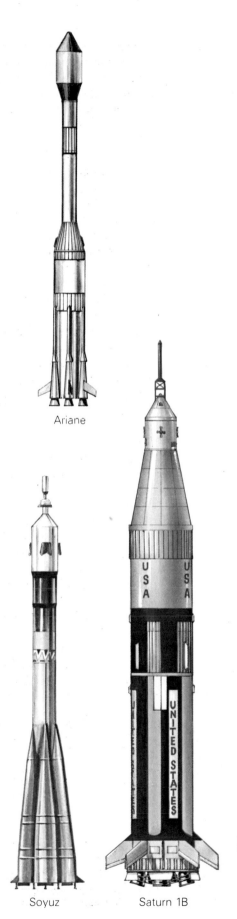

Ariane

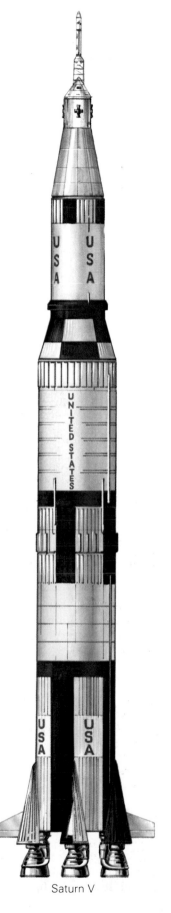

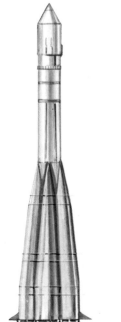

Vostok   Mercury/Atlas   Gemini/Titan   Soyuz   Saturn 1B   Saturn V

NEW MOONS

The V-2 rocket of the Second World War was the second of Hitler's infamous 'revenge weapons' (the V stands for the German word for this). The first was the V-1. This was a small pilotless aircraft powered by a pulse jet engine, the rasping noise of which earned it the nickname 'buzz-bomb'. It was relatively slow, travelling at about 550 kph (350 mph), and vulnerable to attack by aircraft and anti-aircraft guns. Less than half the 7500 V-1s launched against London in 1944 and 1945 reached their target.

The V-2, by contrast, was unstoppable. It climbed to the fringes of Space and then dropped on its target at some 5500 kph (3500 mph) – ten times the speed of the V-1. Fortunately, this terrifying weapon was developed late in the war and so was only in use for seven months.

The V-2 was first successfully tested at Peenemünde in 1942. On the launch pad it stood 14 metres high and weighed about 13 tonnes. It carried a warhead of some 750 kg of high explosive in a nose cone. It was powered by an engine burning alcohol and liquid oxygen.

The space race begins

When the Second World War came to an end in 1945, the V-2 research and development team were split up. Many, including von Braun, went to the United States, while others went to Russia to continue their work. Both countries also gained a supply of V-2s which acted as the springboard for future rocket development. Thus the 'space race' between the United States and Russia began, these two countries having gained an enormous lead over other 'competitors' when they acquired members of the V-2 research team.

By the mid-1950s both countries had built advanced rocket bombs which could travel on ballistic trajectories

over 1000 kilometres to drop their warheads. (A *ballistic trajectory* is the curving flight path followed by the rocket which is propelled and guided only on the upward part of the flight, like a ball thrown into the air.) They were termed *ICBMs* (Inter-Continental Ballistic Missiles). The first American ICBMs were Atlas and Titan. They were preceded by the shorter-range Redstone. All three types were later to feature in the American space programme.

Redstone used the same propellants as the V-2 – alcohol and liquid oxygen. Atlas used the more powerful combination of kerosene (paraffin) and liquid oxygen. And whereas Redstone was a single-stage vehicle, Atlas and Titan had two stages.

The year 1957 was designated International Geophysical Year (IGY) and plans were made to conduct worldwide

Above: *Launch of a V-2 rocket. It climbed up into Space then dropped on its target at 5500 kph (3500 mph).*

research into the Earth and its atmosphere. The United States announced that as part of its activities, it would try to launch an artificial Earth satellite. But it was not successful, and in fact Russia beat them to it.

The Americans were clearly falling behind in rocket technology but they did manage to launch their first satellite, Explorer 1, on 31 January 1958. Though small, it nevertheless made the first major scientific discovery of the Space Age. It detected the presence of bands of intense radiation around the Earth. These are atomic particles from the Sun trapped in Earth's magnetic sphere, and are called the Van Allen belts after the person who devised the experiment which detected them.

The year 1958 is also significant

The first Sputnik

In 1957, Russia, after years of secrecy over its rocket programme, showed its missile might in a spectacular parade to mark the 40th anniversary of the October Revolution (when the Soviet Union was established). And on 4 October 1957 it announced triumphantly that it had successfully launched an artificial satellite, Sputnik 1.

This announcement was dramatic, but, in addition, the weight of Sputnik 1 was an astonishing 83.5 kilograms. This was eight times the weight of the satellite the Americans were planning to put into orbit. Within a month, on 3 November, the world was astounded once again when Russia launched Sputnik 2. This not only weighed a colossal 500 kilograms, but carried the world's first space traveller – a dog known as Laika. For eight days Laika orbited the Earth, kept apparently in good health by a primitive life-support system, until she was put to sleep.

because on 29 July America's National Aeronautics and Space Administration (NASA) came into being, and it was this organization which pioneered important developments in space travel.

Out into Space

Elated with its success with satellite launches, Russia turned its attention to our nearest neighbour in Space. On 2 January 1959 it launched a spacecraft, Luna (or Lunik) 1, towards the Moon. Though it never reached its target, it was nevertheless the first craft to reach Earth-escape velocity (*see page 240*).

Undeterred, Russia launched two more lunar probes later in the year with greater success. Luna 2 was spot on target and crash-landed on the Moon. Luna 3 looped round the far side of the Moon which we cannot see from Earth, and sent back the first photographs of this hidden side.

The Americans, meanwhile, had also been aiming for the Moon with a succession of Pioneer spacecraft, but in vain. However, when they turned their attention to interplanetary flights, they were more successful. Their Pioneer 5 probe was launched into solar orbit in March 1960, and communications were maintained with it over a distance of more than 36 million kilometres.

It was evident that Americans, though they might lack powerful rocket launching vehicles, had developed reliable and sophisticated instrumentation. This is why in subsequent years they gained and maintained the lead in planetary exploration.

Right: *A Titan-Centaur rocket takes off from the Kennedy Space Center in 1974. It carries the Viking Space probe destined to explore the planet Mars.*

ASTRONAUT TRAINING

As the Space Age dawned, with the flight of Sputnik 1 in October 1957, it became clear that it would be only a matter of time before man himself would venture into Space. In 1959 NASA announced the selection of the first seven astronauts (travellers to the stars), for the first American manned space programme, called Project Mercury. It was to be assumed that Russia, too, was embarking upon a manned space programme. Other countries, such as Britain, France and Japan, had begun to design satellites and launch vehicles, but had neither the technology nor the financial resources for a manned programme.

To a large extent manned space flight would be a gigantic leap into the unknown. Who could tell whether a flesh-and-blood human being could withstand the enormous stresses of take-off, endure the prolonged weightlessness in orbit, or survive the searing heat of re-entry?

A certain amount of information about these problems had been gained by sending animals on short rocket flights. They culminated in the orbital flight of the dog Laika in Sputnik 2 in November 1957. Laika survived the ascent and coped with weightlessness.

Animal flights in rockets and in orbiting spacecraft continued, while teams of Americans and Russians began training for the first manned flights. In the event it was a Russian cosmonaut (the Russian term for an astronaut), Yuri Gagarin, who went into orbit first in April 1961.

The American training programme

The first trainee astronauts were all highly experienced jet pilots with at least 1500 hours flying time. They had qualifications in engineering and were in excellent physical condition. Many of them were ex-test pilots, and it was as test pilots, probing the unknown, that they ventured into Space in the flimsiest of capsules. More than once an astronaut had to guide his craft back to Earth using manual controls after the automatic landing systems failed.

As manned space flight became more established, the requirements for astronaut candidates changed. Two different categories of astronauts were needed – pilot-astronauts, who could do the actual flying; and scientist-astronauts, who would be responsible for the experiments carried out during a space mission. The former would still need the advanced flight training of their predecessors, but the latter would be selected primarily on their academic qualifications.

This method of selection was continued in the first selection of astronauts of the space-shuttle era in 1979. They included 15 astronaut-pilots and 20 astronaut-scientists, the latter being known as mission (or payload) specialists. Six of these specialists are the first women to become astronauts in the American space programme. Until them, the only woman astronaut was the Russian Valentina Tereshkova, who flew in Space as early as 1963.

Both pilots and mission specialists spend a lot of their time in the schoolroom, where they attend introductory or refresher courses on all aspects of astronautics including spacecraft and launch vehicle design, guidance and navigation, technology and mathematics, and other relevant sciences. They are also separately briefed on their own specific roles in space flight.

The astronauts also train in survival techniques to prepare for the worst if their craft has to make an emergency landing. They camp out in the desert in makeshift tents, practise parachuting, and rehearse helicopter recovery. Since seas cover most of the globe, there is a good chance that they will come down on water, so water-survival training is included in the programme.

Training becomes intensified after astronauts are assigned to a particular flight. They spend a lot of time inside simulators, which are dummy spacecraft equipped like the real thing and

Below: A close check is kept on the fitness of the astronauts both during training and when they are in Space.

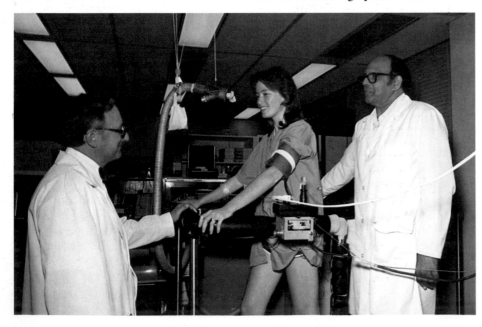

Training for weightlessness

To get the astronauts used to the kind of stresses they will experience at take-off and during re-entry, they train in a whirling centrifuge where centrifugal force is used to mimic rocket acceleration and atmospheric deceleration.

Weightlessness is a difficult thing to train for, but brief weightless periods are obtained in an aircraft flying in a tight arc. Near-weightless conditions can also be experienced by wearing a weighted pressure suit inside a water tank. The astronauts also use the water tank to practise for EVAs – Extra-

Vehicular Activity or space walks. Full-scale mock-ups of the actual craft in which they will fly are built for them to work on inside the tank.

Below: *Astronauts experience weightlessness when they fly in an aeroplane up and over in a tight arc.*

which react in the same way. These devices are similar to those used to train airline pilots. They are linked to computers and projection equipment, which display, on screens, the kinds of views the astronauts would see through the windows of the actual craft as they manoeuvre. While the pilots concentrate on flying, the mission specialists rehearse the experimental procedures they will carry out in orbit.

Every crew member receives cross-training in another's duties so that, should one member of the crew become ill or injured, the mission can still continue as planned. In addition a second, 'back-up' crew duplicates the training of the first so that any member of the latter can be replaced at any time and thus no mission will be endangered for lack of a crew member.

After many months of hard work, the

astronauts are finally ready for their space mission. In the latter stages of their training they will have rehearsed the whole mission in simulators linked to mission control. Mission control will be the nerve centre of the mission, and it is staffed by specialists who supervise every operational stage (*see page 216*). Included in the simulation will be emergency situations for the flight controllers and astronaut crew.

LAUNCH AND RE-ENTRY

The date and time of launch are usually fixed many months ahead. They may be determined by the need to rendezvous with a craft already in orbit, as happened on the Skylab missions and the Apollo-Soyuz test project (*see page 168*). In the case of Apollo, the date was determined by the phase of the Moon. The spacecraft had to arrive at a time when the Moon was nearly full and well lit by the Sun. And during a suitable day there were two 4-hour periods – one at night – when the Kennedy launch site was ideally placed for lift-off. These periods when launching can best take place are known as *launch windows*. Launch windows are particularly critical for launching spacecraft destined to visit distant planets.

A few days before the launch is due, the launch control centre begins the *countdown* – the length of time remaining before lift-off. During the countdown, the complex systems that make up the spacecraft and launching vehicle are checked, tested and re-checked. The launching vehicle has already been assembled and 'rolled out' to the launch pad.

There it is supported and surrounded by a service gantry, fitted with a lift, which gives access to various parts of the structure. The crew compartment is served by a 'white room' in which cleanliness is all-important, to prevent contamination of the spacecraft by dust or germs. A day or so before launch the liquid rocket fuels are pumped into the propellant tanks. All the time the countdown is proceeding. If any faults are discovered during the systems checks, then the countdown is halted until they are put right. If serious problems are revealed, the launching may have to be postponed to a new launch window.

Left: *Apollo 11 on the launch pad at Cape Canaveral before its historic Moon-landing mission in 1969. Work is proceeding inside the 'white room'.*

A few hours before launch the astronauts get kitted out. For earlier space flights they wore their bulky spacesuits to be on the safe side, in case the cabin lost pressure during the ascent into orbit. For the more routine Space Shuttle flights, spacesuits will not be necessary since the Shuttle is fully pressurized like a jet airliner.

Finally the time comes when the service tower swings away, the countdown ends and the launch sequence begins. The powerful rockets ignite and lift the launching vehicle slowly at first off the launch pad. The astronauts are pressed down to their seats as the rocket gathers speed. To withstand the acceleration – g-forces – better, they lie flat on their backs. This reduces the danger of 'blackout' or losing consciousness.

The ride through the lower, thick part of the atmosphere is quite bumpy, but soon they are far above the clouds. They feel a momentary pause in acceleration as the booster rockets separate and then they are thrust even faster as the second-stage rocket fires. The same thing happens as the third-stage fires a few minutes later. This effect is less noticeable in the Space Shuttle since the main engines fire continuously until just before the craft enters orbit. The time elapsed between lift-off and entering orbit is less than a quarter of an hour. During this time the astronauts have been accelerated from rest to a speed of 28 000 kph (17 500 mph).

Re-entry

Returning to Earth from orbit is possibly more dangerous than taking-off. This is because the last part of the flight is unpowered, the returning craft dropping like a stone under the pull of gravity. But before that, the first return, or re-entry, manoeuvre is *retro-fire*. This means decreasing the speed of the craft by firing rockets. To do this the spacecraft is manoeuvred until it is travelling back-to-front, so that its rocket motors will then be pointing forwards.

Above: *After its fiery re-entry through the Earth's atmosphere, the Apollo command module is badly scorched.*

As retro-fire slows the craft down, it begins its approach to Earth. Just before it re-enters the atmosphere, all but the landing capsule housing the crew is jettisoned. As the capsule re-enters the atmosphere, friction with the air generates considerable heat. But the capsule is coated with a bonded plastic material that melts and boils away. In so doing, it disperses the heat and shields the spacecraft and the astronauts inside.

The air brakes the capsule until it is moving slowly enough for parachutes to open. These slow the capsule still more until it is lowered gently to

Earth. The Soviet cosmonauts have always come down on land, in contrast to the American astronauts who, in all the missions from Mercury to Apollo, always splashed down at sea, requiring a complicated recovery operation. From now on, however, American astronauts will be landing on land, too, since the Space Shuttle lands on a runway like an ordinary plane (*see page 228*).

MAN IN SPACE

By the end of the 1950s, American and Russian space scientists were launching Earth satellites and deep space probes with greater confidence. Soon, man himself would venture into Space.

In 1959 the Americans conducted successful tests with monkeys, which were sent into Space on a ballistic trajectory (*see page 200*) and recovered safely. These were by no means the first animal rocket tests. Tests on monkeys and mice had been carried out in the United States since 1948. Russian space scientists had begun rocket tests using dogs in 1955. In 1957 they had put the dog Laika into orbit in their second Sputnik (*see page 201*). And in 1960 they reported that they had successfully recovered two dogs, named Strelka and Belka, from orbit.

The successful flight and recovery of Strelka and Belka was, although no one outside Russia knew it at the time, a full dress rehearsal of man's epic first space flight. This came on 12 April 1961, when Russia announced that 27-year-old Major Yuri Gagarin had made one orbit of the Earth in a Vostok capsule and had been safely recovered. Gagarin reported no impairment of working ability in weightless conditions and ate and drank in orbit without difficulty.

Gagarin's flight stung the United States into renewed effort and, in early May, they sent astronaut Alan Shepard on the first manned flight of the Mercury programme. It was a sub-orbital flight, the spacecraft's path tracing an arc, and reaching a maximum height of 185 kilometres. Shepard splashed down in the Atlantic Ocean some 480 kilometres from the Cape Canaveral, Florida, launching site.

Later the same month President Kennedy urged the United States Congress to support an expanded space effort that would place an American on the Moon 'before this decade is out'.

Even for a nation as prosperous as the United States, this appeared at the time to be a near-impossible task to accomplish. In the event, however, the Americans achieved their goal, with five months of the decade left.

Friendship 7

In July 1961 Virgil Grissom made a further orbital flight in the Mercury programme, getting a ducking when his capsule sank after splashdown. In August, Russia announced their second manned space flight, during which cosmonaut Gherman Titov spent 25 hours in Space.

Not until the following February, on the 20th, did the United States put their first astronaut into orbit. He was ex-fighter pilot John Glenn. His Mercury capsule, Friendship 7, was carried into orbit by a modified Atlas ICBM (*see page 200*), a more powerful vehicle than the Redstone used for the sub-orbital flights. Three further Mercury

Russian pilot Yuri Gagarin became the world's first astronaut when he orbited the Earth on 12 April 1961. He was killed in a flying accident seven years later.

flights took place, the last in May 1963.

No American ventured into space for nearly two years, during which time the Russians continued to forge ahead. In 1963 they launched the first space woman, Valentina Tereshkova, who spent 3 days in orbit — longer than all the previous American astronauts put together! In 1964 Russia launched three cosmonauts in the larger Voskhod spacecraft. During a second Voskhod flight, in March 1965, cosmonaut Alexei Leonov made the first space 'walk', or *EVA* (extra-vehicular activity).

Well behind now in the space race, the Americans began the next phase of their manned programme – Project Gemini. Whereas the Mercury spacecraft carried a single astronaut, the Gemini spacecraft carried two. It was a

Top: *Astronaut John Glenn squeezes into the Mercury capsule Friendship 7 shortly before his successful flight in 1962.*

Right: *Cosmonaut Alexei Leonov during the Apollo-Soyuz joint mission in 1975.*

two-module spacecraft, part of which was jettisoned before re-entry.

The Gemini missions, of which there were nine between March 1965 and November 1966, were successful beyond the wildest dreams of American space scientists. The Gemini astronauts made several successful spacewalks, obviously revelling in the weightless experience. They practised rendezvous manoeuvres with sister spacecraft and also with unmanned target vehicles such as Agena. They also linked up – *docked* – with several of the targets. The success of the rendezvous and docking procedures was vital to the final phase of preparation for the Moon landing.

The Gemini astronauts pioneered space photography, which has since produced some of the most stunning pictures of the century. The flights also showed the superiority of manned space exploration over exploration by remote-controlled robots.

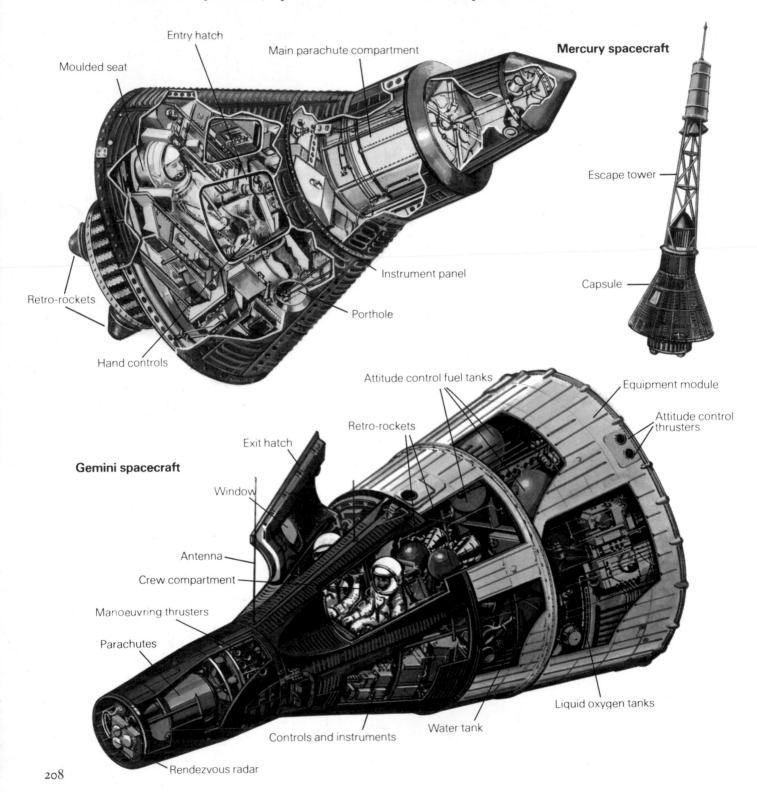

Entry hatch

Moulded seat

Main parachute compartment

Mercury spacecraft

Escape tower

Instrument panel

Capsule

Retro-rockets

Porthole

Hand controls

Attitude control fuel tanks

Equipment module

Retro-rockets

Attitude control thrusters

Exit hatch

Gemini spacecraft

Window

Antenna

Crew compartment

Manoeuvring thrusters

Parachutes

Liquid oxygen tanks

Controls and instruments

Water tank

Rendezvous radar

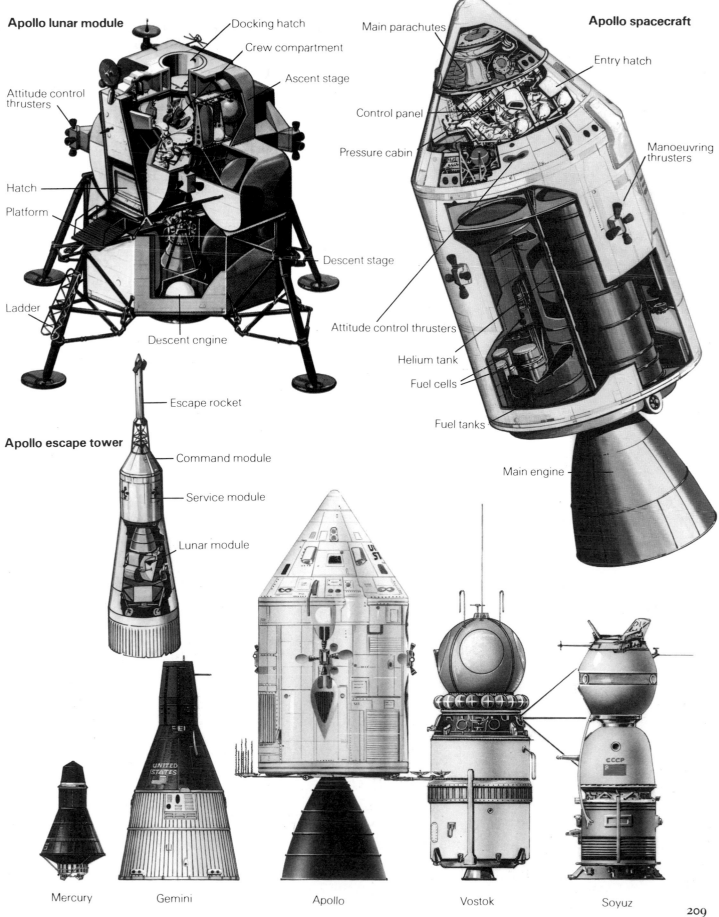

Apollo lunar module

Docking hatch
Crew compartment
Ascent stage

Attitude control thrusters

Hatch
Platform

Ladder

Descent stage

Descent engine

Apollo spacecraft

Main parachutes

Entry hatch

Control panel

Pressure cabin

Manoeuvring thrusters

Attitude control thrusters

Helium tank

Fuel cells

Fuel tanks

Main engine

Apollo escape tower

Escape rocket

Command module

Service module

Lunar module

Mercury

Gemini

Apollo

Vostok

Soyuz

THE GIANT LEAP

The tentative flights of the Mercury astronauts, followed by the triumphant series of flights in the Gemini series, had paved the way for American astronauts to achieve their goal – a manned Moon landing. The Moon-landing mission was called Apollo. By the time the Gemini missions ended in 1966, the *hardware* (mechanical equipment) for the Apollo programme was well advanced. Astronauts had begun training in the Apollo spacecraft.

Then tragedy struck. Three astronauts – Virgil Grissom, Edward White and Roger Chaffee – were killed when a flash fire gutted the crew module in which they were training. The Apollo crew module had to be extensively modified to prevent a recurrence of the disaster. As further emphasis of how dangerous space flight could be, a Russian cosmonaut was killed while returning from the first flight in a new spacecraft, Soyuz.

In 1968 the first manned Apollo flight took place, designated Apollo 7. This flight put the spacecraft through its paces in Earth orbit. In December of the same year three astronauts set off in Apollo 8 for a circumnavigation of the Moon. Their flight was a spectacular success on all counts. The spacecraft worked perfectly, and the flight plan proved flawless, boding well for the Moon landing mission to follow.

The next flight, of Apollo 9 in March 1969, tested all parts of the Apollo spacecraft together for the first time, in Earth orbit. The tests were successful and led to them being repeated in May in lunar orbit, in Apollo 10. Again everything went according to plan. The stage was set for the first lunar landing, which took place on 20 July 1969.

The Apollo spacecraft

The technique selected for the Apollo flights was known as 'lunar orbiter rendezvous'. It called for a spacecraft made up of a number of parts, or modules, which could be separated and jettisoned in turn as the mission progressed. This technique allowed the greatest economy of fuel.

The crew compartment, or *command module*, of the Apollo spacecraft was conical in shape, measuring about 3.6 metres high and about the same in diameter at the base. For most of the time it was attached to the *service module*, which contained the main equipment, fuel cells and rocket motors. The combination was referred to as the *CSM* (command and service modules). The third section of the Apollo craft was the *LM* (lunar module), the part that would descend to the Moon.

The flight proceeded as follows. At launch the CSM was mounted atop the three-stage Saturn V and connected to an escape rocket, which could lift it clear of the rest of the vehicle if the take-off went wrong. The LM was stowed beneath the CSM. The first-stage launched the complete rocket. When its fuel was used, it separated and the second-stage fired, boosting the remaining stages to higher speeds. Then in turn the second stage separated and the third stage fired briefly to thrust itself into orbit. Both the CSM and LM formed part of the third-stage of the rocket. After a complete systems check, the third-stage rocket fired again to put it on to a trajectory that would take it to the Moon.

The CSM then pulled clear, turned around and docked with the LM. It was then in the correct position for the Moon-landing sequence. The whole Apollo craft next separated from the third-stage and in 2–3 days drew close to the Moon. The CSM's motor was

Saturn V

In November 1966 an unmanned Apollo spacecraft made a successful re-entry after the first successful launch by the mighty Saturn V Moon rocket – a 111-metre monster with a thrust of over 3 million kilograms. The Saturn V was the brainchild of the ex-director of Peenemünde, Wernher von Braun.

then fired to slow down the spacecraft so that the Moon's gravity could capture it. It went into lunar orbit.

Two of the three astronauts crawled into the LM, which separated from the CSM, and descended to the Moon. To brake their descent, they had to fire the LM's rocket motor. There was no air to slow them down as there is on Earth.

After their exploration of the Moon the astronauts returned to orbit in the LM in order to rendezvous with the CSM, which had been circling above

them. They flew in the upper part of the LM, using the lower part as a launch pad. After they had transferred to the CSM, the LM was jettisoned. The CSM's motors were fired to thrust it out of lunar orbit into a trajectory that would take it back to Earth.

Just before the CSM reached the Earth's atmosphere, the service module was jettisoned. The tiny command module plunged into the atmosphere at a speed of nearly 40 000 kph. It was prevented from burning up by its thick

Above: *The Apollo command and service module ready for mating with the lunar module and the third stage of the Saturn V rocket.*

heat shield (*see page 205*). The air slowed the craft down until parachutes opened to brake it further. They lowered the scorched cone containing three weary astronauts gently to a splashdown at sea. Within minutes helicopters were on hand to whisk them to a nearby recovery ship.

EXPLORING THE MOON

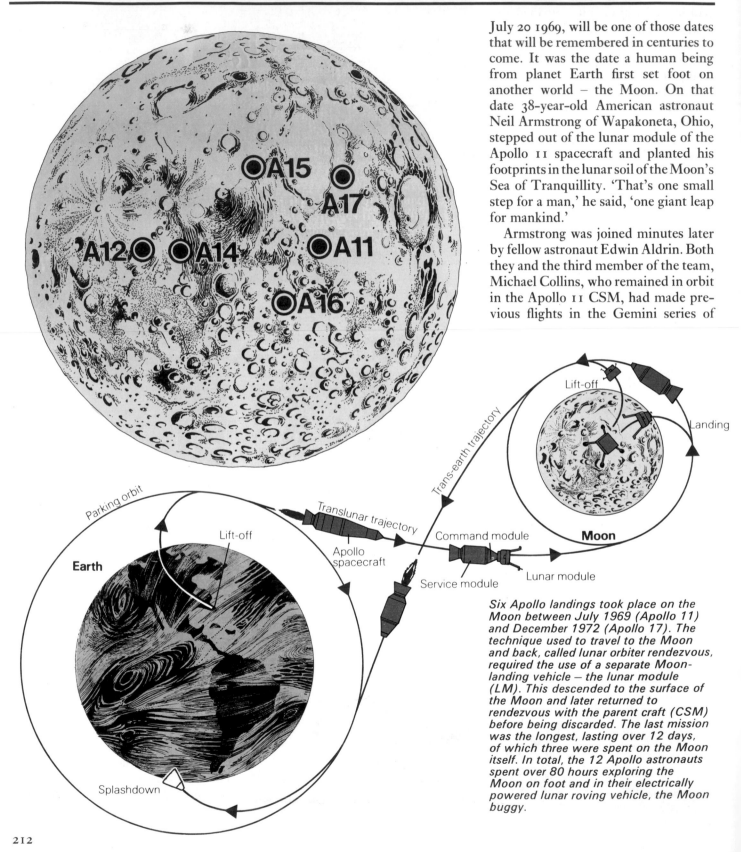

July 20 1969, will be one of those dates that will be remembered in centuries to come. It was the date a human being from planet Earth first set foot on another world – the Moon. On that date 38-year-old American astronaut Neil Armstrong of Wapakoneta, Ohio, stepped out of the lunar module of the Apollo 11 spacecraft and planted his footprints in the lunar soil of the Moon's Sea of Tranquillity. 'That's one small step for a man,' he said, 'one giant leap for mankind.'

Armstrong was joined minutes later by fellow astronaut Edwin Aldrin. Both they and the third member of the team, Michael Collins, who remained in orbit in the Apollo 11 CSM, had made previous flights in the Gemini series of

Six Apollo landings took place on the Moon between July 1969 (Apollo 11) and December 1972 (Apollo 17). The technique used to travel to the Moon and back, called lunar orbiter rendezvous, required the use of a separate Moon-landing vehicle – the lunar module (LM). This descended to the surface of the Moon and later returned to rendezvous with the parent craft (CSM) before being discarded. The last mission was the longest, lasting over 12 days, of which three were spent on the Moon itself. In total, the 12 Apollo astronauts spent over 80 hours exploring the Moon on foot and in their electrically powered lunar roving vehicle, the Moon buggy.

space flights in 1966. Hundreds of millions of television viewers 385 000 kilometres away on Earth watched spellbound as the two 'lunarnauts', clad in bulky spacesuits, plodded and hopped around the grey lunar surface. It was breathtaking, wonderful and altogether incredible. A dream had finally become reality.

Over the next three years, 10 more astronauts trod the lunar surface in further Apollo missions – Apollo 12, 14, 15, 16 and 17. Each mission set down in a different part of the Moon on flat mare regions (plains) like the Sea of Tranquillity and the Ocean of Storms; in the foothills of one of the Moon's towering mountain ranges, the Apennines; and in the rugged lunar highlands.

The astronauts from Apollo 15, 16 and 17 were able to explore further afield, since they brought their own transport. It was a collapsible four-

Above: *On July 20 1969, a human being made footprints on another world – the Moon.*

Below: *Neil Armstrong took this classic picture of fellow lunarnaut Buzz Aldrin.*

wheeled vehicle made from aluminium tubing and wire and stowed folded on the journey out. Called the 'lunar roving vehicle', or Moon buggy, it was powered by electric motors and had a top speed of about 16 kph (10 mph).

If you look at the list of Moon landings, you will notice there is no Apollo 13. This is not because the number was omitted for any superstitious reasons. There was an Apollo 13 mission in April 1970, but as fate would have it, it was unlucky. Apollo 13 blasted off in a perfect launch, but two days into the mission, 300 000 kilometres from Earth, the astronauts radioed back to mission control: 'Houston, we have a problem.'

An oxygen tank in the service module had exploded, ripping a huge hole in the side. This oxygen was needed not only by the fuel cells that powered the craft, but by the life-support system that enabled the astronauts to breathe.

Furious activity ensued at mission control to devise means of getting the astronauts back safely. The Moon landing was cancelled and the lunar module was used as a life-saver. It had independent, although limited, oxygen and power supplies and a rocket engine. This was fired to make the crippled craft loop around the Moon on a return trajectory back to Earth. After three-and-a-half days of nail-biting tension, the crew returned safely.

Astronauts at work

One of the first tasks the astronauts performed on the Moon was to collect rock and soil samples from the area around their landing craft, just in case they had to leave in a hurry. Later they collected further samples as they roamed wider. They also drilled deep into the soil with hollow bits to get 'core' samples. These take the form of a cylinder of the material which has been laid down over millions of years and reveals something of the Moon's history. Altogether the six Apollo missions amassed a total of some 385 kilograms of soil and rocks, excluding the core samples.

The first two Apollo lunarnauts spent only about 2.5 hours on the surface, but nevertheless set up a few experiments, such as a laser reflector and a seismometer to measure 'Moon-quakes'. Later astronauts spent much more time exploring – the Apollo 17 astronauts alone logged over 22 hours. They were able to conduct more experiments and set up automatic scientific stations which would relay information to Earth for years after they had left.

The stations were formed from the Apollo Lunar Surface Experiments Package, or ALSEP for short. They included such instruments as a seis-

mometer, magnetometer (for measuring magnetic forces) and charged-particle detector. They were powered by a nuclear battery, which converts the heat of radioactive decay into electricity. These scientific stations are still operative, although no one is monitoring them any more. The volumes of data acquired by the lunarnauts and by instruments carried on the orbiting mother ships are still being analysed even now.

Above: *Apollo 11 astronaut on the Moon by the lunar module. This was a two-stage craft. Only the upper stage lifted off, the lower stage being used as a launch pad.*

Left: *A chunk of Moon rock brought back by the Apollo 15 astronauts. It is similar to a kind of Earth rock called breccia.*

Far left: *The 16 kph lunar rover proved invaluable on later Apollo missions for transporting astronauts and their equipment.*

MISSION CONTROL

Space rockets and the craft they carry are very complicated pieces of hardware (equipment). To ensure success at lift-off and throughout the mission, the functioning of all critical rocket and spacecraft systems must be continually monitored. Then, if problems start to develop, they can be solved without delay, reducing the risk of damage to launch vehicles, spacecraft and more particularly to any astronauts aboard.

The astronauts, although they are on the spot, have a relatively limited view of their situation. And during a space flight, overall control is exercised by a mission control centre. The actual launching procedures, covering the countdown, lift-off and orbital insertion, are handled by a *launch control centre* at the site of launch. But they hand over to mission control immedi-

ately after the launch.

The main mission control centre for American space flights is located at the Johnson Space Center at Houston, Texas. Its call sign 'Houston' first became familiar to TV viewers during the Apollo missions to the Moon. The centre is staffed, around the clock during a manned mission, by hundreds of engineers and technicians with a wide range of specialist skills. It houses some of the most advanced communications, computer and data display equipment.

The focal point of the mission control centre is the mission operations control room, where teams of flight controllers sit at rows of instrument consoles equipped with video screens. On the wall in front of them is a visual display screen split into sections. On some sections, either television pictures

of astronaut activities or data about systems can be displayed. On the centre section a world map is projected, and superimposed on it is a moving plot showing where the spacecraft is.

The *flight controllers* have responsibilities in three main areas – mission command and control, systems operation and flight dynamics. Mission command and control is headed by the mission director, who is responsible for the overall mission, and the flight director, who is in overall operational control. The person who communicates with the astronauts – '*Capcom*' – is often himself an astronaut. A flight surgeon is available to check the astronauts' medical condition, which is revealed by data sent back by probes attached to their bodies. Another important member of the 'control' group

is the experiments officer who co-ordinates inflight experimental work.

The *systems operation group* keep a constant watch on engineering data fed to them from the various spacecraft systems. If failures occur in the function of any equipment, it is their job to find ways of repairing it or bypassing it. The flight dynamics group is responsible for the overall flight plan of the spacecraft. They are concerned with tracking and trajectories (flight paths) and any spacecraft manoeuvres in orbit. They plan retro-fire manoeuvres to bring down spacecraft from orbit.

The mission control room, however, is only a small part of mission control. Out of sight in other parts of the building are teams of specialists concerned with particular aspects of the mission. They also monitor the incoming data and provide detailed analysis of it for feedback to the appropriate flight controller in the control room. More specialists are available at other NASA space centres if needed.

Communications and tracking

Since a spacecraft circles constantly around the Earth, it can be contacted from a fixed point on the ground only when it is located above that point's horizon. While this may be tolerated for unmanned spacecraft, it is not acceptable for manned missions. Manned spacecraft must be continually tracked and monitored to reduce the dangers always present during flight.

NASA has therefore established tracking and communications ground stations at sites throughout the world, at least one of which is in contact with a spacecraft most of the time. The spacecraft has two basic systems which can be used in combination to satisfy most communications requirements. One is the STDN (Spacecraft Tracking and Data Network), which is operated by the Goddard Space Flight Center near Washington, DC. The other is the DSN (Deep Space Network), operated by the Jet Propulsion Laboratory near Los Angeles. Its main function is communicating with probes to the planets once they are in deep Space. The main 'ears' of the two networks are 26- and 64-metre dish antennae, the largest of which are so sensitive that they can pick up the faint murmur of signals from spacecraft over 1600 million kilometres away.

To link the antennae receiving sites with their respective control centres and Houston, NASA maintains an extensive communications network known as NASCOM (NASA COM-munications). The system uses a combination of commercial telephone and telegraph lines, undersea cables, microwave links and communications satellites to transmit data and voice channels.

Below left: *The American mission control centre at Houston in Texas.*

Below: *Establishing communications was one of the first tasks of the Apollo astronauts.*

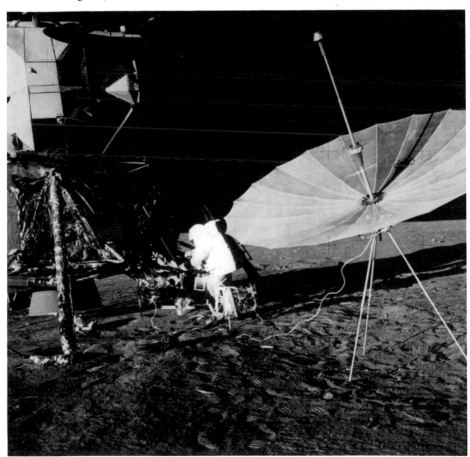

LIVING IN ORBIT

While astronauts are being thrust into orbit by the launching rockets, they experience the forces due to the powerful acceleration. This reinforces the normal pull of gravity on their bodies and increases their weight about three to four times. But when they reach orbit, the acceleration ceases, and the motion of their spacecraft in a circle effectively cancels out Earth's gravity. Suddenly, instead of being over three times as heavy as usual, they have no weight at all!

This state of weightlessness has both advantages and disadvantages. It is easy, for example, to perform gymnastics. But you cannot walk, for there is nothing to keep your feet down on the floor. For that matter there is no floor, because that implies an 'up' and a 'down'. And there is no 'up' or 'down' in orbit. The only way to move is to push and pull yourself along using the sides of the spacecraft. But you must be careful because you cannot stop in mid-air when you want to.

If you are rather on the short side, life in orbit could suit you. Without gravity the spine stretches and you can grow in height because of it. However, your muscles, used to supporting a body weight on Earth of perhaps 75 kilograms, will tend to weaken during long space flights, like those of a person lying in a bed for a long time. And that could mean disaster when you return to normal gravity.

To prevent this problem of flabby muscles regular exercise is prescribed for the astronauts. This may include 'running' for fun round the inside of the spacecraft like a motorcycle on a wall of death, as was done by some Skylab astronauts. But the normal way is to pedal on bicycle exercise machines and to wear special elastic suits, so that the astronauts' muscles have to push against the suits when they move.

The long-duration space station Salyut 6, in which Soviet cosmonauts have spent as much as six months in orbit, is fitted with what is called a KTF, or *comprehensive physical trainer*. This is equipped with apparatus for running, jumping and other exercises. For long-stay cosmonauts a daily exercise plan is vital and has greater importance than every other on-board activity, except in emergencies.

Left: *Two Skylab astronauts who established an 84-day Space endurance record in 1974, suffering no permanent ill-effects.*

Food, drink and relaxation

Weightlessness also interferes with eating and drinking. When you try, for example, to pour liquids out of a bottle, nothing happens. The liquid stays where it is. And if you tried to eat a normal sandwich, the resulting crumbs would float away and get everywhere! So, in Space, liquids are drunk from plastic squeeze bottles placed in the mouth, and crumbly foods are either avoided or coated with edible gelatine to keep them together.

Over the 20 years of manned space flight all manner of foods have been served to the astronauts, some more appetizing than others. As a result of this experience modern space foods take a variety of forms. Some meals served in the Space Shuttle are very similar to those served in ordinary passenger airliners and eaten in much the same way. They consist of precooked or fresh food kept frozen until needed.

Some foods are freeze dried, a process that preserves but does not alter the taste or appearance of foods much, but removes all the water from it. The food is contained in plastic bags fitted with a valve, through which either hot or cold water is squirted to rehydrate (put the water back in) it. Other foods are packaged ready to eat, including bite-sized sandwiches which are rehydrated by the saliva in the mouth as they are chewed.

On long missions there is provision for the crew to enjoy some leisure time and to have rest days. They may take with them video tape recorders to watch films, cassette recorders to listen to concerts, books, chess sets or any other suitable form of recreation.

Astronauts generally sleep in sleeping bags, not placed on a bed – they would soon drift away from it – but hooked to a wall. The men need to be zipped in to prevent them floating away.

Right: *Space Shuttle food is more conventional than the food earlier astronauts had to endure, which came in toothpaste-type tubes.*

Wash and brush-up

In a weightless environment, personal hygiene presents a few problems. Ordinary washing would result in a shower of water droplets, while electric shaving would scatter whiskers everywhere. So wet rub-down cloths are used for washing, while vacuum shavers eliminate the whisker problem. On long duration missions, such as in Skylab and Salyut, showers are provided. They are fitted with a suction device to prevent the escape of water drops.

Suction devices are also fitted to on-board toilets. The waste products are sealed in plastic bags, which are returned to Earth for possible analysis and subsequent disposal. Dumping them into Space would be simpler but would lead to a rather unpleasant form of space pollution.

Below: *Skylab barber at work in orbit.*

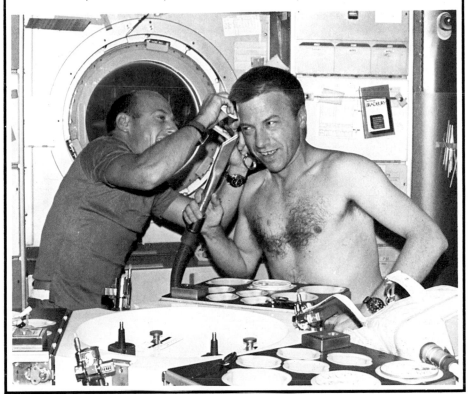

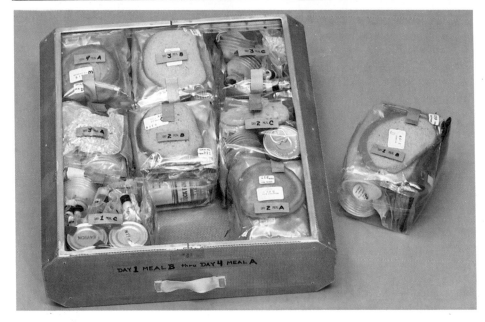

WORKING IN ORBIT

Unmanned spacecraft controlled from Earth, such as weather, Earth-survey and astronomy satellites, can provide an abundance of useful information about the Earth, its environment and outer Space. But they lack flexibility. And if anything goes wrong with them, even a simple thing, they are put out of action.

When instruments are controlled by men in orbit, they become much more useful. They can be pointed in any direction immediately when interesting things are happening. This kind of versatility was demonstrated by the

Below: *Skylab astronaut on an extra-vehicular activity (EVA). His spacesuit is supplied with air by an umbilical tube from the spacecraft's life-support system.*

Skylab astronauts, for example, when they investigated flares and prominences (flaming fountains of gas) that erupted on the Sun while they were in orbit. They were also able to turn their instruments on to the comet Kohoutek when it came within range, acquiring valuable information about the behaviour of comets. And if instruments go wrong, there is a chance that they can be repaired or replaced.

But astronauts in orbit do much more than point instruments at things, though this is an important part of their work. They also conduct many kinds of experiments, all of which advance our scientific knowledge and some of which may pay great dividends in the years ahead.

Experimental work

Among the most interesting experiments performed in orbit are those concerned with materials processing and the life sciences, which include biology and space medicine. Processing materials under zero gravity and in a vacuum, as can be done in Space, results in a purer and more even structure that is much stronger than similar materials which have been processed on Earth. This has been shown by experiments carried out in the Skylab and Salyut space stations. The stations had electric furnaces in which materials could be melted and allowed to cool. The crystals that resulted were

many times bigger than those obtainable on Earth.

The use of supercrystalline metals grown in Space could revolutionize materials technology. They would be used as reinforcement in equipment which undergoes high stresses such as turbines and rocket engines, as well as hypersonic aircraft and spacecraft, which will travel at many times the speed of sound (1060 kph, 660 mph).

But the main use of materials manufactured in Space will be in the development of *semiconductors* and *microelectronics*. Semiconductors, of which the silicon chip is an example, consist of almost pure crystals of substances which conduct electricity only to a limited extent. The greater the purity of the original crystals, the more efficient the semiconductor. Experiments scheduled for Spacelab, the reusable space laboratory (*see page 224*) designed by the European Space Agency, include several connected with manufacturing pure silicon crystals and other semiconductor materials.

Biological experiments are carried out on a variety of plants and numerous species of insects, such as fruit flies, and more lowly forms of life, such as microorganisms (bacteria, viruses and fungi). The way they react to weightlessness and space radiation is studied. Some Salyut astronauts, who grew onions and mushrooms as part of their experimental work, remarked that they found that 'gardening' reduced the mental stress induced by space flight.

In the medical experiments, astronauts test how the body copes with weightlessness. And they carry out routine checks on each other as part of the general health-monitoring programme. They investigate such things as the loss of body calcium that always occurs during space flight, the cause of which is not yet known. They study the effect of weightlessness on the body's balance organs, and on the blood cells and circulation system.

Some in-orbit activities, such as the changing of film in an external camera, may require a crew member to venture outside the spacecraft to carry out

Above: *A spacesuit has to provide the astronaut with a breathable atmosphere and give protection from the hostile environment of Space. On the left the* astronaut is wearing an airtight pressure suit. On the right he is clad in an additional outer garment which gives him protection from solar heat.

EVA (extra-vehicular activity). To perform an EVA, an astronaut has, of course, to wear a spacesuit.

The spacesuit provides him with oxygen to breathe and protects him from the extreme temperatures, dust and dangerous radiation of the hostile Space environment. It is made up of several layers, including water-cooled underwear, an airtight pressure suit, and an insulated outer garment. The transparent space helmet has a gold-tinted visor to reduce the blinding glare of the Sun, which shines continually in Space.

The oxygen is supplied to the suit through an 'umbilical tube', which connects with the on-board life-support system. The umbilical also carries cooling water, electrical connections, and a strong tether. For safety the suit is provided with an emergency life-support pack, just in case the umbilical should accidentally rupture.

When the Space Shuttle becomes fully operational, one of the astronauts' tasks will be to service satellites already in orbit. With this in mind, NASA has developed a manned manoeuvring unit which will give the astronauts the ability to travel to, and inspect, neighbouring craft.

ORBITING STATIONS

By the 21st century – not so very long ahead – space activities will probably be quite different from what they are now. One dominant feature will be the presence in orbit of permanent, manned space stations, far larger than anything launched so far. There will also be a variety of other massive structures in orbit to aid communications on Earth; harness solar power; and provide specialist manufacturing facilities.

Russian space scientists always seem to have concentrated their main efforts in developing orbiting space stations. They launched their first prototype, Salyut 1, in 1971. By 1980 five more Salyuts had been launched, each more sophisticated than the last.

The most successful was Salyut 6, launched in 1977 and still functioning perfectly four years later. Salyut 6 measured about 15 metres long. It had a docking port at each end and with two Soyuz 'ferry craft' docked to it measured over 29 metres. Salyut 6 usually accommodated two cosmonauts, but was regularly visited by other crews of two or three. Some of the visiting crews included men from countries other than Russia, for example Czechoslovakia and the German Democratic Republic.

By 1981 several cosmonauts had spent very long periods working in Salyut 6. In August 1979, Vladimir Lyakhov and Valery Ryumin returned to Earth after a 175-day mission, which was more than twice the length any American astronaut had spent in orbit. Both cosmonauts suffered no ill-effects whatsoever, emphasizing that humans can adapt well to the physical and psychological stresses of prolonged spaceflight. Only seven months later Ryumin returned to Salyut 6 and remained there for a further 184 days!

During the cosmonauts' long periods in Salyut, supplies were delivered both by manned craft and also automatically by unmanned craft of the Progress series. Some of the visiting cosmonauts travelled in an improved version of Soyuz, which had remained virtually unchanged for the previous 10 years. The improved version, the Soyuz T, could carry a three-man crew and also extra cargo.

Above: *This mock-up of Skylab shows the living quarters and experiment room.*

Salyut and Soyuz

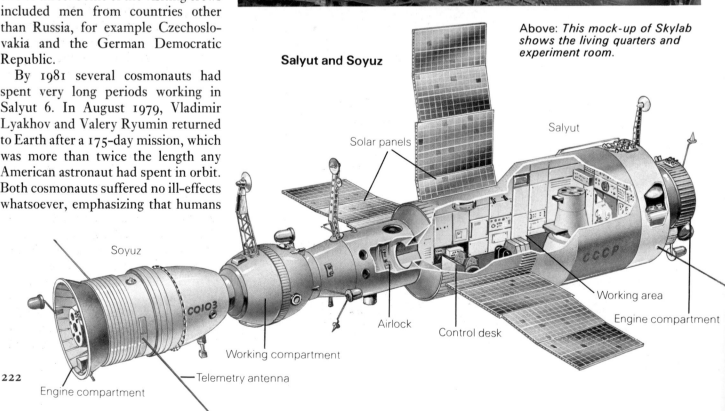

Soyuz

Engine compartment

Telemetry antenna

Working compartment

Airlock

Solar panels

Control desk

Salyut

Working area

Engine compartment

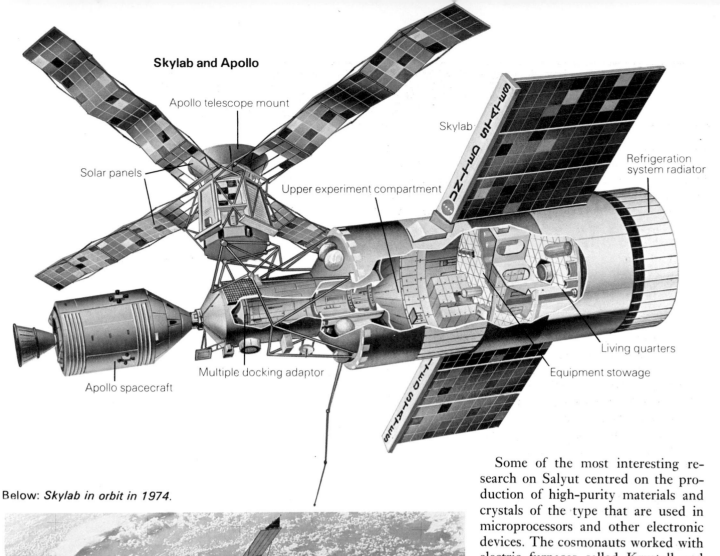

Skylab and Apollo

Apollo telescope mount

Solar panels

Skylab

Refrigeration system radiator

Upper experiment compartment

Living quarters

Apollo spacecraft

Multiple docking adaptor

Equipment stowage

Below: *Skylab in orbit in 1974*.

Some of the most interesting research on Salyut centred on the production of high-purity materials and crystals of the type that are used in microprocessors and other electronic devices. The cosmonauts worked with electric furnaces called Krystall and Splav. They also carried out wide-ranging observations of the heavens with optical, solar and radio telescopes.

The Americans' first attempt at orbiting space stations was their Skylab project. Costing some 2500 million dollars, it began in near disaster, but ended in triumph. It utilized the hardware (equipment) remaining after the Apollo Moon-landing project. A Saturn V rocket launched into orbit a space station consisting of a modified rocket body. The body was fitted out with all kinds of equipment and had extra units attached to provide it with solar power, docking facilities and astronomical instruments. Skylab was visited by three teams of three astronauts, the last team staying in orbit for a record 84 days. The whole Skylab cluster, including the astronauts' Apollo CSM shuttle craft, measured a total of 36 metres long and weighed 90 tonnes.

Tomorrow's space stations

Skylab was a 'one-off' mission, and required the huge and powerful Saturn V to launch it. No such rocket will be available in the future to launch a space station all at once. Instead it will be lifted into orbit in sections, or modules, which will then be linked together. The linking together may well be done automatically. The Russians, for example, routinely dock ferry craft such as Soyuz and Progress with their Salyut space stations by remote control.

American space scientists see the Space Shuttle, or its larger descendants, as ideal for ferrying space-station modules into orbit. Even the present craft can carry cylindrical units up to 18 metres long and 4.5 metres in diameter in its payload bay. The technology already exists for building such mod-ules. The European Space Agency's Spacelab could well be modified and extended for this purpose.

Spacelab is a self-contained space laboratory designed to fit into the Shuttle's cargo bay. It is equipped with all kinds of instruments and apparatus for scientific and engineering experiments. Like the Shuttle, it is re-usable.

Up to four scientists, or payload specialists, can work in Spacelab, using the life-support system and crew facilities of the main craft. They will require only a few weeks special training for their flight, and will be drawn eventually from all nationalities.

The main part of Spacelab is a cylindrical pressurized laboratory module. The other part consists of an open platform, or pallet, which carries instruments that need to be exposed to the space environment. The prime areas of Spacelab activity include zero-gravity studies in the life sciences; medical research; materials technology; Earth surveys; and astronomical observations.

The eventual space station could take a variety of shapes. It could be made up of modules linked end-to-end, or around a central docking unit. This latter arrangement would provide greater flexibility in that modules would be able to come and go more easily. It is envisaged that a basic space station will consist of four main units. In the *habitability module*, the crew will eat, sleep and relax. The *logistics module* will contain bulk cargo and stores. The *subsystem module* will supply electrical power from attached solar cell arrays, life support systems, and the main communications and control equipment. The crew will work in one or more *payload modules*, equipped for carrying out the necessary experiments.

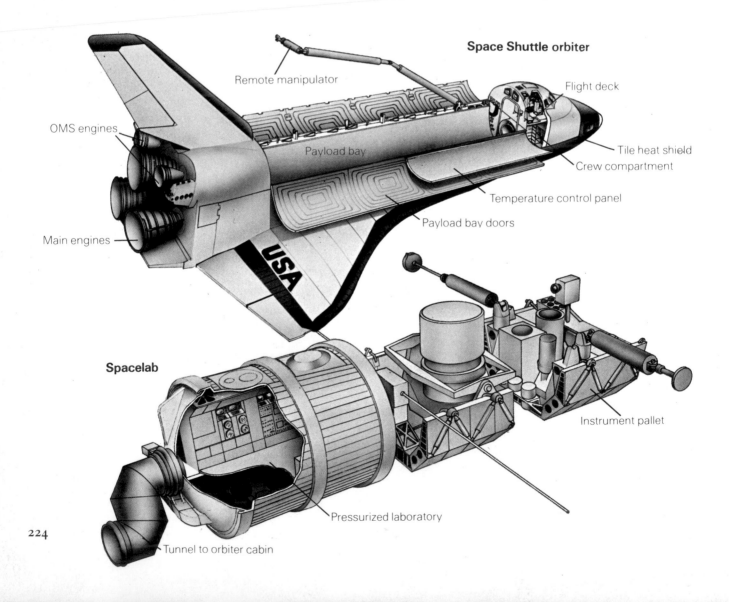

Space Shuttle orbiter

Remote manipulator

Flight deck

OMS engines

Payload bay

Tile heat shield

Crew compartment

Main engines

Temperature control panel

Payload bay doors

Spacelab

Instrument pallet

Pressurized laboratory

Tunnel to orbiter cabin

SPACE COMMUTERS

For the first 25 years of space travel, launching anything into Space was prodigiously expensive. The main reason for this was that everything was expendable. A spacecraft costing up to 100 million dollars was placed on top of a launching vehicle, costing about a fifth of the spacecraft price, and fired off heavenwards. Nothing of what went up came down – at least in usable form. If the launch vehicle misfired or the spacecraft malfunctioned, everything was lost.

For the United States at least, the age of expendable spacecraft is coming to an end. From now on most of its satellites will be launched by a re-usable vehicle – the Space Shuttle. This is a unique vehicle that is part plane, part rocket, which can fly off into Space, operate there, and return intact for re-use. Its main function is to carry spacecraft into orbit.

The fact that it is re-usable guarantees lower launching costs. Further, the Shuttle is manned, and its crew can check that the spacecraft it launches go into the correct orbit and operate satisfactorily there before they return to Earth. They will also be equipped to retrieve from orbit satellites which have reached the end of their working life. And they will be able to service and revitalize long-duration satellites which would otherwise become useless.

As the era of the Shuttle develops, space flight will become almost as routine as airline travel. Except for the pilots, crews for the Shuttle will no longer have to be highly trained and super-fit astronauts, but ordinary men and women with suitable qualifications. The Shuttle is fully pressurized and requires no spacesuits for normal operations.

Right: *Orbiter Columbia being prepared in the Vehicle Assembly Building.*

Below: *The Shuttle stack making its slow journey to the launch pad.*

The hardware

The picture shows the take-off configuration of the Shuttle. The crew occupy the crew module at the front of the delta-winged (*see page 154*) *orbiter*. This is about the size of a modern medium-range airliner, measuring a little over 37 metres in length and having a wingspan of nearly 24 metres. The major part of the orbiter is taken up by the cargo bay, which measures 18 metres long and some 4.5 metres in diameter. Twin doors on top of the bay open to expose the *payload* (cargo) – possibly satellites or other spacecraft – inside.

At the rear of the orbiter is the engine cluster, set beneath a conventional tail. The three main engines burn liquid hydrogen and oxygen. Smaller engines,

of the so-called *orbiter manoeuvring system* (OMS), burn nitrogen tetroxide and UDMH (*see page 196*). The whole orbiter is covered with heat-resistant tiles, which form a shield to protect the aluminium airframe beneath from the heat of re-entry.

On the launch pad the orbiter sits on top of a huge tank, which carries the supply of fuel for its main engines. Attached to the sides of the external tank are twin rocket boosters, which are fuelled by solid propellants. At take-off the Shuttle's main engines and the booster rockets fire together to develop a total thrust of over 3 million kilograms.

At a height of about 45 kilometres the boosters run out of fuel and separate.

Below: *The mobile launch platform carrying the Shuttle cluster is transported by the world's largest tracked vehicle.*

Columbia's maiden flight

In the early morning of 10 April, 1981, astronauts John Young and Robert Crippen climbed into the cockpit of the Space Shuttle *Columbia* on the launch pad at Cape Kennedy and prepared for the Shuttle's first ever lift-off. The minutes ticked away towards the 7.00 am launch, but with only 9 minutes to go the flight was postponed because of trouble with the five on-board computers. Nearly one million spectators in and around the Kennedy Space Center went home disappointed.

Two days later, however, on 12 April, the countdown proceeded smoothly all the way. At T (take-off time) minus 3·5 seconds the main engines were ignited. But bolts still held the Shuttle down to the launch platform. At T plus 2·6 seconds the bolts were severed and the twin, solid-propellant rocket boosters roared into life. *Columbia* emerged from a cloud of steam and soared swiftly into the sky on a pillar of flame and smoke.

After about two minutes, when the Shuttle was lost to view, the solid boosters separated and parachuted back to Earth. The main engines continued to burn for another seven mi ites until the fuel in the exter exhausted. The tank ther nd plummeted back i ntegrating during re-entry into the ocean. *Columbi* had fired its manoeuvring ert it into orbit at a speed (17 500 mph).

In orbit, the as ed the doors of the payloa ecked other spacecraft syst ealed that several heat-sh ome away from the tail s tely this is not a region c by the heat of re-entry, a i- pated any problems. e the case when *Colun* re-entered the atmos later and glided to a pe at Edwards Air Forc Mojave Desert in Calif Shuttle becomes fully will land at, as well as Cape Kennedy. The early flig down at the Mojave site s necessary, the Shuttles could ove the normal runway area without da

After a successful maiden flight in April 1981, Columbia blasted off again the following November, becoming the first spacecraft ever to return to Space. In theory it could make up to 100 trips into Space before being retired.

Above: *Columbia on its ferry craft.*

When they are clear, they deploy parachutes and drop into the sea, for subsequent recovery. The main engines continue to fire until the orbiter reaches orbital velocity. The external tank is then jettisoned and falls back to Earth, but is not recovered. The orbiter then fires the OMS engines for a short time to achieve *orbital insertion*, and once in the correct orbit, the work planned for the flight can be carried out.

Return to Earth

A typical Shuttle mission will last about a week, although it has facilities for food storage etc. so that a mission could be extended to as much as a month. After the mission the orbiter man-

Below: *Columbia makes a smooth touchdown.*

oeuvres into a position where it is travelling engines-first and then fires its OMS engines. This 'retro-fire' slows it down to below orbital velocity, and it thus comes under the influence of Earth's gravity. It resumes a nose-first position for re-entry into the atmosphere. Its heat shield glows red hot due to friction as the air brakes its descent. It adopts a sharp, nose-up position during re-entry, levelling to horizontal only at low altitude prior to landing. During the whole landing sequence the Shuttle is unpowered, gliding to a touch-down on a conventional, but extra-long runway.

Upon landing the orbiter will be taken immediately to a 'deservicing' area where any hazardous materials are removed, and pressurized units are de-pressurized. It next goes to a maintenance and checkout facility where it will be thoroughly inspected for any wear and damage – to the insulation, for

example. When checked out, new payloads will be installed and the orbiter will transfer to the vehicle assembly building. There the orbiter will be lifted into its vertical launch position and mated to a new external tank and rocket boosters. The 'turn-round' time, barring any major problems, should be about a fortnight.

Shuttle missions

The cost of space launchings by Shuttle is low, not only because it is re-usable, but also because it has an enormous payload capacity. It can lift almost 30 tonnes into a near-Earth orbit. This means that it is usually able to carry into orbit a number of satellites at once. And because there is plenty of room in the Shuttle, satellites can be built with standard instruments and technology. Hitherto, sophisticated electronics and miniaturized components have been needed to keep down the weight and size of a satellite.

Even before the Shuttle made its maiden flight the first 40 or so Shuttle flights were fully booked. The payloads include not only large satellites – launched for large corporations such as Intelsat, a multinational communications consortium, and for government agencies – but also small self-contained payloads which NASA calls 'getaway specials'. These are provided by universities, individuals and small companies and are launched for only a small sum of money each. The 'getaway special' facility enables even the smallest

companies to participate in space research.

The majority of civilian Shuttle launches will take place from the Kennedy Space Center at Cape Canaveral, Florida, while a similar site at the Vandenberg Air Force Base in California will be reserved for military missions. At the Kennedy Space Center the Shuttle uses the facilities built originally for the Apollo Moon missions. It is assembled in the mammoth Vehicle Assembly Building, which is said to be large enough to have its own climate! When assembled ready for launch, the Shuttle will be transported to launch complex 39, where the Apollo missions were launched, by the eight-crawler tracked Apollo transporter, still the world's biggest vehicle.

The Shuttle is designed primarily to operate in orbits a few hundred kilometres up. While this is suitable for launching the majority of satellites, it is no use for launching communications satellites that have to reach geostationary orbit (*see page 235*). Launching satellites into high Earth orbits, or alternatively spacecraft to the planets, requires the use of an additional propulsion stage. This is attached to the spacecraft and fired from the Shuttle. In the future a re-usable orbital transfer vehicle may be developed.

Special payloads

Two unusual payloads have been developed especially for launch by the Shuttle. One is Spacelab (*see page 224*) and the other is the space telescope. The space telescope is designed to fit into the Shuttle cargo bay and measures 13 metres long and a little over 4 metres in diameter. The light-gathering mirror of the space telescope has a diameter of 2.4 metres. It will orbit the Earth at about 500 kilometres altitude, where it will be beyond the obscuring and distorting atmosphere that makes viewing difficult for Earth-bound astronomers. Though its mirror is much smaller than those of the world's largest telescopes at Mount Palomar in California, USA,

and Zelenchukskaya in the Caucasus, USSR, its clarity of vision will enable it to see stars 50–100 times fainter than they can. And it will also be able to resolve much finer detail.

The space telescope is designed for a long life. Routine maintenance will be

Above: *This engineering mock-up of Spacelab's interior shows the equipment to be used on missions.*

carried out on it every one or two years in orbit, from a Shuttle craft. About every five years, a Shuttle will return it to Earth for a more extensive overhaul.

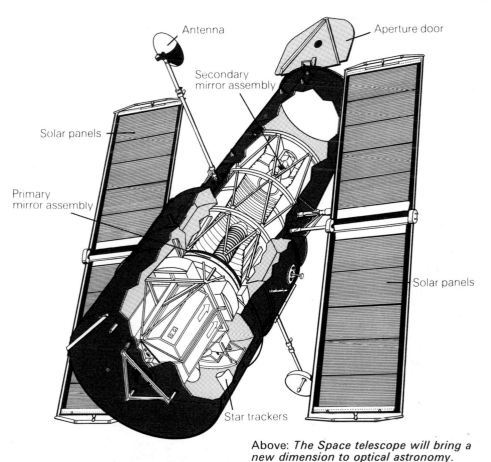

Antenna

Aperture door

Secondary mirror assembly

Solar panels

Primary mirror assembly

Solar panels

Star trackers

Above: *The Space telescope will bring a new dimension to optical astronomy.*

SPACE STRUCTURES

A permanent, manned space station would provide a base for a new generation of space engineers who could put together massive orbiting structures to serve Earth's needs. These structures could include multi-dish aerials for relaying telephone, radio and television signals directly to individual users, no matter where they are on Earth. The aerials would measure more than a kilometre across.

Another possible structure is the solar power satellite. This would most probably take the form of a number of huge reflectors, which would concentrate and focus the Sun's heat on to receivers containing liquid. The liquid would boil, and the vapour would drive a turbogenerator and produce electricity. The electricity would then be converted into microwaves, a form in which it could be beamed to Earth.

At Earth receiving stations, the microwaves would be converted back into electricity and fed into national power grids. Again, such solar power stations would be massive – up to five kilometres across. They would be located 35 900 kilometres up in stationary orbit so that they always remained above the same points on Earth.

At first sight the problems of building such mammoth structures seem overwhelming. But in fact there is nothing fundamentally difficult about their construction since it could be done with existing technology. The main problem is one of scale. But even that problem is not insuperable given sufficient financial resources.

Such structures would be made up of long lengths of aluminium framework

welded together. A machine already exists that can automatically fabricate such beams from narrow aluminium strip. Known as the 'beam builder' and developed at the Marshall Space Flight Center in Alabama, USA, it can turn out triangular, braced beams rigid enough for use in the low-stress conditions of Space. Furthermore, the beam builder was designed from the start to fit into the cargo bay of the Space Shuttle.

Right: *The beam builder makes aluminium beams for use in constructing Space structures in orbit.*

Below: *Mammoth Space structures like this solar power station could be under construction by the end of the century.*

Space colonies

The construction of large space structures will provide the experience for, and lead naturally to, the building of city-sized space habitats, or colonies, farther afield. Current thinking suggests that mining bases will first be set up on the Moon to provide the necessary raw materials. The Moon base would be developed into a space port which would be the starting point for journeys into deep Space, to Mars and the other planets.

With the developments in technology that are expected to occur, space habitats could be built as early as the year 2050 – within the lifetime of children at school today. The habitats would be built, not in orbit but at points in Space about 350 000 kilometres distant from the Earth and at an equal distance from the Moon. Such areas, known as *Lagrangian points*, are regions of gravitational stability where gravitational pull from the Earth is balanced by that from the Moon. When a body is sited there, it tends to remain

locked in position relative to the Moon and the Earth. Siting a space habitat at a Lagrangian point would thus prevent it drifting dangerously off course.

Many shapes have been proposed for a space habitat. The two most favoured are the cylinder and the *torus* or doughnut shape. Professor Gerard O'Neill, professor of physics at Princeton University in the United States, has extensively developed the idea of a cylindrical habitat. A basic habitat would consist of a cylinder about one kilometre in length and 100 metres in diameter. The population of about 10 000 people would live in a hemisphere at one end of the cylinder.

The inside of the cylinder would be used for farming. Three strips of land, separated by three large windows, would run down the length of the cylinder. Sunlight would be reflected into the windows by three large, angled mirrors. The cylinder would be rotated about its longitudinal axis to create an artificial gravity similar to Earth's.

The alternative torus-shaped colony looks like a wheel, with the living area inside an 'inner tube'. To continue the

A NASA-designed Space habitat. People would live in the circular tube, which would rotate to create gravity.

comparison, the inner tube would be protected by an outer 'tyre' of rocky material, which would serve as a shield against harmful radiation. Sunlight would be reflected in through windows on the inside of the tube by a system of mirrors. The whole assembly would be rotated to create artificial gravity: 'up' being towards the hub of the wheel. A population of 10 000 people could be housed in a wheel about 1.6 kilometres in diameter, with a 'tube' measuring about 130 metres across.

Life could be nearly ideal in these spinning habitats, where the perpetual sunshine of Space would guarantee high temperatures all year round. Fast-growing crops would be raised under controlled irrigation and harvested several times a year. Industrial units would be sited in separate modules away from the living area so that there would be no pollution problems.

Right: In this habitat the people would live in the central sphere and farm in the rings at either side.

The mass driver

The basic structure of wheel-shaped habitats would require some 200 000 tonnes of materials. In addition several million tonnes of rocky material would be needed for shielding. To ferry such quantities of materials from the Earth would be impossibly difficult, and so they would be obtained from the Moon.

Suitable ores are known to exist on the Moon from the investigations of the Apollo missions.

The ores would then be transported to the site of the habitat and refined, on the spot, into metal for construction. The ore would not, however, be transported there by conventional rocket-propelled vehicles. It would be flung into Space by means of an electro-magnetic catapult, known as the *mass driver*. This would accelerate a bucketful of ore to a speed of over 8000 kph (5000 mph), which is lunar escape velocity. The ore would be ejected into Space, collected by a net-like catcher and towed to the construction site.

The futuristic mass driver at a lunar mining base.

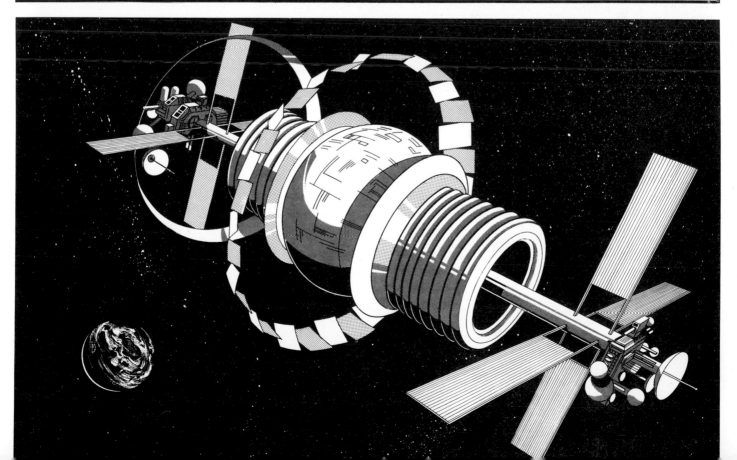

MAN·MADE MOONS

Although most public interest is centred on manned space flight, this is not the most important part of space activities at present. Far more important are the near 100 satellites launched by various countries each year, which are almost unheard of. These satellites are launched for many purposes. Some are military 'spy' satellites designed to observe the activities of rival powers. Some photograph the Earth's surface for different reasons – to survey for minerals, trace the extent of flooding, monitor crop disease, and so on. Some observe the weather, or relay telephone and television signals from continent to continent. Others turn their cameras and instruments outwards to scan the heavens.

From the beginning of the Space Age in 1957, satellites have been launched by expendable rockets. Only now is the American Space Shuttle beginning to change all that, by carry-ing satellites in its voluminous cargo bay and placing them in orbit, often several at a time. However, for some time to come the Russians and the European Space Agency (using Ariane) will continue to launch satellites on conventional rockets.

In orbit

To reach orbit a few hundred kilometres up, a satellite must be boosted to a speed of about 28 000 kph (17 500 mph) in a direction parallel with the ground. At this speed, known as orbital velocity, it will continue to circle the Earth without falling down. The satellite is 'falling' to be sure, but at orbital velocity it falls in a curve which matches the curve of the Earth. And so it effectively remains at the same height, in orbit above the Earth's surface.

A satellite has to be launched into an orbit several hundred kilometres up in order to be above the Earth's atmosphere. Then it will experience no air resistance to slow it down. In practice, however, the atmosphere does not suddenly stop – it gradually fades away into the nothingness of Space. Even at heights of 800 kilometres there are still faint traces of gas. Eventually, these traces will slow a satellite down until it drops below orbital velocity and plummets to the ground.

The lifetime of a satellite about 500 kilometres up is only a few years. The American experimental space station Skylab, orbiting a little lower, remained in orbit for only 6 years. The return of this 90-tonne monster in 1979 caused great alarm among people living under its possible re-entry path, but these fears proved unfounded when it disintegrated and landed over unpopulated regions of Western Australia.

By contrast, a satellite in a high orbit

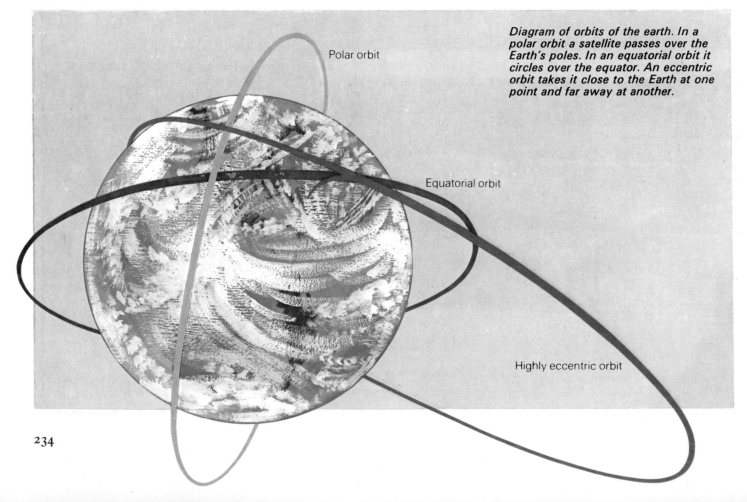

Diagram of orbits of the earth. In a polar orbit a satellite passes over the Earth's poles. In an equatorial orbit it circles over the equator. An eccentric orbit takes it close to the Earth at one point and far away at another.

Polar orbit

Equatorial orbit

Highly eccentric orbit

may remain there for centuries. For example, the small but very heavy American satellite Lageos (launched in 1976), designed to reflect laser beams from ground stations, so that it can measure the drift of continents, will remain in orbit for up to 10 million years. It will stay in orbit for so long that it contains a message to inform Earth's future inhabitants, should they find it, where it came from and when. It tells when it will return to Earth. It also shows pictorially the shape of the Earth's land masses now and what they should look like in about 10 million years time, assuming a steady rate of continental drift.

The higher a satellite's orbit, the longer it takes to complete each orbit. For a satellite about 500 kilometres up the orbital period is a little over 1 hour 30 minutes. At a height of 35 900 kilometres, the period is 23 hours 56 minutes – almost the same as the length of our day – and exactly the time it takes the Earth to spin once. So if a satellite is launched into such an orbit above the Equator, travelling in the direction the Earth is spinning, it will appear to be fixed in the sky. Such a geostationary orbit can be very useful.

The effective lifetime of a satellite – the period during which it performs a useful function – is very much shorter than its stay in orbit. This is not so much because of failure of its complicated electronic systems, but because it runs out of fuel to operate the manoeuvring system that keeps its instruments and antennae pointing in the right direction. Without proper orientation, most satellites become useless. For this reason there are at any time large numbers of useless satellites in orbit around the Earth. This 'space junk' is increased by parts of rocket stages that also remain in orbit for some time. There are currently some 4000 bits and pieces floating uselessly around the Earth, which is already beginning to make satellite tracking a problem. The coming of the Space Shuttle will help alleviate the problem, since it creates less debris and is also able to retrieve satellites that malfunction.

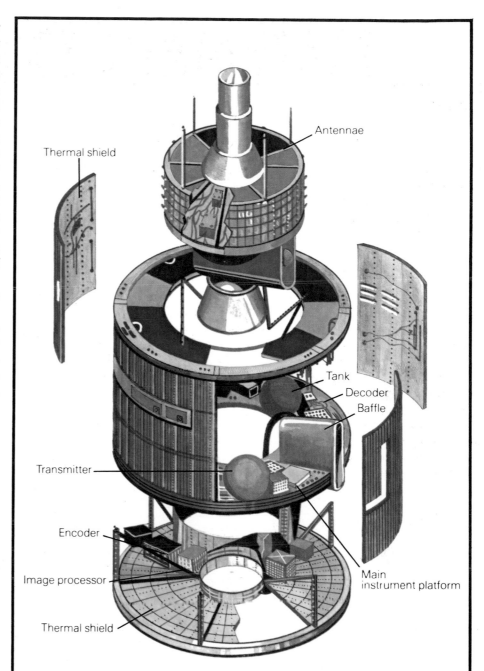

Thermal shield

Antennae

Tank

Decoder

Baffle

Transmitter

Encoder

Image processor

Thermal shield

Main instrument platform

Satellite anatomy

Although every satellite is different, they all have basic systems in common. They have a structural system, usually made of lightweight aluminium alloy, to which other systems are attached. Then there is an instrument system that supports and links all kinds of equipment, from cameras and telescopes to X-ray sensors and magnetometers.

A communications and control unit co-ordinates all the activities of the satellite, acting upon signals transmitted by scientists at ground control stations. The unit switches on instruments, points them in the proper direction, and stores or transmits the data they collect. This process of collecting and transmitting data from a distance is known as *telemetry*. Electrical power for the satellite is obtained from panels of *solar cells*, wafer-thin crystals of silicon which convert sunlight's energy into electricity.

Also carried on board are canisters of gas that is used as propellant for the satellite's manoeuvring system, which keeps it correctly orientated.

SERVING MAN'S NEEDS

Three main types of satellites have brought obvious benefits to people throughout the world – in the fields of communications, weather forecasting and surveying Earth's resources. A fourth main type, in the field of astronomy, has greatly extended our knowledge of the Universe, though not to our immediate benefit.

Long-distance communications have been revolutionized by communica-

Below: *Space satellites are useful for monitoring the weather (1), relaying data (2), national broadcasting (3) and intercontinental communications (4).*

tions satellites. The first ones, like Echo, simply reflected radio signals from one ground station to another. Later ones, like Telstar, received, amplified and then passed on the signals. But they orbited relatively close to Earth and could only relay signals when they were above the horizon for both ground stations.

Most of the latest, and most powerful, communications satellites remain 'fixed' in the sky, so that ground stations can permanently lock their aerials on to them. They are in geostationary orbit 35 900 kilometres up (*see page 235*).

Several such satellites, known as Intelsats after the organization (International Telecommunications Satellite Corporation) which operates them, are in orbit above the Equator over the Atlantic, Pacific and Indian Oceans. They are approximately equidistant and can serve to relay signals between most countries of the world.

Intelsat satellites are financed by an international consortium of 94 nations. The Mark IVa satellites can relay over 6000 two-way telephone circuits and two colour-television channels simultaneously. Individual nations which

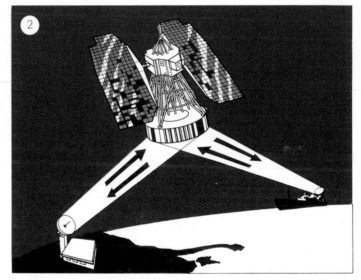

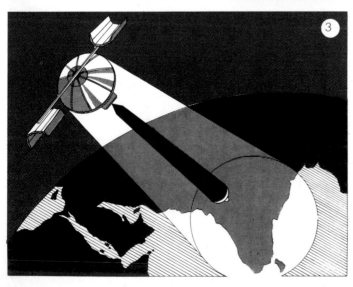

have a population scattered across a large area sometimes finance their own communications satellite systems. Both Canada and Indonesia have such domestic communications satellites. The European Space Agency has also developed a European Communications Satellite which should be operational in the early 1980s. It is built on a modular concept – using a standard satellite configuration but with different electronics and instrumentation.

Though they use complex technology, intercontinental space communications systems have shown many advantages over the old submarine cable links. They are more reliable, they have a much greater capacity, and last but not least they are many times cheaper. This has resulted in enormous growth in overseas telephone calls. Overseas calls from the United States, for example, increased from about 3 million calls a year in 1965 to nearly 200 million in 1980.

Above: *A satellite ground station in Germany relays signals to, and receives them from, orbiting communications satellites.*

Below: *An Intelsat V communications satellite, ready for installation in its Atlas-Centaur launching vehicle.*

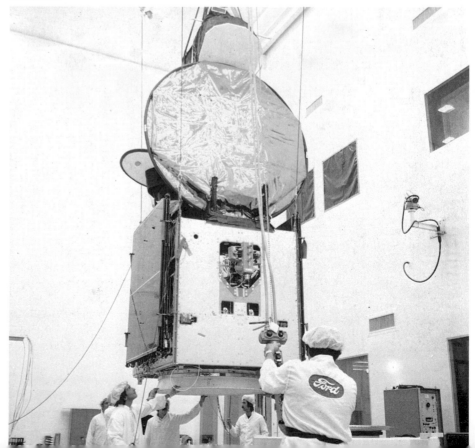

Observing the Earth

Satellites have also been responsible for greater accuracy in weather forecasting, at least for short term forecasts. The first purpose-built weather satellite, Tiros 1, was launched in 1960. The latest in this series of satellites, Tiros N, is still in orbit, and is very much more sophisticated than its early ancestor.

Tiros N and its companion weather satellites (which are designated NOAA after the US National Oceanic and Atmospheric Administration) provide comprehensive information about the Earth's environment. They scan the Earth at both visible and infra-red wavelengths and can record cloud cover during both day and night. They monitor snow and ice cover and determine sea surface temperatures. They

The spectacular launch of the European Space Agency's weather satellite Meteosat.

can also 'sound' the atmosphere, measuring water-vapour distribution, temperatures, and ozone content. Furthermore, they collect and relay data from unmanned meteorological platforms scattered around the world.

Like the other successful series of weather satellites, the Nimbus satellite (notable for its 'moth wing' solar panels), Tiros and NOAA fly in quite low orbit. They pass over the Poles at an altitude of 870 kilometres. In this orbit they can view every part of the Earth twice a day.

By contrast the European Space Agency's Meteosat, launched in 1978, is in fixed, geostationary orbit above the Atlantic. From this vantage point it permanently scans nearly the complete hemisphere which contains the Atlantic Ocean, where European weather is 'born'. It makes a scan every half an hour and supplies photographs of cloud cover plus other meteorological data.

Using data provided by weather satellites enables meteorologists to trace weather patterns more accurately and, particularly, to issue storm and hurricane warnings well in advance to vulnerable populations. Farmers, too, benefit from timely warnings of storms, frost and floods.

One of the most successful series of satellites has been Landsat, formerly known as ERTS (Earth Resources Technology Satellite). These satellites scan the Earth but do not take orthodox photographs, instead recording images *digitally* by the following system. They have a unique oscillating mirror system to direct light reflected from the Earth's surface on to sets of sensors. The light intensity is then converted into digits (numbers) which are transmitted to a ground control station. The digits are there reconverted into images, which reveal the surface details in false colours (for example, vegetation may appear red instead of green). The orbit of the Landsats takes them over the Poles and is *Sunsynchronous*. This means that a satellite passes above the same point at the same time every 18 days. Since lighting conditions are identical each time, surface changes are easy to spot.

The Earth's signatures

From false-colour images, volumes of information can be gleaned. Every type of ground feature, whether rock or plant, reflects light in a different way. We say the feature has a different *spectral 'signature'*, which can be used to identify it. This signature shows up as a characteristic colour on a Landsat photograph. By such means it is possible, for example, to distinguish different crops and even healthy and diseased crops. Urban planners can quickly identify new development areas. Geologists can pinpoint new regions where valuable minerals might occur. Cartographers can update their maps.

In this Landsat picture (above) of the San Joaquin Valley, California, different crops show up in different colours, allowing a crop map (below) to be produced.

Satellites stay relatively close to the Earth's surface and are still subject to its gravitational attraction. To remain in an orbit a few hundred kilometres up, a satellite must travel at a speed of about 28 000 kph (17 500 mph). If we want a spacecraft to travel to the Moon or the planets, we must make it escape from gravity. We do this by speeding it away from the Earth at more than 40 000 kph (25 000 mph). This speed is known as the Earth's *escape velocity*.

Craft travelling to the Moon or to the planets are called lunar and planetary probes respectively. Russian space scientists first dispatched probes to the Moon in 1959. By the year's end one of these craft, called Lunik, or Luna, had crash-landed on the Moon near the prominent crater Archimedes, and another had photographed the far side of the Moon, which can never be seen from Earth. The Russians have since launched more than a score of lunar probes, many of which achieved other

notable 'firsts'. They landed an instrument capsule first (Luna 9, 1966), which took the first close-up photographs of the lunar surface. In the same year Luna 10 became the first probe to go into lunar orbit.

In 1970, Luna 16 soft-landed on the Moon, picked up a sample of soil and returned to Earth. Later that year Luna 17 landed a remote-controlled wheeled vehicle, Lunokhod, which roamed the surface for months. Lunokhod analysed the lunar soil and viewed the landscape with television eyes.

The Americans closely followed the Russians at every stage, soft-landing their Surveyor craft and putting their Lunar Orbiters into orbit. These series of probes returned pictures of great clarity, which enabled space scientists to map the whole Moon for the first time and establish that lunar soil was not treacherous for landing craft.

American exploration of the Moon culminated in the Apollo landings be-

tween 1969 and 1972. Since then such exploration has ceased, although complete analysis of Apollo data will still take many years. The Russians, however, are still active, sending robot sampling craft to different regions of the Moon from time to time.

Launching a probe to the Moon is no simple matter, for the Moon is a moving target. The probe must be launched towards a particular point in the Moon's orbit so that it arrives there at the same time as the Moon. To do this it must be launched at exactly the right angle and at exactly the right speed.

Probes to the planets

The difficulty of actually reaching a distant planet on target is naturally very much greater. Whereas the Moon is less than 400 000 kilometres away, the nearest planet, Venus, never comes closer than 42 million kilometres. Over such distances, an error of a fraction of a degree in aiming, or a deviation in speed of a few kilometres per hour, means the probe would miss its target by a wide margin.

Since our present generation of launching rockets have limited power, probes are boosted to escape velocity and then left to coast to their target unpowered. However, to ensure that its trajectory (path through Space) is absolutely accurate, a probe is equipped with a rocket motor. Then, if the launch team find that it is slightly off course, they can fire the motor for a few seconds either to slow it down or speed it up. Several such trajectory correction manoeuvres are needed on lengthy voyages to Mars and the outer planets, Jupiter and Saturn.

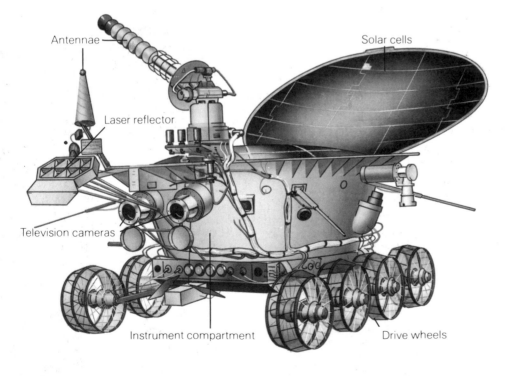

Left: The Russian 'Moonwalker' Lunokhod 1, which explored the Moon in 1970–71. It travelled a total of 10 kilometres, relaying television pictures and sampling the soil in different places.

Antennae

Solar cells

Laser reflector

Television cameras

Instrument compartment

Drive wheels

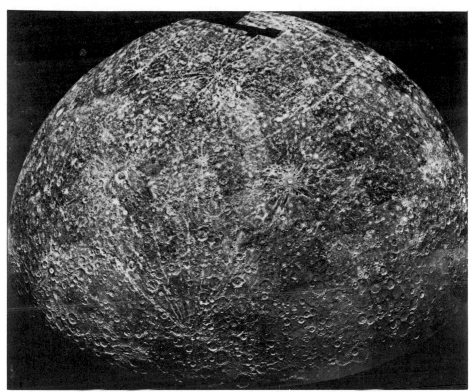

Above: *Mariner 10 photographed the barren surface of Mercury in 1974. This picture shows a mosaic of photographs covering much of the planet's southern hemisphere. The surface resembles that of the Moon.*

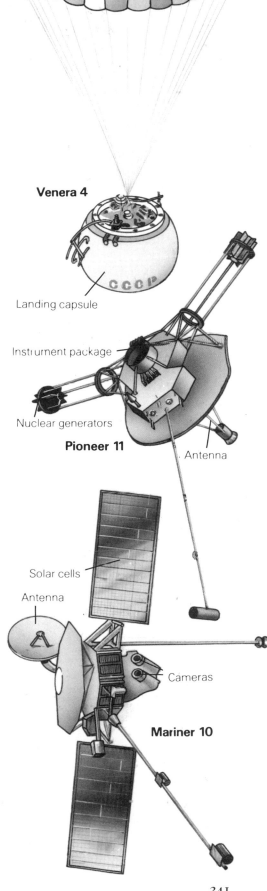

Right: *Three notable Space probes. Venera 4 landed on Venus in 1967. Pioneer 11 took the first close-up pictures of Saturn (1979) after visiting Jupiter. Mariner 10 visited Venus and Mercury (1974).*

Venera 4

Landing capsule

Instrument package

Nuclear generators

Pioneer 11

Antenna

Solar cells

Antenna

Cameras

Mariner 10

A trip to Jupiter, for example, takes nearly two years and involves a journey of some 1000 million kilometres. Yet probes like Pioneer 10 and 11 (1972–74) and Voyager 1 and 2 (1979) have reached the giant planet accurately on target and taken some of the most spectacular pictures of the Space Age.

Pioneer 10 eventually left the Solar System and disappeared into interplanetary Space, while Pioneer 11 used Jupiter's gravity to pull it into a new orbit that took it to Saturn in 1979. Mariner 10 also used this *gravity-assist* method to reach Mercury after surveying Venus, in 1974.

When Pioneer 11 sent back signals from the vicinity of Saturn in 1979, they took over 1.5 hours to travel the intervening distance of some 1600 million kilometres. This illustrates one of the great problems in planetary travel – communications. Signals transmitted over such a distance are incredibly weak but they can nevertheless

be picked up, despite all kinds of background interference, by the huge dish aerials of NASA's space tracking network (*see page 217*).

Even these sensitive aerials can only receive the signals if they are pointing in the correct direction. Trying to locate the exact direction of a tiny probe billions of kilometres away is a task that would be impossible without modern computers, which can store and digest information that can predict the probe's position at any time.

When spacecraft travel to the outer planets, they come across another problem. The sunlight is no longer strong enough to power solar cells for their electrical requirements. So instead of having solar cells like satellites, they have nuclear 'batteries'. Properly termed Radio-isotope Thermal Generators (RTGs), these batteries turn heat, given off by the radio-active metal plutonium, into electricity. They are ruggedly built and long-lasting.

OTHER WORLDS

During the 1970s every planet up to Saturn was observed by probes, which not only took instrument readings but also close-up pictures of the planets' surfaces. The data that the probes returned to Earth expanded our knowledge of the Solar System tremendously. Some of the highlights of the decade of the probes are mentioned below.

Mariner 10 (1974) revealed that Mercury is a barren, rocky planet covered all over in craters. In many respects it resembles the Moon. But its temperature soars to 400°C because it is close to the Sun and has no atmosphere to protect it from the Sun's rays.

The most successful probes to Venus have been the Russian *Venera probes*, two of which, Venera 9 and 10, released instrument capsules that landed and photographed the surface for the first time, in 1975. We can never see the surface of Venus from Earth since it is covered in impenetrable cloud. The Venera probes revealed a rock-strewn but otherwise barren surface, which showed obvious signs of erosion.

This was to be expected since Venus has a very thick atmosphere which must be subject to violent storms. The atmosphere of Venus, near-twin of Earth in size, is totally unlike the Earth's. It is mainly composed of carbon dioxide and exerts 100 times the pressure of Earth's atmosphere. This crushing and suffocating atmosphere traps the Sun's heat like a greenhouse, with the result that the surface of the planet has a temperature of over 450°C – so hot that lead would melt.

Our nearest planetary neighbour, heading away from the Sun, is Mars, well-named the Red Planet after its fiery appearance in the heavens. And close-up pictures of the planet's surface have confirmed its rust-red appearance. Mars was the first planet to be photographed by a space probe, by Mariner 4 in 1965. And it has since been visited by a succession of Mariner probes, the last of which, Mariner 9 (1971), went into Martian orbit and mapped it extensively.

Mariner 9 made many exciting discoveries. They included a Martian 'Grand Canyon', a huge gash that runs

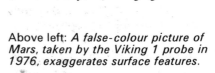

Above left: *A false-colour picture of Mars, taken by the Viking 1 probe in 1976, exaggerates surface features.*

Left: *This Mariner 10 picture of Venus has been computer processed to bring out the swirling cloud patterns in the atmosphere.*

east-west for almost 5000 kilometres. In places it is 50 kilometres across and 2 kilometres deep. Mariner 9 also found a massive extinct volcano that is 25 kilometres high with a base 600 kilometres across. This volcano, named Olympus Mons, is three times the height of Mount Everest.

There were no signs of life on the planet, though there were many channels that could possibly have been made by water. To land and test for life was the aim of the next American Mars probes – *Vikings*. The Viking project can be regarded as the classic interplanetary mission. Each probe was made up of two parts – an orbiter and a lander. On reaching Mars, at different times in 1976, the probes first went into orbit and photographed proposed landing areas.

When a suitable landing site for each probe had been chosen, the lander capsule separated from the orbiter and swooped down to the surface. Since Mars has a slight atmosphere, the

Above: *Close-up of Jupiter taken by Voyager 1, revealing fascinating details of the planet.*

Below: *Few details of Jupiter can be seen through a telescope from Earth.*

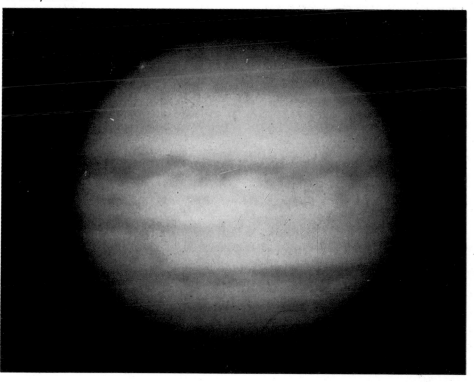

capsule used a parachute for braking, followed by rocket retro-fire to achieve a soft landing. The Viking landers landed in two different regions of Mars and almost immediately began relaying pictures of the landscape. This proved to be dusty, rock-strewn and rust-red at both sites on the planet.

Each lander carried meteorological instruments to measure atmospheric pressure and wind speed, together with a seismometer to measure 'Mars-quakes'. Most importantly, they contained biological instruments with which they could search for life. Samples of Mars soil were scooped up by a movable arm and dropped into the instruments, which subjected the samples to various treatments. If any traces of living organisms had been present, they would have been detected. Alas, no such traces emerged, though the experiments did reveal rather peculiar soil chemistry.

By Jupiter

In 1979, as the Viking mission was successfully drawing to a close, the *Voyager probes* were sending back fantastic pictures of the next planet out after Mars; Jupiter – the giant of the Solar System – and its many moons. The photographs showed in vivid colour the complex system of bands in the Jovian atmosphere and the famous

Red Spot, which is thought to be a centuries-old storm centre. They revealed fascinating surface features of many of Jupiter's moons, including several erupting volcanoes on the large satellite moon, Io. Careful scrutiny of the tens of thousands of images taken by the Voyager probes have led to the discovery of three more small moons, making 16 in all. Also, Jupiter has been shown to have a ring around it, just like its neighbour Saturn. We cannot see it

Left: *The Voyager 1 probe carried 113 kg of scientific instruments, including cameras and particle detectors, to Jupiter and Saturn.*

Above: *Voyager 2 pictures clearly showed Saturn's cloud belts and detail within the planet's beautiful ring system.*

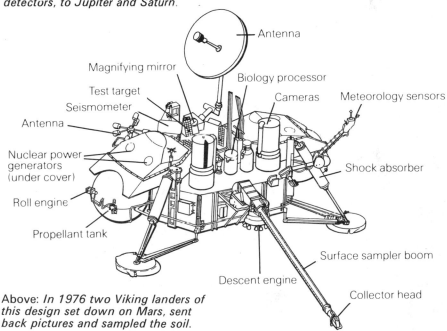

Antenna
Magnifying mirror
Biology processor
Test target
Cameras
Meteorology sensors
Seismometer
Antenna
Nuclear power generators (under cover)
Shock absorber
Roll engine
Propellant tank
Surface sampler boom
Descent engine
Collector head

Above: *In 1976 two Viking landers of this design set down on Mars, sent back pictures and sampled the soil.*

from Earth because it is so thin and Jupiter is so bright.

In 1980 and 1981 Voyagers 1 and 2 travelled further on to take close-up pictures of Saturn's rings, reinforcing the study *Pioneer 11* had made in 1979. Pioneer 11 was launched to study Jupiter in 1974 and then move on to Saturn. Voyager 2 will pass Uranus on

its journey out of the Solar System.

Both the Pioneer and Voyager probes carry messages – the former written, the latter on recorded disc – that tell who sent them. One day, after many years or even centuries of travel away from the Solar System, intelligent beings elsewhere in our Galaxy may intercept the craft and learn something about us.

245

INTO DEEP SPACE

Beyond the Moon, Space is virtually empty until we reach our nearest planetary neighbours Venus and Mars. As we have seen, both planets are impossible to live on. Venus is far too hot and has too thick and too poisonous an atmosphere; Mars is too cold and has too little atmosphere. The chances are, however, that man will visit at least Mars before the middle of next century. This would end, once and for all, speculation as to whether life exists or has ever existed on Mars. To reach Mars, spaceships would need much more powerful rocket motors than they have at present. But experiments have already taken place with advanced nuclear and (charged-particle) propulsion systems, which could supply the necessary power.

The prospects for interplanetary travel next century seem good, but what about the ultimate development in transport – travel to the stars? To make this possible, with a reasonable time-span for the journey, a space ship would have to be accelerated to something near the speed of light (300 000 kilometres per second, 186 000 miles per second). Such speeds at the moment cannot be contemplated. In theory, a rocket that could eventually achieve such speeds is the *photon rocket*. It would emit energetic light beams, as lasers do, and very gradually build up speed.

But for the forseeable future interstellar travel is out of the question. Perhaps it will be achieved eventually by a different means. Some astronomers have theorized that the Universe is far stranger than we think and that it could be permeated with paths, if we can find them, along which time does not exist. If we could find such paths, we could travel instantaneously to other parts of the Universe, or indeed to other universes.

Below: *Artist's impression of Space structures of the future.*

ACKNOWLEDGEMENTS

Photographs

Water
Aerofilms, Boreham Wood 36–37; Stewart Bale, Liverpool 28–29; Jeff Blinn/Moran Towing & Transport Co., New York 45; British Hovercraft Corporation, East Cowes 59, 61; British Petroleum, London 38–39; British Tourist Authority, London 62–63; British Waterways Board, London 49; J. Allan Cash, London 5, 16; Central Gulf Lines, 42–43; Colourviews Picture Library, Birmingham 26; Cunard Leisure, London 28; Cunard Steam-ship Company, London 7, 17; Dover Harbour Board, 16–17; Finnish Tourist Board UK Office, London 10 bottom; Eric S. Greenhalf, Trinity House Lighthouse Service, London 19; David Halford 60; Hamlyn Group Picture Library 15 top left, 48; Kelvin Hughes, Ilford 15 bottom right; Lykes Brothers Steamship Co., 44 top, 44 centre, 44 bottom; National Maritime Institute, Feltham 24 top, 24 bottom; Overseas Containers Limited, London 33, 34–35; P & O Cruises, London 29 left, 29 right; Photo Researchers, New York 10 top, 54, 55; Racal-Decca, New Malden 20; Renegade, Wimborne 30; Rex Features, London 47; Rowan Drilling (UK), Aberdeen 46–47; Royal Netherlands Embassy, London 18–19; Sealink UK 64; Skyfotos, New Romney 27 left, 27 right; Townsend Thoresen, London 31 top, 31 bottom; ZEFA (UK) London – H.J. Edel 53, J. Herman 50–51, Hans Kramartz 51, Orion 22–23, J. Pfaff 11, C. Scheunemann 18.

Land
Bertin & Co., France 95; British Leyland, 105, 106, 108, 108–109, 109 top, 109 bottom, 120; British Rail, London 78–79, 80, 81 top, 82–83, 84–85; J. Allan Cash, London 124 bottom, 128 bottom; Chicago, Burlington & Quincy Railroad 88; Ford Motor Company, South Ockenden 103 bottom; Richard & Sally Greenhill, London 118–119; Hamlyn Group Picture Library 119; David Halford 87 bottom; Handford Photography, Croydon 111; Brian Hawkes, Newnham 75 bottom; Helsinki City Transport 125; Mansell Collection, London 85; Rex Features, London 115; SNCF/Mars, London 71; London Transport 124 top; South African Railways 87 top; Spectrum Colour Library, London 65, 123, 128 top; Terex Ltd., Scotland 122; Tony Stone Associates, London 86 bottom; Nigel Trotter, Leeds 86 top; Union Pacific Railroad 68–69, 72–73; Warrington & Runcorn Development Corporation 126; Washington DC Metropolitan Area Transit Authority 92 bottom; West Virginia University, Morgantown 93 bottom; J. Winkley, Shipley 78; ZEFA (UK), London 73 – M. Mehltretter, 74, 89, 91, J. Millies, 94 bottom.

Air
Air France, London 148 bottom; Associated Press, London 149 bottom; Australian Information Service, London 177 bottom, 184 bottom; BBC Hulton Picture Library, London 139 bottom; British Aerospace, Hatfield 143 top, 143 bottom, 157; British Airways, London 137 bottom, 144, 144 inset, 145 bottom, 146–147, 147, 148 top, 160–161, 164; Central Press, London 149 top; Daily Telegraph Colour Library, London 184 top; Goodyear Tyre & Rubber Co., (Great Britain) Ltd. 135; David Halford 146 bottom, 158 top, 165 top, 165 bottom, 192; Hamlyn Group Picture Library 132–133, 145 top, 152, 173 top, 173 bottom, 177 top, 190 top; High Commissioner for New Zealand, London 176; Illustrated London News Picture Library, London 134, 139 centre; Popperfoto, London 169; RNLI – R.J. Wilson 174; Renegade, Wimborne 186 left; Rex Features, London 131 top, 170–171, 171; Rolls-Royce, Derby 140, 155 top; Royal Scottish Museum, Edinburgh 140; Science Museum, London 136, 137 top, 138, 140; Scott Polar Research Institute, Cambridge 131 bottom; Brian M. Service, Ashford 154–155, 162–163, 178–179; Smiths Industries, Cheltenham 186 right; Spectrum Colour Library, London 129; Michael Taylor, Cheam 172 top, 172 bottom, 185; US Army AAF 153; ZEFA (UK), London – Robert Lorenz 158 bottom, Richard Nicholas 187.

Space
John MacClancy, London 200; NASA, Washington 195 bottom, 202, 203, 204, 205, 207 top, 207 bottom, 210, 211, 213 top, 213 bottom, 214–215, 215 top, 215 bottom, 216–217, 217, 218, 219 top, 219 bottom, 220, 221 left, 221 right, 222, 223, 225 top, 225 bottom, 226, 226–227, 228 top, 228 bottom, 229, 230–231, 233, 237 bottom, 238, 239 top, 239 bottom, 241, 242 top, 242 bottom, 243 top, 243 bottom, 244–245, 245; Novosti Press Agency, London 195 top, 196, 206; Ann Ronan Picture Library, Taunton 194; ZEFA (UK), London – Gerolf Kalt, 237 top.
The photographs on the following pages were kindly supplied by Robin Kerrod: 196, 197, 201, 202, 203, 205, 207 bottom, 210, 214–215, 215 bottom, 216–217, 217, 219 bottom, 222, 225 bottom, 226–227, 228 bottom, 229, 231, 243 bottom.

Title pages
Renegade, Wimborne.

Endpapers
ZEFA (UK) – Damm.

Jacket
Front: motorway in Germany – ZEFA (UK) – Damm.
Inset: Space Shuttle on its carrier aircraft – Brian M. Service, Ashford.
Back: traffic on the Dortmund-Ems Canal, Germany – ZEFA (UK) – J. Herman.

Illustrations
Derek Bunce; David Lewis Management; Linden Artists Ltd; Gerald Whitcomb; John W. Wood.

INDEX

254